About the Author

Wolfgang Sachs is a senior research fellow at the Wuppertal Institute for Climate, Environment and Energy. He has long been active in the German and Italian green movements and is currently chairman of Greenpeace in Germany. Among the various appointments he has held, he has been co-editor of the Society for International Development's journal *Development* in Rome; visiting professor of science, technology and society at Pennsylvania State University in the USA; and a fellow at the Institute for Cultural Studies in Essen. His first book, *For Love of the Automobile: Looking Back into the History of Our Desires*, was published by the University of California Press in 1992. He also edited the immensely influential *Development Dictionary: A Guide to Knowledge as Power*, which was published by Zed Books in the same year and has since been translated into numerous languages. His most recent book (co-authored), *Greening the North: A Post-industrial Blueprint for Ecology and Equity*, marks an important shift of agenda beyond critique to envisaging concrete alternatives and feasible processes of social transition. Wolfgang Sachs travels widely as a public speaker and university lecturer in Europe, North America and the South.

His books published by Zed Books:

The Development Dictionary: A Guide to Knowledge as Power (edited) (1992)

Global Ecology: A New Arena of Political Conflict (edited) (1993)

Greening the North: A Post-Industrial Blueprint for Ecology and Equity (co-authored with Reinhard Loske and Manfred Linz) (1998)

Planet Dialectics: Explorations in Environment and Development (1999)

Planet Dialectics:
Explorations in Environment and Development

Wolfgang Sachs

Fernwood Publishing
HALIFAX, NOVA SCOTIA

Witwatersrand University Press
JOHANNESBURG

Zed Books
LONDON • NEW YORK

Planet Dialectics: Explorations in Environment and Development was first published by Zed Books Ltd, 7 Cynthia Street, London N1 9JF, UK and Room 400, 175 Fifth Avenue, New York, NY 10010, USA in 1999.

Published in southern Africa by Witwatersrand University Press, P.O. Wits, Johannesburg 2050, South Africa, in 1999.

Published in Canada by Fernwood Publishing Ltd, P.O. Box 9409, Station A, Halifax, Nova Scotia, Canada B3K 5S3.

Distributed in the USA exclusively by St Martin's Press, Inc., 175 Fifth Avenue, New York, NY 10010, USA.

Second impression, 2001

Cover designed by Andrew Corbett
Set in Monotype Dante by Ewan Smith, London
Printed and bound in the United Kingdom by Biddles Ltd,
www.biddles.co.uk

A catalogue record for this book is available from the British Library.

ISBN 1 85649 700 3 cased
ISBN 1 85649 701 1 limp

in Southern Africa: ISBN 1 86814 338 4
in Canada: ISBN 1 55266 016 8

Contents

Preface

More than ten years ago, in its first issue for 1989, *Time* magazine declared the planet 'Man of the Year'. While in previous issues Mikhail Gorbachov, Pope John Paul II and other illustrious personalities had stared out at the reader from its covers, this time it was a picture of Planet Earth, shot from outer space, which figured as the leading protagonist in contemporary affairs. With this selection, the editors of *Time* – it can be said in hindsight – hit the mark. Indeed, this image of the blue planet, a gloriously shining sphere floating in the darkness of the universe, has emerged during the last quarter of the twentieth century as the omnipresent icon of our age. The photograph has become so well known because it is so much more than a photograph: it is a symbol that contains the contradictions, the unresolved tensions, of a globalized world. Rich in competing messages, it stands for the ambivalences of a veritable planetary age; it is an outstanding marker in humankind's cultural heritage being transmitted to the twenty-first century.

Time, however, featured the planet as a patient. The planet is shown, in contrast to its overwhelming majesty, as suffering from the onslaught of industrial humankind, hence the healing efforts called for to bring the patient back to health. This metaphor has become the most widespread representation of the planet in recent decades. From the late 1960s, when a spacecraft on its way to the moon made the view available for the first time, the planet has been seen as under threat. Indeed, as one looks at the photograph nothing is more striking than the boundaries that set the luminous earth off against the dark outer space. The closed circle of its boundaries reveal Planet Earth in its finiteness. They offer visual proof of the belief that there are, ultimately, limits to its carrying capacity. In the photograph, the earth, once considered by us as so immense, looks almost fragile, susceptible to being crushed under an excess of burdens. This is the reason why environmentalists have come to cherish this picture as a symbol for their message. It demonstrates so clearly that all effects of human action will inevitably be played out within these limits; any hope of infinity is shown to be nothing but an illusion. After all, the planet was chosen as 'Man of the Year' at the very moment when fear of climate change first erupted among a broader public. The fact that the planet during the last 50 years has lost one-third of its fertile top soil and one-third of its ancient forests pointed in the same direction. From now on, we have to reckon with the finiteness of nature. In this sense, the blue planet has become a symbol for the emergence of bio-physical limits to economic growth in the last quarter of the twentieth century.

A rather different message can be found on the back of a sweatshirt that, above the statement 'Home', displays a picture of the planet. In this case, the photograph conveys a message about the human community rather than nature. The message takes off from an image of the planet as offering within its boundaries a bright and friendly space, a welcoming habitat. In contrast to a hostile universe, the earth appears to be the only place bestowed with light and life where humans – or any living beings for that matter – can find their home. Sharing this one home, and such a magnificent dwelling place at that, binds us together; the blue planet suggests a common destiny for all humanity. The physical unity of the earth, which is so overwhelmingly demonstrated by the photograph, intimates the social unity of all its inhabitants. It seems as if the planet imposes itself as the ultimate container of all human affairs, making all smaller containers that may have bounded people's horizon so far, such as nations or tribes, fade into the background. The picture of the planet has effectively globalized the notion of political community; it stands for the aspiration of creating a world citizenship. It follows almost as a matter of course that both the United Nations and the internet provider America Online use a stylized earth as its logo, and it was against a backdrop of the planet that the well-known Brundtland Report on the environment in 1987 was entitled *Our Common Future*.

However, some inhabitants on this earth of ours are more global than others. To take an example from the news of the day: only in July 1999 did television finally enter the small kingdom of Bhutan, the last television-free country in the world. Over the centuries, country after country, and culture after culture, have been drawn into the orbit of the West. Sometimes violently and sometimes subtly, there has been a process of unification going on in the world, initiated and propelled by the West during colonialism, programmed and engineered during the post-1945 development age, and accelerated and deepened by the lure and the burden of globalization. It is not by accident that photographs of the planet have in recent years become commonplace in the visual marketing language of multinational corporations. Showing the vast globe undivided by nations, cultures and communities, they suggest universal accessibility. With no borders and with distance an irrelevance, the world seems to lie open, waiting to be crossed, conquered and connected. The blue planet thus echoes the message already conveyed by its predecessor, the globe as artefact. Ever since Martin Behaim, the first globemaker, shaped a map into a sizeable ball for demonstrating to the city council of Nuremberg that merchants could in principle circle the earth, the globe has served as a symbol for the West's departure to the ends of the earth. The blue planet is no different. It stands for the unification of the world in the image of the West. The global reach of the West has for its horizons nothing less than the entire planet. After all, 'going global' is a slogan without much meaning for the peasant in the Andes or the shoemaker in Cairo; only the mobile and the powerful are in the position to view the whole world as their arena. Just as Queen Elizabeth I, in a famous painting by Holbein, places her hand on top of a globe to emphasize Britain's claim to worldwide rule, so today's transnational powers stake out their claims when they use this photograph of our planet. In what other terms and under whose hegemony is the unity suggested by this image to be achieved?

  Planet Dialectics explores the ambivalences and ironies, the controversies and conflicts that pervade the terrain of planetary politics. The book pulls together essays that – over a span of ten years – have attempted to make sense of this emerging arena. Most essays adopt a bird's eye view in looking at what are often called 'global issues'; I hope they can add in overview what they lose in detail. More or less all my inquiries turn around one nagging suspicion: that the Western development model is fundamentally at odds with both the quest for justice among the world's people and the aspiration to reconcile humanity and nature. In other words, sustainability (truly conceived) – comprising, it is important to stress, both ecology and social fairness – may be incompatible with the worldwide rule of economism. If there is any truth in this suspicion, then the general thrust of everyday environmental thought and politics since the Brundtland Report has not measured up to the challenge. If anything, what has been achieved is the assimilation of environmental concerns into the rhetoric, dynamics and power structures of developmentalism. This may not be without merit, but it leaves us dangerously unprepared for the turbulence of the twenty-first century. For sustainability is not in the first instance about protecting wetlands or saving whales: it is about global citizenship. To put it squarely, it is the search for civilizations that are capable of extending hospitality to twice as many people on the planet as today without ruining the biosphere for successive generations.

Looking at it this way, it quickly becomes obvious that tinkering here and there will not do. By any stretch of imagination, it will not be possible that all citizens of the world will share in the fossil fuel-based, money-driven development model – with all its attendant paraphernalia – that has come to hold sway in the world today. The biosphere, as we know it, might give way. In other words, there is only one thing worse than the failure of conventional development: namely, its untrammelled success. But what, then, are we to offer the 80 per cent of the world community who so far have not taken part fully in economic progress?

Seen in this light, two things are essential. One is to probe Western-style development, examining its hidden assumptions, its technological glamour, its economic obsessions and the hopes it holds out for a better life. The second is to recognize that, one way or another, we have to leave the Western development model behind. Instead we have to find ways of bringing in other cultures; creating sophisticated but moderate-impact technologies; putting a stop to the reign of relentless accumulation; and appreciating ways of living that are simple in means, but rich in ends. This book aims to keep that debate alive.

A moment of amazement prevails in Part I, entitled 'The Archaeology of the Development Idea'. It turns out that the idea of engineering development worldwide entered the stage of history only in the years after the Second World War. The idea that divides the world into two different categories – developed and underdeveloped countries – so natural for us today, is only a generation old. It came to be a commonplace only as the United States projected its self-image onto the rest of the world. And as a consequence, sure enough, all other cultures suddenly appeared to be deficient, even defective. From there, the march of development took off, eventually drawing even the most remote regions of the planet into the vortex of economic growth – and into a redefinition of what a good society is all about. The essays in this part of the book have been written in close relationship to *The Development Dictionary* (Sachs 1992b), which I edited and which explores the idea of development as a world view now in decline.

Part II, 'The Shaky Ground of Sustainability', takes a closer look at efforts to bend environmentalism to the requirements of developmentalism. Under the banner of 'sustainable development' a major rescue operation for the development idea was set in motion in the 1990s. It only partly succeeded. In the ensuing debate there was a bold attempt to have one's cake and eat it. In trying to square the circle, the question was: how can we protect nature while keeping on competing and growing economically? This has been the implicit agenda of many efforts to reconceptualize development, but it was opposed by those who think instead that growth is the problem, not the solution. The various chapters in this section of the book, therefore, survey 'sustainable development' as contested terrain; they identify political conflicts by tracing shifts and mutations in the discourse on sustainability. The reading of events proposed here is also echoed in another collective work, *Global Ecology* (Sachs 1993), whose rather wary conclusions about the 1992 UN Earth Summit in Rio have unfortunately been amply borne out in the years that followed.

The age of development, in the last 15 years, has given way to the age of globalization. The objective – pursued by both the North and the elites of the South – of refashioning the world in the image of the West has not changed, but the method has. In this view, the sovereignty of nations matters less than the sovereignty of multinational corporations, and the formation of national economies less than the expansion of a global consumer class. That famous photograph of the planet symbolizes the gravitation of everything towards this one world; Part III of the book, entitled 'In the Image of the Planet', sets out to deconstruct the message of unity implied. The liberal hope of creating one world conflicts with any renaissance of a plurality of cultures. Although quite a few environmentalists look to a more or less homogeneous world civilization, it is likely that a plurality of cultures and civilizations offers a better chance of eventually keeping economic development within limits.

Finally, Part IV of the book, 'Ecology and Equity in a Post-development Era', launches ideas and proposals for moving towards societies that are able to cope gracefully with finiteness. As a point of departure, the search for justice has to start with changing the rich – not with changing the poor, as the development discourse implied. After all, the appropriation by 20 per cent of the world's population of 80 per cent of the world's resources makes marginalization of the majority world inevitable. Turning the affluent into good global neighbours, therefore, requires building economies which weigh much less heavily on the planet and on other nations. Such a transition amounts to a civilizational change of sorts, calling for both greater efficiency and greater sufficiency. While efficiency is about doing things right, sufficiency is about doing the right things. Most essays in this part were written in the context of *Greening the North*, a major study carried out with colleagues from the Wuppertal Institute (Sachs et al. 1998).

They highlight, just as that study does, the two main paths for a transition towards a post-fossil fuel society: resource-light technologies and new models of wealth.

Writings are dialogues in disguise. They respond to positions taken by others, they put a message across to an imaginary audience, and they are also the author's conversations with himself. As has often been noted, what looks like a solitary occupation is in fact a social act. In particular, any intellectual effort – consciously, unconsciously – grows out of a web of 'relevant others'. Like any author, I am indebted to friends and colleagues, to their ideas and, above all, to their sympathy and companionship. My first thanks go to Ivan Illich, the master, who has given direction to my inner compass; I have fond memories of our 'gang' at Foster Avenue, just off the campus at Pennsylvania State University, including Barbara Duden, Jean Robert, Majid Rahnema, Lee Swenson and Frederique Apffel-Marglin. I am grateful to my friends from the South, such as Smitu Kothari, Ashis Nandy, Vandana Shiva, Ramachandra Guha, Ashok Khosla, Farida Akhter, Tariq Banuri, Gustavo Esteva and Grimaldo Rengifo, who have widened my horizon immensely. I have drawn much of value from our annual *Crottorf Conversations* with, among others, Hermann von Hatzfeldt, Joan Davis, Christine von Weizsäcker, Nicholas Hildyard, Michiel Schwarz, Susan George, Bruce Rich, Barbara Unmuessig and Christine Merkel. I owe much to Satish Kumar and, over the years, the students of Schumacher College, as I do to those friends who make up my Italian network, including Giuseppe Onufrio, Gianfranco Bologna, Tonino Perna, Alberto Magnaghi, Alberto Tarozzi, Franco Travaglini, Karl-Ludwig Schibel, and the late Alexander Langer. Moreover, conversations running for many years link me to Helmut Spitzley, Otto Ullrich and Marianne Gronemeyer, while, more recently, I have shared in the knowledge and friendship of colleagues at the Wuppertal Institute, including Willy Bierter, Friedrich Schmidt-Bleek, Hermann Ott, Manfred Linz, Reinhard Loske, Stefanie Boege, Fritz Hinterberger, Gerhard Scherhorn and Ernst Ulrich von Weizsäcker. Finally, I consider myself fortunate in having found in Robert Molteno of Zed Books an editor who gently, but with insistence, calls his authors to the task.

Melania Cavelli has seen all of these essays grow. From a small flat in Boston's Back Bay to an apartment looking toward the Gianicolo Hill in Rome, she has participated in both the vibrations of the places and the humours that are present in these essays. I thank her.

Wolfgang Sachs
Wuppertal/Rome

Bibliographical Note

The essays in the Part I, 'The Archaeology of the Development Idea' were originally published in English by *Interculture* (Montréal), Fall 1990. 'Global Ecology and the Shadow of "Development"' appeared first in W. Sachs (ed.), *Global Ecology: A New Arena of Political Conflict*, London: Zed Books, 1993. 'The Gospel of Global Efficiency' was first published in *IFDA-Dossier*, November–December 1987, while 'Environment and Development' and 'One World – Many Worlds?' were first printed in W. Sachs (ed.), *The Development Dictionary. A Guide to Knowledge as Power*, London: Zed Books, 1992. 'Sustainable Development: On the Political Anatomy of an Oxymoron' is also available in F. Fischer and M. Hajer (eds), *Living with Nature. Environmental Politics as Cultural Discourse*, New York: Oxford University Press, 1999, and longer extracts from 'The Blue Planet: On the Ambiguity of a Modern Icon' have been published in *The Ecologist*, vol. 24, September–October 1994. A shorter version of 'Ecology, Justice, and the End of Development' appeared in *Development*, June 1997, and an earlier version of 'Speed Limits' in *New Perspectives Quarterly*, Winter 1997. All other essays appear here for the first time.

I

The Archaeology of the Development Idea

1

The Archaeology of the Development Idea

A Guide to the Ruins

Ruined buildings hide their secrets under piles of earth and rubble. Archaeologists, shovels in hand, work through layer upon layer to reveal underpinnings and thus discover the origins of a dilapidated monument. But ideas can also turn out to be ruins, with their foundations covered by years or even centuries of sand.

I believe that the idea of development stands today like a ruin in the intellectual landscape, its shadows obscuring our vision. It is high time we tackled the archaeology of this towering conceit, that we uncovered its foundations to see it for what it is: the outdated monument to an immodest era.

A world power in search of a mission Wind and snow stormed over Pennsylvania Avenue on 20 January 1949 when, in his inauguration speech before Congress, US President Harry Truman defined the largest part of the world as 'underdeveloped areas' (Truman 1950: 1366). There it was, suddenly a permanent feature of the landscape, a pivotal concept that crammed the immeasurable diversity of the globe's south into a single category: underdeveloped. For the first time, the new world view was announced: all the peoples of the earth were to move along the same track and aspire to only one goal – development. And the road to follow lay clearly before the president's eyes: 'Greater production is the key to prosperity and peace.' After all, was it not the USA that had already come closest to this Utopia? According to that yardstick, nations fall into place as stragglers or lead runners. And 'the United States is pre-eminent among nations in the development of industrial and scientific techniques'. Clothing self-interest in generosity, Truman outlined a programme of technical assistance designed to 'relieve the suffering of these peoples' through 'industrial activities' and 'a higher standard of living'.

3

Looking back after 40 years, we recognize Truman's speech as the starting-gun in the race for the South to catch up with the North. But we also see that the field of runners has been dispersed, as some competitors have fallen by the wayside and others have begun to suspect that they are running in the wrong direction.

The idea of defining the world as an economic arena originated in Truman's time – it would have been completely alien to colonialism. True, colonial powers saw themselves as participating in an economic race, with their overseas territories a source of raw materials. But it was only after the Second World War that these territories had to stand on their own and compete in a global economic arena. For Britain and France during the colonial period, dominion over their colonies was first of all a cultural obligation that stemmed from their vocation to a civilizing mission. British imperial administrator Lord Lugard had formulated the doctrine of the 'double mandate': economic profit, of course, but above all the responsibility to elevate the 'coloured races' to a higher level of civilization. The colonialists came as masters to rule over the natives; they did not come as planners to start the spiral of supply and demand.

Development as imperative According to Truman's vision, the two commandments of the double mandate converge under the imperative of 'economic development'. A change in world view had thus taken place, allowing the concept of development to rise to a standard of universal rule. In the British Development Act of 1929, still influenced by colonial frameworks, 'development' applied only to the first duty of the double mandate: the economic exploitation of resources such as land, minerals and wood products; the second duty was defined as 'progress' or 'welfare'. At this time it was thought that only resources, not people or societies, could be developed (Arndt 1981). It was in the corridors of the State Department during the Second World War that 'cultural progress' was absorbed by 'economic mobilization' and development was enthroned as the crowning concept. A new world view had found its succinct definition: the degree of civilization in a country could be measured by the level of its production. There was no longer any reason to limit the domain of development to resources only. From now on, people and whole societies could, or even should, be seen as the objects of development.

Truman's imperative to develop meant that societies of the Third World were no longer seen as diverse and incomparable possibilities of human living arrangements but were rather placed on a single 'progressive track', judged more or less advanced according to the criteria of the Western industrial nations. Such a reinterpretation of global history was not only politically flattering but also unavoidable, since underdevelopment can be recognized only in looking back from a state of maturity. Development without predominance is like a race without direction. So the pervasive power and influence of the West was logically included in the proclamation of development. It is no coincidence that the preamble of the UN Charter ('We, the peoples of the United nations ...') echoes the Constitution of the USA ('We the people of the United states ...'). Development meant nothing less than projecting the American model of society onto the rest of the world.

Truman really needed such a reconceptualization of the world. The old colonial world had fallen apart. The United States, the strongest nation to emerge from the war, was obliged to act as the new world power. For this it needed a vision of a new global order. The concept of development provided the answer because it presented the world as a collection of homogeneous entities, held together not through the political dominion of colonial times, but through economic interdependence. It meant that the independence process of young countries could be allowed to proceed, because they automatically fell under the wing of the USA anyway when they proclaimed themselves to be subjects of economic development. Development was the conceptual vehicle that allowed the USA to behave as herald of national self-determination while at the same time founding a new type of world-wide domination: an anti-colonial imperialism.

Regimes in search of a raison d'état   The leaders of the newly founded nations – from Nehru to Nkrumah, Nasser to Sukarno – accepted the image that the North had of the South, and internalized it as their self-image. Underdevelopment became the cognitive foundation for the establishment of the nations throughout the Third World. The Indian leader Nehru (incidentally, in opposition to Gandhi) made the point in 1949: 'It is not a question of theory; be it communism, socialism or capitalism, whatever method is more successful, brings the necessary changes and gives satisfaction to the masses, will establish itself on its own ... Our problem today is to raise the standard of the masses.' Economic development as the primary aim of the state; the mobilization of the country to increase output: this beautifully suited the Western concept of the world as an economic arena.

As in all types of competition, this one rapidly produced its professional coaching staff. The World Bank sent off the first of its innumerable missions in July 1949. Upon their return from Colombia, the 14 experts wrote: 'piecemeal and sporadic efforts are apt to make little impression on the general picture. Only through a generalized attack throughout the whole economy on education, health, housing, food and productivity can the vicious circle of poverty, ignorance, ill health and low productivity be decisively broken' (IBRD 1950: xv). To increase production at a constant level, entire societies had to be overhauled. Had there ever existed a more zealous state objective? From then on, an unprecedented flowering of agencies and administrations came forth to address all aspects of life – to count, organize, mindlessly intervene and sacrifice, all in the name of 'development'. Today the scene appears more like collective hallucination. Traditions, hierarchies, mental habits – the whole texture of societies – have all been dissolved in the planner's mechanistic models. But in this way the experts were able to apply the same blueprint for institutional reform throughout the world, the outline of which was most often patterned on the American way of life. There is no longer any question of letting things 'mature for centuries', as in the colonial period. After the Second World War, engineers set out to develop whole societies, and to accomplish the job in a few years or at the most a couple of decades.

Shocks and erosion   In the late 1960s, deep cracks began to appear in the building: the trumpeted promises of the development idea were built on sand! The international elite, which had been busy piling one development plan on another, knitted its collective brow. At the International Labour Office and the World Bank, experts suddenly realized that growth policies were not working. Poverty increased precisely in the shadow of wealth, unemployment proved resistant to growth, and the food situation could not be helped through building steel works. It became clear that the identification of social progress with economic growth was pure fiction.

In 1973, Robert McNamara, the president of the World Bank, summed up the state of affairs: 'Despite a decade of unprecedented increase in the gross national product ... the poorest segments of the population have received relatively little benefit ... The upper 40% of the population typically receive 75% of all income.' No sooner had he admitted the failure of Truman's strategy than he immediately proclaimed another development strategy with its new target group – rural development and small farmers. The logic of this conceptual operation is obvious enough: it meant that the idea of development did not have to be abandoned; indeed, its field of application was enlarged. Similarly, in rapid succession during the 1970s and 1980s, unemployment, injustice, the eradication of poverty, basic needs, women and the environment were turned into problems and became the object of special strategies.

The meaning of development exploded, increasingly covering a host of contradictory practices. The development business became self-propelling: whatever new crisis arose, a new strategy to resolve it could be devised. Furthermore, the background motive for development slowly shifted. A rising environmental chorus noted that development was meant not to promote growth, but to protect against it. Thus the semantic chaos was complete, and the concept torn to shreds.

A concept full of emptiness So development has become a shapeless amoeba-like word. It cannot express anything because its outlines are blurred. But it remains ineradicable because it appears so benign. They who pronounce the word denote nothing but claim the best of intentions. Development thus has no content but it does possess a function: it allows any intervention to be sanctified in the name of a higher evolutionary goal. Watch out! Truman's assumptions travel like blind passengers under its cover. However applied, the development idea always implies that there are lead runners who show the way to latecomers; it suggests that advancement is the result of planned action. Even without having economic growth in mind, whoever talks of development evokes notions of universality, progress and feasibility, showing him- or herself unable to escape Truman's influence.

This heritage is like a weight that keeps one treading in the same spot. It prevents people in Michoacan, Gujarat or Zanzibar from recognizing their own right to refuse to classify themselves as under-developed; it stops them rejoicing in their own diversity and wit. Development always entails looking at other worlds in terms of what they lack, and obstructs the wealth of indigenous alternatives.

Yet the contrary of development is not stagnation. From Gandhi's Swaraj to Zapata's Ejidos, we see that there are striking examples of change in every culture. Distinctions such as backward/advanced or traditional/modern have in any case become ridiculous given the dead end of progress in the North, from poisoned soil to the greenhouse effect. Truman's vision will thus fall in the face of history, not because the race was fought unfairly, but because it leads to abyss.

The idea of development was once a towering monument inspiring international enthusiasm. Today, the structure is falling apart and is in danger of total collapse. But its imposing ruins still linger over everything and block the way out. The task, then, is to push the rubble aside to open up new ground.

The Discovery of Poverty

I could have kicked myself afterwards. Yet my remark had seemed the most natural thing on earth at the time. It was six months after Mexico City's catastrophic earthquake in 1985 and I had spent the whole day walking around Tepito, a dilapidated quarter inhabited by ordinary people but threatened by land speculators. I had expected ruins and resignation, decay and squalor, but the visit had made me think again: I witnessed a proud neighbourly spirit, vigorous building activity and a flourishing shadow economy. But at the end of the day the remark slipped out: 'It's all very well but, when it comes down to it, these people are still terribly poor.' Promptly, one of my companions stiffened: 'No somos pobres, somos Tepiteños!' (We are not poor people, we are Tepitans). What a reprimand! Why had I made such an offensive remark? I had to admit to myself in embarrassment that, quite involuntarily, I had allowed the clichés of development philosophy to trigger my reaction.

Inventing the low-income bracket 'Poverty' on a global scale was discovered after the Second World War; before 1940 it was not an issue. In one of the first World Bank reports, dated 1948–49, the 'nature of the problem' is outlined:

> Both the need and potential for development are plainly revealed by a single set of statistics. According to UN Bureau of Statistics, average income per head in the United States in 1947 was over $1400, and in another 14 countries ranged between $400 and $900. For more than half of the world's population, however the average income was less – and sometimes much less – than $100 per person. The magnitude of this discrepancy demonstrates not only the urgent need to raise the living standards in the underdeveloped countries, but also the enormous possibilities to do just this.

Whenever poverty was mentioned at all in the documents of the 1940s and 1950s, it took the form of a statistical measurement of per capita income whose significance rested on the fact that it lay ridiculously far below the US standard.

When size of income is thought to indicate social perfection, as it does in the economic model of society, one is inclined to interpret any other society that does not follow that model as 'low-income'. This way, the perception of poverty on a global scale was nothing more than the result of a comparative statistical operation, the first of which was carried out only in 1940 by the economist Colin Clark.

As soon as the scale of incomes had been established, order was imposed on a confused globe: horizontally, such different worlds as those of the Zapotec people of Mexico, the Tuareg of north Africa and Rajasthanis of India could be classed together, while a vertical comparison to 'rich' nations demanded relegating them to a position of almost immeasurable inferiority. In this way 'poverty' was used to define whole peoples, not according to what they are and want to be, but according to what they lack and are expected to become. Economic disdain had thus taken the place of colonial contempt.

Moreover, this conceptual operation provided a justification for intervention: wherever low income is the problem, the only answer can be 'economic development'. There was no mention of the idea that poverty might also result from oppression and thus demand liberation, or that a culture of sufficiency might be essential for long-term survival, or, even less, that a culture might direct its energies towards spheres other than the economic. No, as it was in the industrial nations so it was to be in all the others: poverty was diagnosed as a lack of spending power crying to be banished through economic growth. Under the banner of 'poverty' the enforced reorganization of many societies into money economies was subsequently conducted like a moral crusade. Who could be against it?

Descent to the biological minimum Towards the end of the 1960s, when it was no longer possible to close one's eyes to the fact that 'economic development' was patently failing to help most people achieve a higher standard of living, a new conception of 'poverty' was required. 'We should strive', Robert McNamara of the World Bank stated in 1973, 'to eradicate absolute poverty by the end of the century. That means, in practice, the elimination of malnutrition and illiteracy, the reduction of infant mortality and the raising of life expectancy standards to those of the developed nations.'

Anyone who lived below an externally defined minimum standard was declared absolutely poor; the yardstick of per capita income was thrown onto the trash-heap of development concepts. Two shifts in the focus of international discussion of poverty were responsible for this. On the one hand, attention switched to yawning social gulfs within societies, which had been completely blurred by national averages. On the other, income revealed itself to be a rather blunt indicator of the living conditions of those not fully integrated into a money economy.

These new efforts to understand poverty in terms of quality of life emerged out of disappointment at the results of the stimulation of growth, but they brought their own form of reductionism. Since the first attempts in England at the turn of the century, the calculations of an absolute poverty line has been based on nutrition: the absolute poor are those whose intake of foods does not exceed a certain minimum of calories. The trouble with such definitions is that they reduce the living reality of hundreds of millions of people to an animalistic description. In an attempt to find an objective and meaningful criterion, the ground was clear for a conception of reality that reduces the rich variety of what people might hope and struggle for to one bare piece of data about survival. Can a lower common denominator be imagined? It is no wonder that the measures taken in response – ranging from deliveries of grain to people who eat rice to literacy campaigns in regions where the written word is altogether uncommon – have all too often been insensitive and have shown no regard for people's self-esteem. Reducing whole ways of life to calorie levels does, to be sure, make the international administration of development aid a lot easier. It allows a neat classification of the clientele (without which worldwide strategies would be pointless) and it serves as permanent proof of a state of global emergency (without which doubt might be cast on the legitimacy of some development agencies).

This readjusted idea of poverty enabled the development paradigm to be rescued at the beginning of the 1970s. In its official version, the fulfilment of basic needs strictly called for economic growth, or at least growth 'with redistribution'. The link to the previous decade's dogma of growth was thus established.

Poor is not necessarily poor Binary divisions, such as healthy/ill, normal/abnormal or, more pertinently, rich/poor are like steamrollers of the mind: they level a multiform world, completely flattening anything that does not fit. The stereotyped talk of poverty has disfigured the different, indeed contrasting, forms of poverty beyond recognition. It fails to distinguish, for example, between frugality, destitution and scarcity.

Frugality is a mark of cultures free from the frenzy of accumulation. In these, the necessities of everyday life are won mostly from subsistence production, with only the smaller part being purchased on the market. To our eyes, people have rather meagre possessions – perhaps a hut and some pots and a Sunday costume – with money playing only a marginal role. Instead, everyone usually has access to fields, rivers and woods, while kinship and community duties guarantee services that elsewhere must be paid for in hard cash. Despite being in the 'low-income bracket' nobody goes hungry. What is more, large surpluses are often spent on jewellery, celebrations or grandiose buildings.

In a traditional Mexican village, for example, the private accumulation of wealth results in social ostracism; prestige is gained precisely by spending even small profits on good deeds for the community. Here is a way of life maintained by a culture that recognizes and cultivates a state of sufficiency; it turns into demeaning 'poverty' only when pressurized by an accumulating society.

Destitution, on the other hand, becomes rampant as soon as frugality is deprived of its foundation. Along with community ties, land, forest and water are the most important prerequisites for subsistence without money. As soon as they are taken away or destroyed, destitution lurks. Again and again, peasants, nomads and tribals have fallen into misery after being driven from their land, savannas and forests. Indeed the first state policies on poverty, in sixteenth-century Europe, were a response to the sudden appearance of vagabonds and mendicancy provoked by enclosures of the land; it had traditionally been the task of communities to provide for widows and orphans, the classical cases of unmaintained poor people. Scarcity derives from modernized poverty. It affects mostly urban groups caught up in the money economy as workers and consumers whose spending power is so low that they fall by the wayside. Not only does their predicament make them vulnerable to the whims of the market, but they also live in a situation where money assumes an ever-increasing importance. Their capacity to achieve through their own efforts gradually fades, while at the same time their desires, fuelled by glimpses of high society, spiral towards infinity; this scissor-like effect of want is what characterizes modern poverty. Commodity-based poverty, still described as 'the social question' in the nineteenth century, led to the welfare state and its income and employment policy after the world economic crisis of 1929. Precisely this view of poverty, influenced by Keynes and the New Deal, shaped the development ideas of the post-war era.

More frugality, less destitution Up until the present day, development politicians have viewed 'poverty' as the problem and 'growth' as the solution. They have not yet admitted that they have been largely working with a concept of poverty fashioned by the experience of commodity-based need in the northern hemisphere. With the less well-off *homo economicus* in mind, they have encouraged growth and often produced destitution by bringing multifarious cultures of frugality to ruin. For the culture of growth can only be erected on the ruins of frugality, and so destitution and dependence on commodities are its price.

Is it not time after 40 years to draw an obvious conclusion? Whoever wishes to banish poverty must build on sufficiency; a cautious handling of growth is the most important way of fighting poverty. It seems my friend from Tepito knew of this when he refused to be labelled 'poor'. His honour was at stake, his pride too; he clung to his Tepito form of sufficiency, perhaps sensing that without it there loomed only destitution or never-ending scarcity of money.

Technology as a Trojan Horse

There are two entirely different principles that can shape a society's image of itself. Either a person-to-person or a person-to-things relationship predominates. In the first case, events are examined in the light of their significance with regard to neighbours or relatives, ancestors or gods; in the second, they are judged according to what they contribute to the acquisition and ownership of things. The modern epoch, whose thoughts and aspirations revolve mainly around property, production and distribution, devotes itself to the cult of things; the use of technology is thus its beatifying ritual.

It was not until after the Second World War, precisely in the 'age of development', that the Third World countries moved into focus within this world view: they were perceived for the first time from a material-centred viewpoint. Spurred on by the experience of societies investing all their physical and mental energies in the propagation of things, development strategists perused the world and, lo and behold, discovered an appalling lack of useful objects wherever they looked. However, what was of primary importance in many villages and communities – the tissue of relationships with neighbours, ancestors and gods – more or less melted into thin air under their gaze. The popular image of the Third World was one of have-nots desperately battling for mere survival; whatever constituted their strength, their honour or their hope remained out of sight.

Although such a definition fails to capture the realities of the lives of many people, it still provided the basis for programmes of global goodwill. A classic example of this occurred when John F. Kennedy called upon Congress in March 1961 to finance the 'Alliance for Progress'. 'Throughout Latin America,' he said, 'millions of people are struggling to free themselves from the bonds of poverty, hunger and ignorance.' In the wake of such an exposition, in material-centred terms, of the aspirations of people throughout Latin America – from traders on the Gulf of Mexico to cattle-farmers of the pampa – the strategic conclusion was self-evident. 'To the North and the East,' Kennedy continued, 'they see the abundance which modern science can bring. They know the tools of progress are within their reach.'

From Truman's pledge to provide scientific and technical aid, to the hopes of some countries in recent years to leapfrog the outdated industrial nations with the help of bio-techniques and information technology, the 'tools of progress' have been regarded as the guarantors of successful development. Indeed, if ever there was a single doctrine uniting North and South it was this: more technology is always better than less.

The popularity of this doctrine derives from the tragic fallacy that modern technologies possess the innocence of tools. Are they not basically comparable to a hammer that one can choose to pick up or not but that, when used, immensely increases the power of one's arms? Throughout all classes, nationalities and religions the consensus was for 'more technology' because technology was viewed as powerful but neutral, entirely at the service of the user. Modern technology seemed to be applicable to any cultural project. In reality, of course, a model of civilization follows hot on the heels of modern technology. Like the entry of the Trojan horse, the introduction of technology into the Third World paved the way for a conquest of society from within.

Not a tool but a system   Commercial artists love to represent modern technologies as the triumphant heirs of primitive techniques. The jungle drum is pictured as the precursor of intercontinental computer mail, the search for medicinal plants compared to the synthesis of antibiotics, or the striking of fire from flint revealed as an under-developed form of nuclear fission. Hardly any piece of fiction has contributed more to hiding the true nature of technical civilization than that of seeing in modern technology nothing more than a mere tool, even if a particularly advanced one.

Take the example of an electric mixer. Whirring and slightly vibrating, it mixes ingredients in next to no time. A wonderful tool! So it seems. But a quick look at cord and wall-socket reveals that what we have before us is rather the domestic terminal of a national, indeed worldwide, system: the electricity arrives via a network of cables and overhead utility lines fed by power stations that depend on water pressures, pipelines or tanker consignments, which in turn require dams, offshore platforms or derricks in distant deserts. The whole chain guarantees an adequate and prompt delivery only if every one of its parts is overseen by armies of engineers, planners and financial experts, who themselves can fall back on administrations, universities, indeed entire industries (and sometimes even the military).

As with a car, a pill, a computer or a television, the electric mixer is dependent on the existence of sprawling, interconnected systems of organization and production. Someone who flicks a switch is not using a tool. They are plugging into a combine of running systems. Between the use of simple techniques and the use of modern equipment lies the reorganization of a whole society.

However innocent they appear to be, the products of the modern world function only as long as large parts of society behave according to plan. This entails the suppression of both individual will and chance, apart from odd remnants of spontaneity. After all, the aforementioned mixer would not make one revolution were it not assured that, in the whole system chain, everything happens at the right time and place and is of the right quality. Coordination and scheduling, training and discipline, not just energy, are the elixir of life for these exceedingly compliant devices. They appear helpful and labour-saving, yet call for the predictable performance of many people in distant places; the tools function only if people themselves turn into tools.

But, especially in developing countries, things often don't work that way. In almost any developing country you can find unused equipment, rusting machinery and factories working at half their capacity – for the 'technical development' of a country demands putting into effect that multitude of requirements that have to be fulfilled to set the interconnected systems whirring. And this generally amounts to taking apart traditional society step by step in order to reassemble it according to functional requirements. No society can stay the same; there can be no mixers without remodelling the whole. It is not astonishing, in view of this Herculean task, that the development debate has incessantly repeated the phrase 'comprehensive planning instead of piecemeal solutions' since the early 1960s.

Not a tool but a world view   Any technical device is much more than an aid: it is culturally potent. The overwhelming effects of its power dissolve not only physical resistance but also attitudes to life. Technologies shape feelings and fashion world views; the traces they leave in the mind are probably more difficult to erase than the traces they leave in the landscapes.

Who has not experienced the thrill of acceleration at the wheel of a car? A slight movement of the ball of the foot suffices to unleash powers exceeding those of the driver many times over. This incongruity between gentle effort and powerful effect, typical of modern technology, gives rise to the exhilarating feelings of power and freedom that accompany the triumphant forward march of technology. Be it a car or plane, telephone or computer, the specific power of modern technology lies in its ability to remove limitations imposed on us by our bodies, by space and by time.

There is more to it, though, than the shaping of feelings. Something new becomes real: it is probably no exaggeration to say that the deep structures of perception are changing with the massive invasion of technology. A few key words probably suffice: nature is viewed in mechanical terms, space is seen as geometrically homogeneous and time as linear. In short, human beings are not the same as they used to be – and they feel increasingly unable to treat technologies like tools that leave the user unaffected.

Through the transfer of technology, generations of development strategists have worked hard to get Southern countries moving. Economically they have had mixed results, yet culturally – quite involuntarily – they have been a resounding success. The flood of machines that has poured into many regions may or may not have been beneficial, but it has certainly washed away traditional aspirations and ideals. Their place has been taken by aspirations and ideals ordered on the coordinates of technological civilization – not only for the limited number who benefit from it, but also for the far larger number who watch its fireworks from the sidelines.

Fragile magic   As everyone knows, magic consists in achieving extraordinary effects through the manipulation of powers that are not of this world. Cause and effect belong to two different spheres; in magic, the sphere of the visible is fused with the sphere of the invisible. Anyone who puts their foot down on an accelerator or pulls a lever also commands a remote, invisible world in order to bring about an event in the immediate, visible everyday world. All of a sudden, incredible power or speed become available, whose actual causes lie hidden far beyond the horizon of direct experience.

In this separation of effect and cause, in this invisibility of the systems that pervade the society and produce technical miracles, lies the reason for the magic technology that, especially in the Third World, holds so many people spellbound. The power of the car excites the driver precisely because its prerequisites (pipelines, streets, assembly lines) and its consequences (noise, air pollution, greenhouse effect) remain far beyond the view from behind the windscreen. The glamour of the moment is based upon a gigantic transfer of its cost: time, effort and the handling of consequences are shifted onto the systems running in the background of society. So the appeal of technical civilization often depends on an optical illusion.

The 40 years of development have created a paradoxical situation.

Today the magic 'tools of progress' dominate the imagination in many countries, but the construction of the underpinning systems has got stuck and, indeed, may never be completed in view of the shortage of resources and the environmental crisis. It is this rift between the newly acquired ideal and the reality lagging behind that will shape the future of developing countries. There was no way to shove the Greeks back into the wooden horse after they had appeared right inside Troy.

The Economist's Blind Eye

'Should India ever resolve to imitate England, it will be the ruin of the nation.' In 1909, while still in South Africa, Mohandas Gandhi formulated the conviction upon which he then, over a period of 40 years, fought for the independence of India. Although he won the fight, the cause was lost: no sooner was independence achieved than his principle fell into oblivion. Gandhi wanted to drive the British out of the country in order to allow India to become more Indian; Nehru, on the other hand, saw independence as the opportunity to make India more Western. An assassin's bullet prevented the controversy between the two heroes of the nation from coming into the open, but the decade-long correspondence between them clearly demonstrates the issues.

Gandhi was not won over to technical civilization with its machines, engines and factories because he saw in it a culture that knew no more sublime end than that of minimizing bodily effort and maximizing physical well-being. He could only shrug his shoulders at such an obsession with gaining comfort; as if a good life could be built on that! Didn't India's tradition, undisturbed for thousands of years, have more substantial things to offer? Although far from being a traditionalist on many issues, Gandhi insisted on a society that, in accordance with Hindu tradition, gave priority to a spiritual way of life. An English style of industrialism is out of place if *swaraj*, the calm freedom to follow personal truth, is to rule. Gandhi pleaded for a renewal of countless villages of India and for a form of progress to be judged accordingly. In his eyes, India was committed to an idea of the good and proper life that contradicted the ideals prevalent in England during the age of automation. For this reason, a wholesale imitation of the West was simply out of question. Individual elements should, in his mind, be adopted only if they could help give better expression to India's aspirations.

Nehru disagreed. He saw no alternative but to introduce the young nation to the achievements of the West as soon as possible and to take the road towards an economic civilization. Even in the early days, and in spite of his great admiration for the man, he found Gandhi 'completely unreal' in his vision. Although he intended to avoid the excesses of capitalism, he still envisaged Indian society defining itself in terms of its performance in providing goods.

From an economic viewpoint, however, the nature of humanity, the function of politics and the character of social reform all assume a particular meaning. People are seen as living in a permanent situation of scarcity, since they always have less than they desire. The most noble task of politics is therefore to create the conditions for material wealth, and this in turn requires the reorganization of society from a host of locally based subsistence communities into a nationwide economy.

Nehru thus fostered precisely the Western self-delusion that was also at the core of the development idea: that the essential reality of a society consists in nothing else than its functional achievements; the rest is just folklore or private affairs. From this viewpoint the economy overshadows every other reality; the laws of economy dominate society and not the rules of society the economy. This is why, whenever development strategists set their sights on a country, they see not a society that has an economy, but a society that *is* an economy. Taking this conquest of society by the economy for granted is a burden inherited from nineteenth-century Europe that has been passed on to the rest of the world over the last 40 years.

When production is not God Observing a group of Maya Indians who work their fields in the mountains around Quiche in Guatemala, and seeing the barren ground, the primitive tools and scanty yield, one might easily come to the conclusion that nothing in the world is more important to them than increasing productivity. Remedies could swiftly be found: better crop rotation, improved seeds, small machines, privatization, and anything else the cookbook of management might recommend.

All this is not necessarily wrong, but the economic viewpoint is notoriously colour-blind: it recognizes the cost–yield relation with extreme clarity, but is hardly able to perceive other dimensions of reality. For example, economists have difficulty in recognizing that the land bestows identity upon the Maya since it represents the bridge to their ancestors. Similarly, economists often fail to note the central importance of collective forms of labour, in which the village community finds visible expression. The outlook of the Maya is incompatible with that of the economists: for them, land and work are not mere factors of production waiting to be optimally combined.

To put this in the form of a paradox: not everything that looks like an economic activity is necessarily a part of economics. Indeed, economics offers only one of the many ways of looking at goods-oriented activities and putting them in a larger context. In every society things are produced, distributed and consumed, but only in modernized Westernized societies are prices and products, and conditions of ownership and work, predominantly shaped by the laws of economic efficiency. Elsewhere different rules are valid, other models prevail (Gudeman 1986).

The Bemba in Zambia, for example, see a good harvest or a successful hunting expedition as a gift from their ancestors; they court the ancestors' favour in the hope of higher production. Even the haggling and chaotic hustle and bustle in the souks of an Arab medina have nothing to do with undercutting the competition. Who pursues which of the many trades is determined by factors of social and geographical origin as well as by one's religious allegiance. Then there are the cycles of cultivation practised by the farmers in Maharashtra, which neatly fit into the yearly round of weddings, festivals and pilgrimages. New methods of cultivation can soon disrupt this social calendar.

In societies that are not built on the compulsion to amass material wealth, economic activity is also not geared to slick, zippy output. Rather, economic activities like choosing an occupation, cultivating the land, or exchanging goods are understood as ways of enacting that particular social drama in which the members of the community happen to see themselves as the actors. That drama's story largely defines what belongs to whom, who produces what and how it is exchanged. The 'economy' is closely bound up with life but it does not stamp its rules and rhythms on the rest of society. Only in the West does the economy dictate the drama and everyone's role in it.

An invention in the West   As late as 1744, *Zedler's Universal Encyclopaedia* unwittingly gave a naive definition of the term 'market': 'that spacious public place, surrounded by ornate buildings or enclosed by stands, where, at certain times, all kinds of victuals and other wares are offered for sale; hence the same place is also called market place'. The market, heralded both as blessing and as bane over the last two centuries, this powerful idea – nothing more than a location! The author of the *Encyclopaedia* seemed to be thinking only of crowds, stands and baskets. There is no mention of 'market shares', 'price fluctuations' or 'equilibrium'. Between then and now a far-reaching change has taken place in the self-image of society.

Adam Smith was the first thinker who, when using the term 'market', no longer envisaged a locally determinable outlet for goods, but that society-wide space throughout which all prices intercommunicate. This innovation was no accident, but mirrored a new social reality: an economy of national scope. Before then, a domestic market was not something to be taken for granted; even in Europe at the end of seventeenth century, there was hardly any trade between different regions of the same country. Of course from time immemorial there has been trade – one need only think of the North German Hanseatic League or the splendour of Venice – but this was trade with distant countries, which remained limited to a few cities as bridgeheads. History knows markets in all shapes and sizes, but they were local and temporary places of exchange between towns and the surrounding countryside (Polanyi 1977).

In Adam Smith's century, however, the nation-state drew a web of trade relations over the whole of society and established the domestic market. Like today's developing countries, the young states of that time pushed hard to make economic principles prevail everywhere, be it only to finance their own existence. That was the birth of the national economy, even on a lexical level – while the term 'economy' had formerly been applied to the 'domestic economy' of the prince, now the whole nation was transformed into a 'political economy'. And Smith became the theoretician of a society governed by the rules of the market.

Alternatives to the economy? The transformation of society into a political economy was, of course, achieved only after a prolonged struggle demanding many sacrifices. After all, people were not shaped by a commercial ethos: it did not influence how they regarded work or property, their idea of good conduct or their sense of time. The merchant was not yet an entrepreneur, land was not saleable, competition was frowned upon, usury was disreputable, and those who worked for wages lived on the fringes of society. As a result, the progress of capitalism was punctuated by bitter disputes about whether and to what extent land and forest, grain and money, and workers themselves, could be treated as commodities.

In the last decades, similar radical changes have taken place in large parts of the Third World as the economic ideology has tightened its grip. Traditions of sufficiency have been pushed aside, local exchange relations dissolved, collective forms of ownership broken up, and subsistence economies wiped out. For a long time the guiding light of international development policy was to create societies of paid workers and consumers everywhere. Experts scrutinized countries to identify 'obstacles to development' that were hampering the free mobility of 'production factors'. No cost was too high and few sacrifices were too great in the quest to turn societies into smoothly running political economies.

Without any doubt, miracles were thus wrought, and a great tide swept through the countries of the southern hemisphere. History had taken an enormous leap. However, it is becoming ever clearer that disaster is in the offing. At the very moment the economy has finally achieved worldwide dominion, social disruptions and environmental destructions have become rampant. The dominance of the economy is showing its menacing side. Societies find themselves cornered: they cannot afford to surrender to this monster, but they cannot escape from it either. In fact the economy, during its rise to the top, has stamped out alternatives that are not so hazardous for both humans and nature.

How is it possible to reinvent economic institutions that allow people to live gracefully without making them prisoners of the pernicious drive to accumulate? Maybe there will be more creative power in the Third World to meet this historical challenge, simply because, in spite of everything, many people there still remember a way of life in which economic performance was not paramount.

From 'Development' to 'Security'

The Greek philosopher Heraclitus provides two quotations that are apt here. 'All things flow: nothing abides' was the formula he used to describe the continuous coming and going of existence. However, as history does not always flow slowly and quietly, but sometimes surges forward impetuously, Heraclitus coined another phrase: 'War is the mother of all things.'

Heraclitus was referring to the clash between opposites in general, but there is considerable truth in the meaning that people generally give it: wars very often accelerate history, precipitate events and create new perspectives. My opinion is that the Gulf War of 1991 marked the final curtain on the era in which the relationships between North and South could be considered in terms of 'development'. In its place, a new era is dawning in which relationships with the Third World will be dominated by the concept of 'security'.

From the common road to global apartheid The Gulf War made clear one essential fact: a terrifying technological divide today, more than ever, separates the richer countries from all the others. This is a divide that expresses itself in macabre statistics: 115 American soldiers lost their lives as opposed to 100,000 Iraqis, a 1:1000 ratio that must be unique in the history of war. In spite of the efforts Iraq made to arm itself to the teeth, its army was wiped out because, technologically, it had remained at the level of the 1970s. The defeat of Saddam Hussein, however desirable it might have been, became the symbol of the speed of innovation in the First World and of the powerlessness of the Third.

It is no longer possible to deny it: the idea that all the countries in the world were marching along a common road was but a post-Second World War illusion. It is no longer possible to say that everyone is moving in an interdependent economic space. On the contrary, the international super economy of the North and the poor economies in the South appear to be separated by a wall.

Much time has passed since, as in the Brandt Report of 1980, the North was considered the South's engine of growth. It is still longer since the North was dependent on raw materials, agricultural commodities and cheap labour – all things that a highly technologized economy can substitute with increasing ease. The North no longer needs the South: it can prosper on the exclusion of the rest of the world. To quote Alvin Toffler, the world is divided no longer between capitalism and communism, but between fast economies and slow economies. In the wake of the Gulf War it has become obvious that the nations of the world are not at different points on the same road, as the image of 'development' implies, but are separated in a situation of planetary apartheid.

From developing countries to risk zones The way the peoples of the South are perceived is changing as a result. For Truman, Third World societies were indeed poor, but also full of potential. They were 'young' and 'emerging' nations, whose future was to shine more splendidly than their present. Such optimism is implicit in the very idea of development: where should the road of progress lead, if not to the promised land?

In a situation of world apartheid, this concept collapses. No one speaks any more of a radiant tomorrow; the future appears grim and the South is seen as the breeding ground of all crises. In a world divided, the countries of the South are looked at no longer with hope but with suspicion. In the cynical eye of the privileged, development aid is done for and the job at hand is to keep a latent explosive force under control. The Gulf War made it clear, once and for all, that Third World countries are now risk zones. All kinds of dangers are to be found there, as the newspapers and television keep telling us: violence keeps exploding, the mafia is in command, epidemics are spreading, deserts are advancing, ideologies are rampant, and everywhere the demographic bomb is looming. And even the stronghold of the North is not immune from the threat of immigration, the greenhouse effect, drug traffic, terrorism and war: the 'one world' is discovering the boomerang effect of degradation. The more the threatening dangers strike fear into people's minds, the more the image of 'The Other' takes on a different colouring. During the centuries it has been identified with the pagan, then with the savage, then with the indigenous and finally with the poor, who today embody the 'risk factor'.

From aid for progress to aid for prevention   In these circumstances, the 'development' concept loses its reassuring connotations for the future: slowly it is being substituted by the concept of 'security' – from the North's viewpoint, naturally. There are already many development projects that have little to do with taking a country along the road to progress and simply content themselves with trying to prevent the worst on a once-only basis. Once, the order of the day was to 'catch up' with the North. Now the aim must be to avoid being engulfed by disaster and to engage in 'security for survival'.

At the international level, too, the change of theme has been under way for some time. Whereas, in the past, the discussion at conferences was about how to give the South more opportunities to enter into the world's economic growth, today conferences analyse how to keep the excesses of such growth under control. Governments are concerned about the signs of weakness in the biosphere – pollution of the seas, the ozone hole, global warming. Who should eliminate emissions, and how much, and in what timespan? Who can claim what compensation? The focus of international negotiations has changed: the division of wealth has been replaced on the agenda by the division of risks.

From hegemony for the sake of prosperity to hegemony for the sake of stability   Amidst all this, the way in which the North perceives itself has had to change too. Truman was proud to consider US dominance not from a colonial viewpoint, as the trustee of peoples who are still under age, but rather in terms of the economic prosperity of the whole world. It was in line with this that institutions for 'aid' and 'cooperation' were set up. Little has remained of all this under planetary apartheid: today, for reasons of self-defence, the North must stop itself being pulled down by the collapse of the South. From now on, the North will claim that it is obliged to dominate so as to protect the stability of the world system.

On 1 April 1991 *Time* magazine dedicated its front cover to fears about security, showing a uniformed body wearing a sheriff's badge marked 'Global Cop'. The new attitude has its military expression in the present planning of a multinational intervention force. Whether this belongs to the Western European Union, NATO or the UN is of secondary importance. What is under way is an epoch-making re-orientation of the military apparatus towards war of low and medium intensity in the South (and in the East, which is slowly slipping towards the South).

In a more charity-orientated variation, troops are being sent to relieve people who are struck by natural disasters, as in Bangladesh and Kurdistan, while one is beginning to hear talk of 'green helmets' who will intervene in the case of ecological disasters. And people are talking about the planetary environmental crisis in terms of 'ecological security'. Ecology, once the rallying cry for new public virtues, has become a problem of security policy. Satellites are launched that keep an eye on far-away countries – veritable environmental spies.

Global security is beginning to justify anything, just as it united the international community against the dictator of Baghdad. Rich countries are now increasing their diplomatic, charity and military instruments for risk prevention. But where there is no justice, there cannot be peace. Security has replaced development as the global guiding light – another tragic consequence of the continuing arrogance of power.

II

The Shaky Ground of Sustainability

2

Global Ecology and the Shadow of 'Development'

The walls in the Tokyo subway used to be plastered with advertising posters. The authorities, aware of Japan's shortage of wood-pulp, searched for ways to reduce this wastage of paper. They quickly found an 'environmental solution': they mounted video screens on the walls and these now continuously bombard passengers with commercials – paper problem solved.

This anecdote exemplifies an approach to the environmental crisis that was also very much on the minds of the delegates who in 1992 descended upon Rio de Janeiro for the 'Earth Summit' (the UN Conference on Environment and Development) to reconcile 'environment' and 'development'. To put the outcome of UNCED in a nutshell: the governments at Rio came round to recognizing the declining state of the environment, but insisted on the relaunching of development. Indeed, most controversies arose from some party or another's heated defence of its 'right to development'; in that respect, Malaysia's resistance to the Forest Statement or Saudi Arabia's attempt to sabotage the Climate Convention trailed not far behind President Bush's cutting remark that the lifestyle of the USA would not be up for discussion at Rio. It is probably no exaggeration to say that the rain-dance around 'development' kept the conflicting parties together and offered a common ritual that comforted them for any sacrifice made in favour of the environment. At the end, the Rio Declaration ceremoniously emphasized the sacredness of 'development' and invoked its significance throughout the document wherever possible. Only after 'the right to development' has been enshrined does the document proceed to consider 'tine developmental and environmental needs of present and future generations' (Principle 3). In fact, the conference inaugurated environmentalism as the highest state of developmentalism.

Reaffirming the centrality of 'development' in the international

27

discussion on the environment surely helps to secure the collaboration of the dominating actors in government, economy and science, but it prevents the rupture required to head off the multifaceted dangers to the future of humankind. It locks the perception of the ecological predicament into the very world view that stimulates the pernicious dynamics, and hands the action over to those social forces – governments, agencies and corporations – that have largely been responsible for the present state of affairs. This may turn out to be self-defeating. After all, the development discourse is deeply imbued with Western certainties like progress, growth, market integration, consumption and universal needs, all notions that are part of the problem, not of the solution. They cannot but distract attention from the urgency of public debate on our relationship with nature, for they preclude the search for societies that live graciously within their means, and for social changes that take their inspiration from indigenous ideas of the good and proper life. The incapacity to bid farewell to some of the certainties that have shaped the development era was the major shortcoming of Rio. The great divide between development enthusiasts and development dissenters will be at the root of future conflicts about global ecology.

Truman and What Followed

Epochs rise slowly, but the development era opened at a certain date and hour. On 20 January 1949, it was President Harry Truman who, in his inauguration speech before Congress, drawing the attention of his audience to conditions in poorer countries, for the first time defined them as 'underdeveloped areas'.[1] Suddenly, a seemingly indelible concept was established, cramming the immeasurable diversity of the South into one single category – the underdeveloped. That Truman coined a new term was not a matter of accident but the precise expression of a world view: for him all the peoples of the world were moving along the same track, some faster, some slower, but all in the same direction. The Northern countries, in particular the USA, were running ahead, while he saw the rest of the world – with its absurdly low per capita income – lagging far behind. An image that the economic societies of the North had increasingly acquired about themselves was thus projected onto the rest of the world: the degree of civilization in a country is to be indicated by the level of its production. Starting from that premise, Truman conceived of the world as an economic arena where nations compete for a better position on the GNP scale. No matter what ideals inspired Kikuyus, Peruvians or Filipinos, Truman recognized them only as stragglers whose historical task was to participate in the development race and catch up with the lead runners. Consequently, it was the objective of development policy to bring all nations into the arena and enable them to run in the race.

Turning the South's societies into economic competitors required not only the injection of capital and transfer of technology, but a cultural transformation, for many 'old ways' of living turned out to be 'obstacles to development'. The ideals and mental habits, patterns of work and modes of knowing, webs of loyalties and rules of governance in which the South's people were steeped were usually at odds with the ethos of an economic society. In the attempt to overcome these barriers to growth, the traditional social fabric was often dissected and re-assembled according to the textbook models of macro-economics. To be sure, 'development' had many effects, but one of its most insidious was the dissolution of cultures that were not built around a frenzy of accumulation. The South was thus precipitated into a transformation that had long been going on in the North: the gradual subordination of ever more aspects of social life under the rule of the economy. In fact, whenever development experts set their sights on a country, they fell victim to a particular myopia: rather than a society that *had* an economy, they saw a society that *was* an economy. As a result, they ended up revamping all kinds of institutions, such as work, schools or the law, in the service of productivity, degrading the indigenous style of doing things in the process. But the shift to a predominantly economic society involves a considerable cost: it undermines a society's capacity to secure well-being without joining unconditionally the economic race. The fact that the unfettered hegemony of Western productivism has made it more and more impossible to take exit roads from the global racetrack dangerously limits the space of manoeuvre for countries in times of uncertainty. Also in that respect, the countries of the North provide an ambiguous example. they have been so highly trained in productivism that they are incapable of doing anything but running the economic race.

After 40 years of development, the state of affairs is dismal. The gap between front-runners and stragglers has not been bridged – on the contrary, it has widened to the extent that it has become inconceivable that it could ever be closed. The aspiration of catching up has ended in a blunder of planetary proportions. The figures speak for themselves: during the 1980s, the contribution of developing countries (where two-thirds of humanity live) to the world's GNP shrank to 15 per cent, while the share of the industrial countries, with 20 per cent of the world population, rose to 80 per cent. Admittedly, closer examination reveals that the picture is far from homogeneous, but neither the South-East Asian showcases nor the oil-producing countries change the result that the development race has ended in disarray. The truth of this is more sharply highlighted if the destiny of large majorities of people within most Southern countries is considered: they live today in greater hardship and misery than at the time of decolonialization. The best one can say is that development has created a global middle class of individuals with cars, bank accounts, and career aspirations. It is made up of the majority in the North and small elites in the South, and its size roughly equals that 8 per cent of the world population that owns a car. The internal rivalries of that class make a lot of noise in world politics, condemning to silence the overwhelming majority of the people. At the end of development, the question of justice looms larger than ever.

A second result of the development era has come dramatically to the fore in recent years: it has become evident that the race-track leads in the wrong direction. While Truman could still take for granted that the North was at the head of social evolution, this premise of superiority has today been fully and finally shattered by the ecological predicament. For instance, much of the glorious rise in productivity is fuelled by a gigantic throughput of fossil energy, which requires mining the earth on one side and covering it with waste on the other. By now, however, the global economy has outgrown the earth's capacity to serve as mine and dumping ground. After all, the world economy increases every two years by about the size ($60 billion) it had reached by 1900, after centuries of growth. Although only a small part of the world has experienced large-scale economic expansion, the world economy already weighs down nature to an extent that it has in part to give in. If all countries followed the industrial example, five or six planets would be needed to serve as 'sources' for the inputs and 'sinks' for the waste of economic progress. Therefore, a situation has emerged where the certainty that ruled two centuries of growth economy has been exposed as a falsehood: growth is by no means open-ended. Economic expansion has already come up against its bio-physical limits; recognizing the earth's finiteness is a fatal blow to the idea of development as envisaged by Truman.

Ambiguous Claims for Justice

The UNCED process unfolded against this background of 40 years of post-war history. Any consideration of global ecology has to respond to both the crisis of justice and the crisis of nature. While the Northern countries' main concern was about nature, the South, in the run-up to the conference, managed to highlight the question of justice. In fact, during the debates leading up to UNCED, attentive spectators wondered if they had not seen it all before. Slogans that had animated the 1970s discussions on the 'New International Economic Order' kept creeping back to the forefront. Suddenly, calls for better terms of trade, debt relief, entry to Northern markets, technology transfer and aid, aid, and more aid drowned the environmentalist discussion. Indeed, it was difficult to overlook the regressive tendencies in the controversy that opened up. The South, deeply hurt by the breakdown of development illusions, launched demands for further rounds of development. Already, in the June 1991 Beijing Declaration of the Group of 77, the point was made clearly and bluntly:

> Environmental problems cannot be dealt with separately, they must be linked to the development process, bringing the environmental concerns in line with the imperatives of economic growth and development. In this context, the right to development for the developing countries must be fully recognized.[2]

After the South's years of uneasiness in dealing with the environmental concerns raised by the North, the plot for Rio had finally thickened. Since the North expects environmentally good behaviour worldwide, the South, grasping this opportunity, discovered environmental concessions as diplomatic weapons. Consequently, the South reiterated the unfulfilled demands of the 1970s and opposed them to the North's ecological impositions.

If matters look bad with respect to the environment, according to Southern countries they look worse with respect to development. It was along these lines that they succeeded, after the 'lost decade' of the 1980s, in putting the North–South division squarely back on the international agenda. The spotlight was thus largely focused on the North's willingness to come up with $125 billion of yearly assistance, to fulfil its long overdue promise of allocating 0.7 per cent of its GNP to development aid, and to provide clean technologies or access to bio-industrial patents. On the diplomatic level this was hardly surprising, since most of the Third World, trapped by the failure of the politics of catching up, fears that the world will eternally be split between the North's super-economy and the South's wretched economies. But on a deeper level, the continuing commitment to run the development race leaves the Southern countries in an untenable position. In fact, the Rio documents make clear that the South has no intention of abandoning the Northern model of living as its implicit Utopia. In using the language of development, the South continues to subscribe to the notion that the North shows the way for the rest of the world. As a consequence, however, the South is incapable of escaping the North's cultural hegemony, for development without hegemony is like a race without a direction. Apart from all the economic pressures, adherence to 'development' puts the South, culturally and politically, in a position of structural weakness, leading to the absurd situation in which the North can present itself as the benevolent provider of solutions to the ecological crisis.

Needless to say, this plays into the hands of the Northern countries. With the blessing of 'development', the growth fatalists in the North are implicitly justified in rushing ahead on the economic race-track. The cultural helplessness of the industrial countries in responding adequately to the ecological predicament thus turns into a necessary virtue. After all, the main concern of the Northern elites is to get ahead in the competitive struggle between the USA, Europe and Japan, achieving an ecological modernization of their economies along the way. They are light-years away from the insight that peace with nature eventually requires peace in economic warfare; consequently, a country such as Germany, for instance, manages to pose as a shining example of environmentalism, while pushing ahead with such ecologically disastrous free-trade policies as the European common market and the reform of GATT. The fact that 'development', that race without a finishing line, remains uncontested allows the North to continue the relentless pursuit of overdevelopment and economic power, since the idea of societies that settle for their already accomplished stage of technical capacity becomes unthinkable. Indeed, such matters as limits to road-building, to high-speed transport, to economic concentration, to the production of chemicals, to large-scale cattle-ranching, and so on, were not even pondered in Rio.

The unholy alliance between development enthusiasts in the South and growth fatalists in the North, however, works not only against the environment but also against greater justice in the world. In most countries, while development has benefited rather small minorities, it has done so at the expense of large parts of the population. During the development era, growth was expected to abolish poverty. Instead, it led to social polarization. In many cases, communities that guaranteed sustenance have been torn apart in the attempt to build a modern economy. Southern elites, however, often justify their pursuit of development by ritual reference to the persistence of poverty, cultivating the worn-out dogma that growth is the recipe against poverty. Locked into their interests of power and fixed on the lifestyle of the affluent, they fend off the insight that securing livelihoods requires a careful handling of growth. Yet the lesson to be drawn from 40 years of development can be stated bluntly: the issue of justice must be delinked from the perspective of 'development'. In fact, both ecology and poverty call for limits to development. Without such a change in perspective, the struggle for redistribution of power and resources between North and South, which is inevitably renewed in facing environmental constraints, can be only what it was in the 1970s: a quarrel within the global middle class on how to divide the cake.

Earth's Finiteness as a Management Problem

'Development' is, above all, a way of thinking. It cannot, therefore, be easily identified with a particular strategy or programme, but ties many different practices and aspirations to a common set of assumptions. Whatever the theme on the agenda in the post-war era, the assumptions of 'development' – like the universal road, the superiority of economics, the mechanical feasibility of change – tacitly shaped the definition of the problem, highlighted certain solutions and consigned others to oblivion. Moreover, as knowledge is intimately related to power, development thinking inevitably featured certain social actors (for example, international agencies) and certain types of social transformation (for example, technology transfer), while marginalizing other social actors and degrading other kinds of change.[3]

Despite alarming signs of failure throughout its history, the development idea has survived. When it became clear in the 1950s that investments were not enough, 'manpower development' was added to the aid package; as it became obvious in the 1960s that hardship continued, 'social development' was discovered; and in the 1990s, as the impoverishment of peasants could no longer be overlooked, 'rural development' was included in the arsenal of development strategies. And so it went on, with further creations like 'equitable development' and the 'basic needs approach'. Again and again, the same conceptual operation was repeated: degradation in the wake of development was redefined as a lack that called for yet another strategy of development. All along, the myth of the efficacy of 'development' remained impervious to any counter-evidence, but the concept showed remarkable staying power: it was repeatedly stretched until it included both the strategy that inflicted the injury and the strategy designed for therapy. This strength of the concept, however, is also the reason for its galloping exhaustion; it no longer manifests any reactions to changing historical conditions. The tragic greatness of 'development' consists in its monumental emptiness.

'Sustainable development', which UNCED enthroned as the reigning slogan of the 1990s, has inherited the fragility of 'development'. The concept emasculates the environmental challenge by absorbing it into the empty shell of 'development', and insinuates the continuing validity of developmentalist assumptions even when confronted with a drastically different historical situation. In Rachel Carson's *Silent Spring*, the book that gave rise to the environmental movement in 1962, development was understood to inflict injuries on people and nature. Since the 'World Conservation Strategy' in 1980 and later the Brundtland Report (WCED 1987), development has come to be seen as the therapy for the injuries caused by development. What accounts for this shift?

First, in the 1970s, under the impact of the oil crisis, governments began to realize that continued growth depended not only on capital formation or skilled manpower, but also on the long-term availability of natural resources. Foods for the insatiable growth machine – oil, timber, minerals, soils, genetic material – seemed on the decline and concern grew about the prospects of long-term growth. This was a decisive change in perspective: not the health of nature but the continuous health of development became the centre of concern. In 1992, the World Bank summed up the new consensus in a laconic phrase: 'What is sustainable? Sustainable development is development that lasts.'[4] Of course, the task of development experts does not remain the same under this imperative, because the horizon of their decisions is now supposed to extend in time, taking into account also the welfare of future generations. But the frame stays the same: 'sustainable development' calls for the conservation of development, not for the conservation of nature.

Even bearing in mind a very loose definition of development, the anthropocentric bias of the statement springs to mind: it is not the preservation of nature's dignity that is on the international agenda, but the extension of human-centred utilitarianism to posterity. Needless to say, the naturalist and bio-centric current of present-day environmentalism has been cut out by this conceptual operation. With 'development' back in the saddle, the view on nature changes. The question now becomes: which of nature's 'services' are to what extent indispensable for further development? Or the other way around: which 'services' of nature are dispensable or can be substituted by, for example, new materials or genetic engineering? In other words, nature turns into a variable, albeit a critical one, in sustaining development. It comes as no surprise, therefore, that 'nature capital' has already become a fashionable notion among ecological economists.[5]

Second, a new generation of post-industrial technologies suggested that growth was not invariably linked to the squandering of ever more resources, as in the time of smoke-stack economies, but could be pursued through less resource-intensive means. While in the past innovations were largely aimed at increased productivity of labour, it now appeared possible that technical and organizational intelligence could concentrate on increasing the productivity of nature. In short, growth could be delinked from a rising consumption of energy and materials. In the eyes of developmentalists, the 'limits to growth' called not for abandoning the race, but for changing the running technique. After 'no development without sustainability' had spread, 'no sustainability without development' also gained recognition.

Third, environmental degradation has been discovered to be a worldwide condition of poverty. While formerly the developmentalist image of the 'poor' was characterized by lack of water, housing, health and money, they are now seen to be suffering from lack of nature as well. Poverty is now exemplified by people who search desperately for firewood, find themselves trapped by encroaching deserts, are driven from their soils and forests, or are forced to endure dreadful sanitary conditions. Once the lack of nature is identified as a cause of poverty, it follows neatly that development agencies, since they are in the business of 'eliminating poverty', have to diversify into programmes for the environment. But people who are dependent on nature for their survival have no choice other than to pursue the last remaining fragments of its bounty. As the decline of nature is also a consequence of poverty, the poor of the world suddenly entered the stage as agents of environmental destruction. Whereas in the 1970s the main threat to nature still appeared to be industrial man, in the 1980s environmentalists turned their eyes to the Third World and pointed to the vanishing forests, soils and animals there. With the shifting focus, environmentalism took on, in part, a different colour: the crisis of the environment is no longer perceived as the result of building affluence for the global middle class in both North and South, but is seen as the result of human presence on the globe in general. No matter if nature is consumed for luxury or survival, no matter if the powerful or the marginalized tap nature, it all becomes one for the rising tribe of ecocrats. And so it could be that, among other things, an 'Earth Summit' was called to reach decisions that should primarily have been the concern of the OECD – or even the G7.

The persistence of 'development', the newly found potentials for less resource-intensive growth paths, and the discovery of humanity in general as the enemy of nature – these notions were the conceptual ingredients for the type of thinking that received its diplomatic blessings at UNCED: the world is to be saved by more and better managerialism. The message, which is ritually repeated by the many politicians, industrialists and scientists who have recently decided to slip on a green coat, goes as follows: nothing should be (the dogmatic version) or can be (the fatalist version) done to change the direction the world's economies are taking; problems along the way can be solved, if the challenge for better and more sophisticated management is taken up. As a result, ecology, once a call for new public virtues, has now become a call for new executive skills. The UNCED document *Agenda 21*, for example, overflows with such formulae as 'integrated approach', 'rational use', 'sound management', 'internalizing costs', 'better information', 'increased coordination' and 'long-term prediction', but by and large fails (except for some timid phrases in the hotly debated chapter 'Changing Consumption Patterns') to consider any reduction of material standards of living and any attempts to slow down the accumulation dynamics. In short, alternatives to development are black-balled, alternatives within development are welcome.

Nevertheless, it was an achievement for UNCED to have delivered the call for environmental tools from a global rostrum, an opening that will give a boost to environmental engineering worldwide. But the price for this achievement is the reduction of environmentalism to managerialism, for the task of global ecology can be understood in two ways: it is either a technocratic effort to keep development afloat against the drift of plunder and pollution, or it is a cultural effort to shake off the hegemony of ageing Western values and gradually retire from the development race. These two ways may not be exclusive in detail, but they differ deeply in perspective. In the first case, the paramount task becomes the management of the bio-physical limits to development. All powers of foresight have to be mustered in order to steer development along the edge of the abyss, continuously surveying, testing, and manoeuvring the bio-physical limits. In the second case, the challenge consists in designing cultural/political limits to development. Each society is called upon to search for indigenous models of prosperity, which allow society's course to stay at a comfortable distance from the edge of the abyss, living graciously within a stable or shrinking volume of production. It is analogous to driving a vehicle at high speed towards a canyon – either you equip it with radar, monitors and highly trained personnel, correct its course and drive it as hard as possible along the rim, or you slow down, turn away from the edge and drive here and there without too much attention to precise controls. Too many global ecologists, implicitly or explicitly, favour the first choice.

Bargaining for the Rest of Nature

Until some decades ago, quite a few tracts of the biosphere remained untouched by the effects of economic growth. It is really over the last 30 years that the tentacles of productivism have closed on the last virgin areas, leaving no part of the biosphere untouched. More often than not, the human impact grows into a full-scale attack, tearing up the intricate webs of life. Since time immemorial humanity has defended itself against nature, and now nature must be defended against humanity. In particular danger are the 'global commons' – the Antarctic, ocean beds, tropical forests – with many species threatened by the voracious growth of demand for new inputs, while the earth's atmosphere is overburdened with the residues growth leaves behind. For that reason, the 1980s saw the rise of a global environmental consciousness, expressed by many voices, all deploring the threats to the earth's biosphere and the offence to the generations to come. The collective duty to preserve the 'common heritage of humankind' was invoked, and *Caring for the Earth*[6] became an imperative that agitated spirits worldwide. Respect for the integrity of nature independently of its value for humans, as well as a proper regard for the rights of humanity, demanded that the global commons be protected.

International environmental diplomacy, however, is about something else. The rhetoric that ornaments conferences and conventions ritually calls for a new global ethic, but the reality at the negotiating tables suggests a different logic. There, for the most part, one sees diplomats engaged in the familiar game of accumulating advantages for their countries, eager to out-manoeuvre their opponents, shrewdly tailoring environmental concerns to the interests dictated by their particular nation's economic position. Their parameters of action are bounded by the need to extend their nation's space for 'development'; in their hands environmental concerns turn into bargaining chips in the struggle of interests. In that respect, the thrust of UNCED's negotiations was no different from the thrust of previous negotiations about the Law of the Sea, the Antarctic, or the Montreal protocol on the reduction of CFCs. Forthcoming negotiations on climate, animal protection or biodiversity are unlikely to be any different.

The novelty of Rio, if there was one, lay not in commitments on the way to a collective stewardship of nature, but rather in international recognition of the scarcity of natural resources for development. The fragility of nature came into focus, because the services it offers as a 'source' and a 'sink' for economic growth have become inadequate; after centuries of availability, nature can no longer be counted upon as a silent collaborator in the process of 'technical civilization'. In other words, environmental diplomacy has recognized that nature is finite as a mine for resources and as a container for waste. Given that 'development' is intrinsically open-ended, the logic underlying international negotiations is pretty straightforward. First, limits are to be identified at a level that permits the maximum use of nature as mine and container, right up to the critical threshold beyond which ecological decline would rapidly accelerate. This is where scientists gain supremacy, since such limits can be identified only on the basis of 'scientific evidence'; endless quarrels about the state of knowledge are therefore part of the game. Once that hurdle has been overcome, the second step in the bargaining process is to define each country's proper share in the utilization of the 'source' or the 'sink' in question. Here diplomacy finds a new arena, and the old means of power, persuasion and bribery come in handy in order to maximize the share of one's own country. And finally, mechanisms have to be designed to secure all parties' compliance with the norms stated by the treaty, an effort that calls for international monitoring and enforcement institutions. Far from 'protecting the earth', environmental diplomacy that works within a developmentalist frame cannot but concentrate its efforts on rationing what is left of nature. To normalize, not eliminate, global overuse and pollution of nature will be its unintended effect.

Four major lines of conflict cut through the landscape of international environmental diplomacy, involving: rights to further exploitation of nature; rights to pollution; rights to compensation; and overall, conflict over responsibility. In the UNCED discussions on the Biodiversity Convention, for example, the rights to further exploitation of nature held centre stage. Who is entitled to have access to the world's dwindling genetic resources? Can nation-states exert their sovereignty over them, or are they to be regarded as 'global commons'? Who is allowed to profit from the use of genetic diversity? Countries rich in biomass but poor in industrial power were thus counterposed against countries rich in industrial power but poor in biomass. Similar issues arise with respect to tropical timber, to the mining of ocean beds, or to wild animals. Regarding the Climate Convention, on the other hand, diplomatic efforts were aimed at optimizing pollution rights over various periods of time. Oil-producing countries were not happy about any ceilings for CO_2 emissions, while small island states, understandably, hoped for the toughest limits possible. Moreover, the more economies are dependent on a cheap fuel base, the less the respective representatives were inclined to be strong on CO_2: the USA was in the forefront, followed by the large newly industrialized countries, while

Europe along with Japan could afford to urge stricter limits. In both cases, claims to compensation were voiced by an insistent chorus. How much compensation for retrospective development can the South demand? Who carries the losses incurred by a restrained exploitation of nature? Who should foot the bill for transferring clean technologies? Obviously, here the South was on the offensive, led by countries with potentially large middle classes, while the North found itself on the defensive. In all these matters, however, the conflict over responsibilities loomed large – again, the North was under pressure. After all, didn't the industrialized countries fell their own forests to feed development? Haven't they in the past used the entire world as the hinterland for their industrialization? With regard to greenhouse gases, is it appropriate or even justifiable to lump together methane emissions from India's rice fields with the CO_2 emissions from US car exhausts? In sum, a new class of conflicts has thrown into disarray the diplomatic routines: while in the 1970s, particularly, multilateral conferences focused on how to achieve a broader participation of the South in the growth of world economy, in the 1990s these conferences are dealing with how to control the pollution produced by this growth. As the bio-physical limits to development become visible, the tide of the post-war era turns: multilateral negotiations centre no longer on the redistribution of riches but on the redistribution of risks.[7]

Efficiency and Sufficiency

Twenty years ago, 'limits to growth' was the watchword of the environmental movement worldwide; today the buzzword of international ecology experts is 'global change'. The messages implied are clearly different.[8] 'Limits to growth' calls on *homo industrialis* to reconsider his project and to abide by nature's laws. 'Global change', however, puts humankind in the driver's seat and urges it to master nature's complexities with greater self-control. While the first formula sounds threatening, the second has an optimistic ring: it believes in a rebirth of *homo faber* and, on a more prosaic level, lends itself to the belief that the proven means of modern economy – product innovation, technological progress, market regulation, science-based planning – will show the way out of the ecological predicament.

The cure for all environmental ills is called 'efficiency revolution'. It focuses on reducing the throughput of energy and materials in the economic system by means of new technology and planning. Be it for the light-bulb or the car, for the design of power plants or transport systems, the aim is to come up with innovations that minimize the use of nature for each unit of output. Under this prescription, the economy will supposedly gain in fitness by keeping to a diet that eliminates the overweight in slag and dross. The efficiency scenario, however, seeks to make the circle square: it proposes a radical change through redirecting conventional means. It confronts modern society with the need to reduce drastically the utilization of nature as a mine for inputs and a deposit for waste, promising to reduce the physical scale of the economy. Conversely, it holds out the prospect of achieving this transformation through the application of economic intelligence, including new products, technologies and management techniques; in fact, this scenario proposes the extension of the modern economic imperative, that is, the optimization of the means–ends relationship,[9] from the calculation of money flows to the calculation of physical flows. 'More with less' is the motto for this new round in the old game. Optimizing input, not maximizing output, as in the post-war era, is the order of the day, and one already sees economists and engineers taking a renewed pleasure in their trade by puzzling out the minimum input for each unit of output. The hope that goes along with this strategic turnabout is again concisely stated by the World Bank: 'Efficiency reforms help reduce pollution while raising a country's economic outputs.'[10]

No doubt an efficiency revolution would have far-reaching effects. Since natural inputs were cheap and the deposition of waste mostly free of charge, economic development has for long been skewed towards squandering nature. Subsidies encouraged waste, technical progress was generally not designed to save on nature, and prices did not reflect environmental damages. There is a lot of space for correcting the course, and *Agenda 21*, for example, provides a number of signposts that indicate a new route. But the past course of economic history in the East, West and South – though with considerable variations – suggests that there is little room for efficiency strategies in earlier phases of growth, whereas they seem to work best, and are affordable, when applied after a certain level of growth has been attained. Since in the South the politics of selective growth would be a much more powerful way to limit the demand for resources, to transfer the 'efficiency revolution' there wholesale makes sense only if the South is expected to follow the North's path of development.

Even for the North scepticism is in order. Those who hail the rising information and service society as environment-friendly often overlook the fact that these sectors can grow only on top of the industrial sector and in close symbiosis with it. The size of the service sector in relation to production has its limits, just as its dependence on resources can be considerable for such sectors as tourism, hospitals or data-processing.[11] Even commodities without any nature content – for example patents, blueprints or money – derive their value from the command over a resource base they provide. More specifically, gains in environmental efficiency often consist in substituting high-tech for energy/materials, a process that presupposes the presence of a resource-intensive economy. In short, the efficiency potential that lies in well-tuned engines, bio-technological processes, recycling technologies or systems thinking is indigenous to the Northern economies. But the efficiency obviously plays into the North's hands: this way, they can again offer the South a new selection of tools for economic progress, at a price that will scarcely differ from that paid in the decades of technology transfer.

Environmentalists who refer exclusively to efficient resource management concentrate social imagination on the revision of means, rather than on the revision of goals. Their ingenuity lies in advocating a strategy that emphasizes what business has always been best at, and their strength is to propose a perspective that is far from putting the growth imperative into question. But the magic words 'resource efficiency' have a shady side, and staring at them for too long leads to blindness in one eye. Many environmentalists have already succumbed to this malady. In praising 'resource efficiency' alone, they obscure the fact that ecological reform must walk on two legs: scrutinizing means as well as moderating goals. This omission, however, backfires, and threatens the ecological project. An increase in resource efficiency alone leads to nothing, unless it goes hand-in-hand with an intelligent restraint of growth. Instead of asking how many supermarkets or how many bathrooms are enough, one focuses on how all these – and more – can be obtained with a lower input of resources. If, however, the dynamics of growth are not slowed down, the achievements of rationalization will soon be eaten up by the next round of growth. Consider the example of the fuel-efficient car. Today's vehicle engines are definitely more efficient than in the past, yet the relentless growth in number of cars and miles driven has cancelled out that gain. And the same logic holds across the board, from energy saving to pollution abatement and recycling, not to mention the fact that continuously staving off the destructive effects of growth in turn requires new growth. In fact, what really matters is the overall physical scale of the economy with respect to nature, not only the efficient allocation of resources. Herman Daly has offered a telling comparison: even if the cargo on a boat is distributed efficiently, the boat will inevitably sink under too much weight – even though it may sink optimally![12] Efficiency without sufficiency is counterproductive; the latter must define the boundaries of the former.

However, the rambling development creed impedes any serious public debate on the moderation of growth. Under its shadow, any society that decides, at least in some areas, not to go beyond certain levels of commodity-intensity, technical performance or speed appears to be backward. As a result, the consideration of zero-options – that is, choosing *not* to do something that is technically possible – is treated as a taboo in the official discussion on global ecology, even to the point of exposing some agreements to ridicule. Take, for example, *Agenda 21*'s (Chapter 9) section on transport: although the 'population' of cars grows at the present rate four times faster than the population of humans, *Agenda 21*'s authors were incapable of suggesting any strategies for avoiding and reducing traffic, or, of course, any option for low-speed transport systems. There are many reasons for this failure but, on a deeper level, it shows that the development syndrome has dangerously narrowed the social imagination in the North as well as in the South. As the North continues to set its sight on an infinite economic future, and the South cannot free itself from its compulsive mimicry of the North, the capacity for self-mobilized and indigenous change has been undermined worldwide. Politics that choose intermediate levels of material demand remain outside the official consensus; the search for indigenous models of prosperity, which de-emphasize the drive for overdevelopment, has become an apostasy. Clearly, such a perspective would in the first place be at the expense of the wealthy, but without a politics of sufficiency there can be neither justice nor peace with nature.

The Hegemony of Globalism

'Sustainable development', although it can mean many things to many people, nevertheless contains a core message: keep the volume of human extraction/emission in balance with the regenerative capacities of nature. That sounds reasonable enough, but it conceals a conflict that has yet to win public attention, even though such fundamental issues as power, democracy and cultural autonomy are at stake. Sustainability, yes, but at what level? Where is the circle of use and regeneration to be closed? At the level of a village community, a country, or the entire planet? Until the 1980s, environmentalists were usually concerned with the local or the national space; ideas like 'eco-development' and 'self-reliance' had aimed to increase the economic and political independence of a place by reconnecting ecological resource flows.[13] But in subsequent years, they began to look at things from a much more elevated vantage-point: they adopted the astronaut's view, taking in the entire globe at one glance. Today's ecology is in the business of saving nothing less than the planet. That suggestive globe, suspended in the dark universe, delicately furnished with clouds, oceans and continents, has become the object of science, planning and politics.

Modesty hardly seems to be the hallmark of such thinking. The 1989 special issue of the *Scientific American*, with the programmatic title 'Managing Planet Earth', sets the tone:

> It is as a global species that we are transforming the planet. It is only as a global species – pooling our knowledge, coordinating our actions and sharing what the planet has to offer – that we may have any prospect for managing the planet's transformation along the pathways of sustainable development. Self-conscious, intelligent management of the earth is one of the great challenges facing humanity as it approaches the 21st century.[14]

Perceiving the earth as an object of environmental management is, on the cognitive level, certainly an outcome of space travel, which has turned the planet into a visible object, a revolution in the history of human perception.[16] But there are political, scientific and technological reasons as well. Politically, it was only in the 1980s that acid rain, the ozone hole and the greenhouse effect drove home the message that industrial pollution affects the entire globe across all borders. The planet revealed itself as the ultimate dumping ground. Scientifically, ecological research, after having for years mainly focused on single and isolated ecosystems like deserts, marshes and rainforests, recently shifted its attention to the study of the biosphere, that envelope of air, vegetation, water and rocks that sustains life globally. Technologically, as often in the history of science, it was a new generation of instruments and equipment that created the possibility of collecting and processing data on a global scale. With satellites, sensors and computers, the technology available in the 1990s permits the biosphere to be surveyed and modelled. As these factors have emerged simultaneously, human arrogance has discovered the ultimate dominion: Planet Earth.

Only a few years ago, invoking the wholeness of the globe meant something else. Environmentalists waved around the picture of the earth taken from outer space, in order to remind the public of its majestic finiteness and to spread the insight that there is in the end no escape from the consequences of human action. While they appealed to the reality of the planet, inviting people to embrace humility, a new tribe of global ecocrats is ready to act upon the newly emerged reality of the planet, imagining that they can preside over the world. Research on the biosphere is rapidly becoming big science: spurred by a number of international programmes[16] 'planetary sciences', including satellite observation, deep-sea expeditions and worldwide data processing, are being institutionalized in many countries.

With this trend, sustainability is increasingly conceived as a challenge for global management. The new experts set out to identify the balance between human extractions/emissions on the one side, and the regenerative capacities of nature on the other, on a planetary scale, mapping and monitoring, measuring and calculating resource flows and bio-geochemical cycles around the globe. According to *Agenda 21*: 'This is essential, if a more accurate estimate is to be provided of the carrying capacity of the planet Earth and of its resilience under the many stresses placed upon it by human activities.'[17]

It is the implicit agenda of this endeavour to be eventually able to moderate the planetary system, supervising species diversity, fishing grounds, felling rates, energy flows and material cycles. It remains a matter of speculation which of these expectations will ever be realized, but there is no doubt that the linkage of space travel, sensor technology and computer simulation has vastly increased the power to monitor nature, to recognize human impact and to make predictions. The management of resource budgets thus becomes a matter of world politics.

Satellite pictures scanning the globe's vegetative cover, computer graphs running interacting curves through time, threshold levels held up as worldwide norms are the language of global ecology. It constructs a reality that contains mountains of data, but no people. The data do not explain why Tuaregs are driven to exhaust their water-holes, or what makes Germans so obsessed with high speed on freeways; they do not point out who owns the timber shipped from the Amazon or which industry flourishes because of a polluted Mediterranean sea; and they are mute about the significance of forest trees for Indian tribals or what water means in an Arab country. In short, they provide a knowledge that is faceless and placeless, an abstraction that carries a considerable cost: it consigns the realities of culture, power and virtue to oblivion. It offers data, but no context; it shows diagrams, but no actors; it gives calculations, but no notions of morality; it seeks stability, but disregards beauty. Indeed, the global vantage-point requires ironing out all the differences and disregarding all circumstances; rarely has the gulf between observers and the observed been greater than between satellite-based forestry and the *seringueiro* in the Brazilian jungle. It is inevitable that the claims of global management are in conflict with the aspirations for cultural rights, democracy and self-determination. Indeed, it is easy for an ecocracy that acts in the name of 'one earth' to become a threat to local communities and their lifestyles. After all, has there ever, in the history of colonialism, been a more powerful motive for streamlining the world than the call to save the planet?

Yet the North faces a problem, for the bid for global management has been triggered by a new historical constellation. Ever since Columbus arrived in Santo Domingo the North has by and large remained unaffected by the tragic consequences that followed his expansion overseas – others had borne the burden of sickness, exploitation and ecological destruction. Now this historical tide seems about to turn, and for the first time the Northern countries themselves are exposed to the bitter results of Westernizing the world. Immigration, popuation pressure, tribalism with mega-arms, and above all, the environmental consequences of worldwide industrialization threaten to destabilize the Northern way of life. It is as if the cycle which had been opened by Columbus is about to be closed at the end of this century. As a result, the North devises ways and means for protection and risk management worldwide. The rational planning of the planet becomes a matter of Northern security.

The celebrated control of (Western) humankind over nature leaves much to be desired. Science and technology successfully transform nature on a vast scale, but so far, with unpleasant as well as unpredictable consequences. In fact, only if these consequences were under control would it be possible to speak of having accomplished domination over nature. It is here that technocratic environmentalism comes in. Seen from this angle, the purpose of global environmental management is nothing less than control of a second order; a higher level of observation and intervention has to be installed, in order to control the consequences of the control over nature. Such a step becomes the more imperative as the drive towards turning the world into a closely interrelated and expanding economic society continues unabated. Given that the continuing force of the development syndrome is an impediment to restraining the dynamics of worldwide industrialization, the obvious task is to prepare for regulating the transformation of nature globally in an optimal fashion. It is in that light that the *Scientifc American* can elevate the following questions to key issues for future decision-making:

> Two central questions must be addressed: What kind of planet do we want? What kind of planet can we get? ... How much species diversity should be maintained in the world? Should the size or the growth rate of the human population be curtailed ...? How much climate change is acceptable?[18]

If there are no limits to growth, there surely seem to be no limits to hubris.

Notes

1. See the entry for 'underdeveloped' in the *Oxford English Dictionary* (1989), vol. XVIII, p. 960. Extensive inquiries into the history of the development discourse can be found in Sachs 1992b.

2. Beijing Ministerial Declaration on Environment and Development, 19 June 1991.

3. For these reasons, I do not follow proposals to make a distinction between growth and development. It seems to me that 'development' cannot be purified of its historical context. For a distinction, see Daly 1990.

4. World Bank 1992: 34.

5. See for instance El Serafy 1991.

6. The title of a major document, published jointly by IUCN, UNEP and WWF in Gland, Switzerland, in 1991.

7. This change has been observed for the domestic scene by Ulrich Beck (Beck 1987).

8. Buttels et al. 1990.

9. Karl Polanyi has identified the optimization imperative as the core of modern economic thinking (Polanyi 1977).

10. World Bank 1992: 114.

11. Goodland et al. 1991: 14.

12. Daly 1990: 35.

13. For instance Sachs 1980; or *What Now?* (1975), the report of the Dag Hammarskjöld Foundation.

14. Clark 1989.

15. For an elaborate analysis of this aspect, see Sachs 1992c.

16. For an overview see Malone 1986.

17. Chapter 35.1 in the section 'Science for Sustainable Development'.

18. Clark 1989: 48.

3

The Gospel of Global Efficiency

It's raining reports about the state of the planet. The *Gaia Atlas* and the Worldwatch Institute's *State of the World* are circulating in more than a dozen languages, the Annual Report of the World Resources Institute is within easy reach of enlightened UN officials, and environmentalists across the world hail the report of the Brundtland Commission as high-level testimony to their claims.

I should feel gratitude and relief. The curtain of silence has finally been pulled away from the global survival crisis and a series of data and tables reveal the vast panorama of today's threats and perils. The evidence is indeed uncontestable, and the appeal for urgent responsible action, long overdue, cannot but command consent. Conversion is indeed indispensable. Yet my admiration for the reports is increasingly tempered by mistrust of their effects. The proposed policies of resource management, I am afraid, ignore the option of intelligent self-limitation and reduce ecology to a higher form of efficiency. Such a reductionism, in my opinion, implicitly affirms the universal validity of the economic world view and will eventually spread further the Westernization of minds and habits, a cultural fall-out that in the long run also endangers the overall goal of sustainability.

More out of Less

Each of the eighty-odd Worldwatch papers, for example, paints a picture of the global state of affairs that looks roughly like this: on the one hand we see how more and more people with increasing needs for food, shelter, health care or energy are demanding to be recognized, as the population grows and some inequality is levelled. On the other hand we are shown how economies squander their potential to meet these demands as they deplete resources, ruin the environment and drive up costs. The available means are diminishing, while needs become more pressing: what looms large in the picture is a global sustainability squeeze. Fossil fuels, for instance, use up in one year what took a million years to produce, overburden the atmosphere with carbon dioxide, and prove to be more costly than investing in saving energy. The misuse of water supplies deprives humans, animals and plants of a basic means of survival and pollutes the earth's reserves for a long time to come, and new water works carry a multi-billion-dollar price tag. Examples abound. Fortunately enough, the World-watch people say, the picture is not completely gloomy, but shows a streak of light in the distance. Shifting to less harmful means and concentrating on efficiency signals for them the way out of the dilemma. Renewable fuels and fine tuning through conservation and careful management are typical responses that point to the desired target: resource efficiency. Indeed, if one were to suggest a motto to be engraved above the entrance of the Worldwatch Institute, the obvious choice would be 'More out of less'.

I do not doubt the necessity of this approach, nor do I wish to quarrel with the soundness of the alternative solutions suggested. But I should like to draw attention to a hidden reductionism that turns ecological politics from a call for new public virtues into a set of managerial strategies. As with a pair of pliers, where pressure is relieved by yielding the grip of both parts, there are two possible ways out of the dangerous squeeze between growing demand and insufficient means: to consider an enlightened restraint of demand on the one hand, and to deal diligently with the available means on the other. The world watchmen, however, highlight only the second alternative and allow the first to sink into oblivion. In their reports they stress the efficiency of means, elevating the rules of micro-economics to imperatives for national (and even global) policy. Certainly, by doing so they spearhead the transition from an output-centred to an input-centred economy where resources are not all lavished on boosting the GNP but utilized with utmost efficiency in order to obtain growth without slag and dross. Under the new prescriptions economies are supposed to 'work out' until they reach overall fitness instead of simply putting on more muscle until they break some record, as in the decades after the war. Optimizing, not maximizing, is the order of the day, and both engineers and economists take renewed pleasure in their trade puzzling out the minimum input for each unit of output.

Yet disregard for the first alternative – the consideration of an enlightened restraint of supply-oriented demands – traps the world watchmen into the economic world view. In such a perspective, each society puts production highest on its list of values and seeks the good life through expanding and accelerating the economic apparatus. As the reports rarely question the predominant position of the economy in society, they implicitly take for granted that the world's cultures converge in the steady desire for more material production. This prejudice bars the way to examining closer – even for the over-industrialized countries of the North – a politics of intelligent self-limitation, which attempts to adapt level, volume, structure and velocity of production/consumption to society's overarching goals. In their failure to do that, the reports seem to consider less commodity-intensive, less professionalized, less speedy societies inherently deficient. Since they are unable to imagine diverse cultures that intentionally live on intermediate levels of material demand, they cannot but make the economic outlook appear as the natural mode of human living. Consequently, the view on the globe they propose continues (in the tradition of 'development') to assume that all circumstances have first to be judged according to the imperative of production, be it even environmentally rational production. But ecological policies that take the steady growth in demand for granted, and limit themselves to propagating efficient means, fall into the trap of pushing, in the name of ecology, for the further rationalization of the world.

Resources Everywhere

The myopia of conventional economists has become proverbial. While staring at the role of capital and labour, they ignore many other sources of wealth and well-being, from the unpaid labour of women backing up the world of production to the silent workings of nature replenishing water, nutrients and energy. Eco-developers set out to overcome this tunnel vision, and prospect the broad range of life-supporting factors to assure the sustainability of yields over the long term. Through their glasses, numerous things and actions thus far taken for granted as part of ordinary life acquire a new, dramatic significance: they change into valuable resources. Cow dung, for example, kindled by the Senegalese peasant to heat water in the cooking pot, suddenly becomes an energy resource; the scrap metal used by a Peruvian squatter to build an annex to his hut takes on the dignity of a recoverable input; Kenyan women cultivating village fields are discovered to be human resources for boosting food production. Under Worldwatch eyes, more and more parts of the world assume a new status, and are disembedded from their local context and redefined as resources.

In what new light, however, do actions, things and people appear

when they are redefined as 'resources'? Obviously they acquire importance because they are considered useful for some higher purpose. They
count not because of what they are but because of what they can
become. They are stripped of their own worth in the present in order
to be stripmined for somebody else's use in the future. A resource is
something that has no value until it has been made into something
else. Whatever its intrinsic value, it fades away under the claim of
superior interests. For more than a hundred years the term 'resource'
has been used to survey the world for useful inputs into industry.
Consequently, perception has been trained to look at forests and see
lumber, at rocks and see ore, at landscapes and see real estate, at
people and see human resources. To call something a 'resource' means
to place it under the authority of production. The old-fashioned
synonym for 'resources' reveals clearly how language can impart
destiny: what can you do with 'raw materials' except finish them in a
manufacturing process? But not just any productive use can make
something a resource. While the peasant in Gujarat may use cow
dung to fertilize his plot, it becomes a resource only in the framework
of national production. It is in national (or global) accounting books
that resources are specified, measured and assessed according to their
relative productivity; it is the capacity to boost GNP that constitutes a
resource. Calling something a resource endows it with the availability
to be exploited for the national interest.

In a non-economic perspective, things often have a meaning that
makes them resistant to unlimited availability. For instance, in a Hindu
village there is always a holy tree or a sacred grove that is untouchable.
Gods are said to reside in their shadow; to cut them as timber would
deprive the village of mighty protection. Consider another example:
from Bolivia to ancient Germany, mines were regarded as wombs of
Mother Earth where metals grow in slow gestation. Entering this
underground world with its mysteries meant crossing a threshold into
a domain that does not rightfully belong to humans. Responsibility
and care were required, and rituals were performed in order to ask for
Mother's generosity. Cooperation of nature also had to be obtained by
the North American Cree when they went hunting deer. For them,
animals were not game out there to be killed, but had to be persuaded,
in a dialogue of rites and offerings, to present themselves to the
hunters. Indeed, hunting was an exchange between animals and man
that was governed by friendship, coercion or love, like an ordinary
human relationship. In sum, understanding trees, rocks or animals as
animated beings in a wider cosmos, where each element possesses its
separate but related identity, entailed intrinsic limits on exploitation.

Labelling things as 'resources' takes off whatever protective identity they may have and opens them up to intervention from the outside. Looking at water, soils, animals, people in terms of resources reconstitutes them as objects for management by planners and for prizing by economists. Even if they are renamed 'resources' in order to maximize their efficient use, because of the cultural fall-out from the all-embracing economic cloud, it will, in the future, be much more difficult to have any intrinsic respect for them.

Never Enough

The clock, we are warned, shows five minutes to twelve. Or even later. Be it Gaia, Worldwatch or Brundtland, they set off the alarm and seek to alert us against the threat to the survival of the planet. The message is fully credible. But the conclusion is highly double-edged: 'securing survival' is the proclaimed target for all responsible planning. However, has there ever been a society whose primary concern was survival? Probably not. Nomads might have fled droughts, Florentine citizens may have hidden from the plague, soldiers in Verdun might have mobilized their last reserves, but when has it ever been proposed that society's structure should be geared towards securing survival? Of course, previous cultures never deliberately neglected the requirements of survival, but neither did they pay them much attention. Whatever their customs, whatever their obsessions and fantasies, the conditions of physical existence were met in the course of the culture's pursuit of higher goals. Survival was nothing else than the by-product of greater achievements. It was not an explicit concern, but a given banality. Yet, precisely in the historical epoch where riches have been amassed as never before, eco-developers from all four winds raise their voice and call upon people and governments to put survival first.

A glance at the various Worldwatch papers and yearbooks reveals the most recent part of the story: how plenty vanished and scarcity assumed command. A short time ago it could be taken for granted that the great cycle of evaporation, condensation and precipitation fully replenished our sources of water, but overpumping for irrigation, which makes the water level drop, and pollution from industry, which renders it unsafe, have today turned fresh water into a scarce good. Since time immemorial, legions of insects and worms have renewed the topsoil, but pesticides and overuse of marginal land now accelerate the rate of erosion. And so it goes for global rainfall (forests), sun radiation (ozone hole) or temperature (greenhouse effect). Plenty turned into scarcity as industrial and agricultural production were intensified and generalized around the globe. The threat to survival is the result – I am embarrassed to state the obvious – of the increasing identification of the good life with the availability of material products. Scarcity, therefore, is one side of a coin whose reverse side is called open-ended production.

An emerging tribe of eco-experts, however, defines its field of expertise by focusing the spotlight on the first side of the coin, leaving the second in the shadow. As the World Resources Institute programmatically states on the first page of its 1987 report: 'The global environment is an interconnected web ... The human race relies on the environment and therefore must manage it wisely.' Clearly, the 'therefore' is the crux of the matter: the scarcity of what was once plenty is sealed and meant to be the base for a new type of management. While the supposition in the statement holds true for all cultures, its conclusion highlights the hidden axiom of the economic world view: there will be no boundaries to material progression. It is only when this axiom reigns that water, air and soil become and remain scarce. Taking the scarcity of natural riches for granted, however, is the base for the eco-developer's intervention: it becomes his or her task to monitor and manage what has now turned into a scarce resource. And it will require all his or her professional skill to steer a course along that optimal level of exploitation that does not jeopardize the sustainability of future growth. To rally around 'survival' happens only in a society driven by the imperative of continuously testing the limits of nature. Any other couldn't care less.

By putting on the glasses of micro-economics, i.e. the technique for selecting the most efficient means for a given end, eco-developers cannot escape the axiom of infinite growth. Since the time of W. St. Jevron and Léon Walras, the founders of neo-classical economics, means are for the economist principally insufficient; their scarcity appears as part of the natural order of things and no longer as caused by some particular, transient constellation where ends happen to outstrip means. Instead, the presumptuous expectation of nineteenth-century Europe – that wants, along the supposedly linear course of history, will continuously expand, rendering means insufficient – has entered the nature of things as an implicit axiom, whenever economists seek to make the best out of so-called scarce means. They will never tell you what ends you will finally achieve by 'managing wisely' your means; for them ends are faceless, they have only one, formal character: they are infinite.

For the economic world view, needs will always translate into claims on material production. Well-being, in this perspective, is recast as well-having. Society's welfare therefore depends in the first place on material output. Setting out to manage 'global resources', world watchmen take the worldwide victory of this specifically modern outlook as a *fait accompli*. What separates them from the conventional economist is their straightforward recognition of environmental limits to production; what ties them nevertheless to the economic world view is the failure to appreciate cultural limits to the predominance of production, cultural limits that render production less important and consequently also relieve environmental pressure. For them as well as for the conventional economists, nature's riches are doomed to be insufficient, because both the affluent and the impoverished part of the world will inevitably grow in their attachment to material growth. The many different ways to the good life are implicitly reduced to the one single race-track towards a higher standard of living. If societies always expended all their energies on pushing production, there would never have been the strikingly coloured fabrics of Senegal, or the extravagant Moghul gardens of India, or any Gothic cathedral in France. As diverse as these societies have been, they had, nevertheless, one thing in common: they aspired to something other than producing and spent their surplus on whatever grand design they had in mind. The West has decided to spend it on multiplying output, and eco-developers tacitly accept that formula for the entire globe.

Always Rational

Throughout the Worldwatch papers, one frequently meets persons of a particular virtue. The Utopia of a sustainable world appears to be populated by a fairly recent version of *homo sapiens*, the efficiency-conscious individual. Disposing of glass bottles in separate containers, replacing open fires with stoves, introducing minimum tillage in place of soil-breaking ploughing, or installing drip irrigation instead of canals – all these suggestions, as reasonable as they may be, propagate the gospel of efficiency. A. L. Lovins, the American guru of eco-efficiency, provided a striking illustration of the eco-developer's mood when he presented his audience with two light-bulbs. The lights were equally bright, although the conventional model used 75 and the new one only 18 watts. He explained: 'We should get used to seeing the purchase of an electricity-saving device like constructing a tiny power plant in the home. The new bulb, in fact, is producing 57 negawatts, i.e. unused watts. And the saved electricity can be sold to another client, making new power plants superfluous.' Indeed, this could nicely express the efficiency ethos in a nutshell: 'Produce negawatts!'

Undoubtedly, the message is charming in its elegance – and this tends to blur the shift from the housekeeping to the efficiency ethos. Good housekeeping is the traditional ideal of subsistence-oriented households. Food is stored, tools are carefully maintained, furniture is handed down from generation to generation. Necessary possessions are fully used, while outside purchases are kept to a minimum. Each coin is turned over twice before it is spent, each transaction is carried out prudently, sometimes even with misgivings. However, the point of good housekeeping is not economizing for the sake of investment, but saving for the sake of independence. Choice of an efficient means has nothing to do with keeping expenses down, but aims at obtaining a higher return in order to liberate funds for further investments. Saving, in contrast, intends to keep market involvement at a low level in order to shield the domestic economy against pressure from the larger economy. Efficiency looks for opportunities, saving looks for security. While the former implies infinite progression, the latter derives from a sense of 'enoughness'. These attitudes can easily come into conflict as soon as a gain in efficiency requires money; the Indian peasant may, therefore, prefer to burn piles of cow dung, which involves no money expense, rather than buy a bio-digester, although it uses less cow dung to obtain the same amount of heat.

More fundamentally, the peasant might not want to care at all, because he or she has other preferences in life. After all, the efficiency imperative demands leaving nothing idle and selecting – in terms of money, effort and environmental consequences – the least costly way to achieve a goal. Our peasant, however, might not be happy with the waterproof roof the 'development' agency provided and replace it with the traditional roof of leaves and branches, which requires major repairs each year. After all, this roof repair is the occasion of the village's weeklong festival! He or she is ready to be effective but not efficient. Since people are not fools, they will always intend to be effective and act so as to achieve a certain result. Yet efficiency can be way off, because the activity is embedded in a web of other concerns. They may, for instance, use hours every day to pay customary visits to family members, or spend most of their money on elaborate festivities. The call to efficiency disrupts the other priorities that deflect or retard the (technically) one best way. Actions are often over-determined and serve a host of purposes; to turn mere effectiveness into efficiency means to delete the other concerns and to privilege the naked means–end relationship. Once that privilege is erected, means count only as means; any consideration of context, quality, style or aesthetics tends to become irrelevant. The model of rational choice, in fact, is based on the assumption that means have been purified of any context, since they are considered to be interchangeable according to the highest return and calculable according to a single yardstick, generally either money or energy. Efficiency behaviour spreads at the expense of culture-guided behaviour; it undermines non-economic notions of the good and proper life.

Certainly, interpreting the state of the world chiefly in terms of 'resources', 'management' and 'efficiency' may appeal to planners and economists. But it continues to promote development as a cultural mission and to shape the world in the image of the West. The reports do more than simply propose new strategies; they also tell people how to see nature, society and their own actions. The more their language is adopted around the globe, the more difficult it will be to see nature in terms of respect and not as a resource, society in terms of the common good and not of production, and action in terms of virtue and not of efficiency. To put it in a nutshell: such reports promote the sustainability of nature and erode the sustainability of cultures. And this, for sure, will not benefit nature either.

4

Environment and Development: The Story of a Dangerous Liaison

The journey of Apollo 11 to the moon brought us under the spell of a new image – not of the moon but of the earth. Looking back from the spaceship to distant earth, Neil Armstrong shot the pictures that now adorn the cover of almost every report about the future of the planet – a small and fragile ball, shining blue against the dark of outer space, delicately covered by clouds, oceans, greenery and soils. Never before had the planet been visible to the human eye in its full shape; it was space photography that imparted a new reality to the planet by turning it into an object lying right there before our eyes. In its beauty and vulnerability, the floating globe arouses wonder and awe. For the first time it has become possible to speak of our planet.

But the possessive noun reveals at the same time a deep ambivalence. On the one hand, 'our' can imply participation and highlight humankind's dependence on an encompassing reality. On the other hand, it can imply ownership and emphasize the human vocation to control this common property. Consequently, the image of 'our' planet conveys a contradictory message: it can call either for moderation or for megalomania.

The same ambivalence characterizes the career of the concept 'environment'. While it was originally advanced to put development politics under indictment, it is now raised like a banner to announce a new era of development. Indeed, after 'ignorance' and 'poverty' in previous decades, 'survival of the planet' is likely to become a well-publicized emergency in the 1990s, in whose name a new frenzy of development will be unleashed. Significantly, the report of the World Commission on Environment and Development (Brundtland Report), having evoked the image of the planet floating in space, concludes the opening paragraph by stating: 'This new reality, from which there is no escape, must be recognized – *and managed*' (WCED 1987; emphasis added).

Setting the Stage for the Brundtland Report

For better or worse, the vicissitudes of the international development debate follow closely the rise and fall of political sensibilities within the Northern countries. Unfettered enthusiasm for economic growth in 1945 reflected the West's desire to restart the economic machine after a devastating war; the emphasis on manpower planning echoed American fears after the shock of Sputnik in 1957; the discovery of basic needs was stimulated by President Johnson's domestic war on poverty in the 1960s, and the concern about worldwide inequality. What development means depends on how the rich nations feel. 'Environment' is no exception to this rule.

The UN Conference on the Human Environment held in Stockholm in June 1972, the occasion on which the 'environment' arrived on the international agenda, was first proposed by Sweden, which was worried about acid rain, pollution in the Baltic, and the levels of pesticides and heavy metals in fish and birds. What could be called massive accidental internationalization cast its shadow before it: industrial wastes escape national sovereignty, they do not show up at customs posts or travel with passports. Countries discovered that they were not self-contained units, but contingent on actions taken by others. Thus a new category of problems, the 'global issues', emerged. The Stockholm Conference was the prelude to a series of large UN meetings throughout the 1970s (on population, food, human settlements, water, desertification, science and technology, renewable energy) that set out to alter the post-war perception of an open global space where many nations can individually strive to maximize economic growth. Instead a different view began to be promoted: from now on, the concept of an interrelated world system, which is seen as operating under a number of common constraints, took hold.

The cognitive furniture for this shift was provided by a particular school of thought that had gained prominence in interpreting the significance of pollution and man-made disasters. In the USA during the 1960s, environmental issues forced their way into public consciousness: Los Angeles smog and the slow death of Lake Erie, oil spills and the planned flooding of the Grand Canyon led to articles on the environment in the *New York Times* sky-rocketing from about 150 in 1960 to about 1,700 to 1970. Local incidents, which were increasingly seen as adding up to a larger picture, were put into a global perspective by scientists who borrowed their conceptual framework from eco-systems theory in order to interpret the predicament of a world rushing towards industrialization. Infinite growth, they maintained, is based on a delusion, because the world is a closed space, finite and of limited carrying capacity. Perceiving global space as a system whose stability rests on the equilibrium of its components, like population, technology, resources (including food) and environment, they foresaw – echoing Malthus' early challenge to the assumption of inevitable progress – an imminent disruption of the balance between population growth (exacerbated by technology) on the one hand, and resources and en-vironment on the other. Besides Ehrlich's *Population Bomb* (1968) or *The Ecologist* magazine's *A Blueprint for Survival* (1972), it was in particular the Club of Rome's *Limits to Growth* (Meadows et al. 1972) that made it seem natural to imagine the future of the globe as the result of the interaction of quantitative growth curves operating in five dimensions.

The global ecosystems approach was not without competitors, but both the biocentric and the humanist perspectives were foreign to the perceptions of the international development elite. Attributing absolute value to nature for its own sake, as environmentalists in the tradition of Henry D. Thoreau, Ralph Emerson and John Muir did, would have barred the way to continuing, albeit in a more sophisticated and flexible manner, the exploitation of nature. And recognizing the offences against nature as just another sign of the supremacy of technological expansion over people and their lives, as humanist authors like Lewis Mumford or Ernst Friedrich Schumacher suggest, would go against the grain of development aspirations and could hardly please the guardians of the growth machine. In fact, only an interpretation that magnified rather than undermined their managerial responsibilities could raise their spirits, even in spite of dim prospects. It was the global ecosystems approach that perfectly suited their vantage-point at the summits of international organizations, for it proposed the global society as the unit of analysis and, by denouncing population growth, put the Third World at the centre of attention. Moreover, the model rendered intelligible what would otherwise have appeared as a messy situation by removing resource conflicts from any particular local or political context. The language of aggregate data series suggests a clear-cut picture, abstract figures lend themselves to playing with scenarios, and a presumed mechanical causality among the various components creates the illusion that global strategies can be effective. And even if the ideal of growth crumbled, there was, for those who felt themselves in charge of running the world, still some objective to fall comfortably back on: stability.

However, there was still a long way to go before, in 1987, the Brundtland Report finally announced the marriage between the craving for development and concern for the environment. As the adamant rejection of all 'no-growth' positions, in particular by Third World governments at the Stockholm Conference demonstrated, the compulsion to drive up the GNP had turned many into cheerful enemies of nature. It was only in the course of the 1970s, under the additional impact of the oil crisis, that it began to dawn on governments that continued growth depended not only on capital formation or skilled manpower but also on the long-term availability of natural resources. Worried first of all about the conservation of inputs for future growth, development planners gradually adopted what had been a strand of thought as far back as the introduction of forest management in Germany around 1800 and the American Progressive movement after 1900: that – in the words of Gifford Pinchot, the steward of Theodore Roosevelt's conservation programme – 'conservation means the greatest good for the greatest number for the longest time'. Tomorrow's growth was seen to be under the threat of nature's revenge. Consequently it was time to extend the attention-span of planning and to call for the 'efficient management of natural resources' as part of the development package: 'We have in the past been concerned about the impacts of economic growth upon the environment. We are now forced', concludes the Brundtland Report, 'to concern ourselves with the impacts of ecological stress - degradation of soils, water regimes, atmosphere, and forests – upon our economic prospects' (WCED 1987: 5).

Another roadblock on the way to wedding 'environment' to 'development' had been an ossified vision of growth. The decades of smoke-stack industrialization had left the impression that growth was to be invariably linked to squandering ever more resources. Under the influence of the appropriate technology movement, however, this univocal notion of development began to crumble and give way to an awareness of the availability of technological choices. It was, after all, in Stockholm that NGOs had gathered for the first time to stage a counter-conference calling for alternative paths in development. Later on, initiatives like the Declaration of Cocoyoc and *What Now?* of the Dag Hammarskjöld Foundation helped – perhaps unwittingly – to challenge the assumption of an invariable technological process and to pluralize the roads to growth. Out of this awareness of technological flexibility grew, towards the end of the 1970s, a new perception of the ecological predicament: the 'limits to growth' are seen no longer as an insurmountable barrier blocking the surge of growth, but as discrete obstacles forcing the flow to take a different route. Soft-path studies in areas from energy to health-care proliferated and charted new riverbeds for the wrongly directed stream.

Finally, environmentalism was regarded as inimical to the alleviation of poverty throughout the 1970s. The claim to be able to abolish poverty, however, has been – and still is – the single most important pretension of the development ideology, in particular after its enthronement as the official number one priority after World Bank President Robert McNamara's speech at Nairobi in 1973. Poverty was long regarded as unrelated to environmental degradation, which was attributed to the impact of industrial man; the world's poor entered the equation only as future claimants to an industrial lifestyle. But with spreading deforestation and desertification all over the world, the poor were quickly identified as agents of destruction and became the targets of campaigns to promote 'environmental consciousness'. As soon as blaming the victim entered the professional consensus, the old recipe could also be offered for meeting the new disaster: since growth was supposed to remove poverty, the environment could be protected only through a new era of growth. As the Brundtland Report puts it: 'Poverty reduces people's capacity to use resources in a sustainable manner; it intensifies pressure on the environment ... A necessary but not sufficient condition for the elimination of absolute poverty is a relatively rapid rise in per capita incomes in the Third World' (WCED 1987: 49–50). The way was thus cleared for the marriage between 'environment' and 'development': the newcomer could be welcomed to the old-established family.

'No development without sustainability; no sustainability without development' is the formula that establishes the newly formed bond. 'Development' emerges rejuvenated from this liaison, the ailing concept gaining another lease on life. This is nothing less than the repeat of a proven ruse: every time in the past 30 years when the destructive effects of development were recognized, the concept was stretched in such a way as to include both injury and therapy. For example, when it became obvious, around 1970, that the pursuit of development actually intensified poverty, the notion of 'equitable development' was invented so as to reconcile the irreconcilable: the creation of poverty with the abolition of poverty. In the same vein, the Brundtland Report incorporated concern for the environment into the concept of development by erecting 'sustainable development' as the conceptual roof for both violating and healing the environment.

Certainly, the new era requires development experts to widen their attention span and to monitor water and soils, air and energy utilization.

But development remains what it always comes down to, an array of interventions for boosting the GNP: 'given expected population growth, a five- to ten-fold increase in world industrial output can be anticipated by the time world population stabilises sometime in the next century' (WCED 1987: 15). Brundtland thus ends up suggesting further growth, but not, as in the old days of development, in order to achieve the happiness of the greatest number, but to contain the environmental disaster for the generations to come. The threat to the planet's survival looms large. Has there ever been a better excuse for intrusion? New areas of intervention open up, nature becomes a domain of politics, and a new breed of technocrats feels the vocation to steer growth along the edge of the abyss.

A Successful Ambivalence

Ecology is both computer modelling and political action, scientific discipline as well as all-embracing world view. The concept joins two different worlds. On the one side, protest movements all over the globe wage their battles for the conservation of nature, appealing to evidence allegedly offered by the scientific discipline that studies the relationships between organisms and their environment. On the other side, academic ecologists have seen with bewilderment how their hypotheses have both become a reservoir for political slogans and been elevated to principles for some post-industrial philosophy. The liaison between protest and science can hardly be called a happy one. While the researchers have resented being called on to testify against the rationality of science and its benefits for humankind, activists have, ironically enough, adopted theorems like the 'balance of nature' or the 'priority of the whole over its parts' at a moment when they had already been abandoned by the discipline.

However, without recourse to science, the ecology movement would probably have remained a bunch of nature freaks and never acquired the power of a historical force. One secret of its success lies precisely in its hybrid character. As a movement highly suspicious of science and technical rationality, it plays anew the counter-melody that has accompanied the history of modernity ever since Romanticism. But as a science-based movement, it is capable of questioning the foundations of modernity and contesting its logic in the very name of science. In fact, the ecology movement seems to be the first anti-modernist movement attempting to justify its claims with the enemy's own means. It not only resorts to the arts (like the Romantics), to organicism (like the conservatives), to the glory of nature (like preservationists), or to a transcendental creed (like fundamentalists), although all these themes are present, but it bases its challenge on ecosystems theory, which integrates physics, chemistry and biology. This unique achievement, however, cuts both ways: the science of *ecology* gives rise to a scientific anti-modernism that has succeeded largely in disrupting the dominant discourse, yet the *science* of ecology opens the way for the technocratic recuperation of the protest. It is this ambivalence of ecology that, on the epistemological level, is responsible for the success as well as the failure of the movement.

While its roots go back to eighteenth-century natural history, ecology was successful in becoming a full-fledged discipline – with university chairs, scholarly journals and professional associations – only during the first two decades of the twentieth century. It inherited from its precursors in the nineteenth century a predilection for looking at the world of plants (and later animals) in terms of geographically distributed ensembles. The tundra in Canada is evidently different from the rainforest in Amazonia. Consequently, pre-ecology organized its perception of nature, following the core themes of Romanticism, around the axiom that place constitutes community. From an emphasis on the impact of climatic and physical circumstances on communities, the attention shifted, around the turn of the century, to the processes within these communities. The competitive/cooperative relations between organisms in a given environment and, under the influence of Darwinism, their adaptive change through time ('succession') emerged as the new discipline's field of study. Impressed by the mutual dependency of species in biotic communities, the ecologists began to wonder just how real these units were. Is a given ensemble only the sum of individual organisms or does it express a higher identity? Up to the Second World War, the latter conception was clearly dominant: plant/ animal societies were seen as super-organisms that evolve actively, adapting to the environment. In opting for organicism – the postulate that the whole is superior to its parts and an entity in its own right – the ecologists were able firmly to constitute the object of their science.

This anti-reductionist attitude was doomed after the war when, across disciplines, mechanistic conceptions of science again prevailed. Ecology was ripe for a restructuring along the lines of positivist methodology; like any other science, it was supposed to produce causal hypotheses that are empirically testable and prognostically relevant. The search for general laws, however, implies concentrating attention on a minimum of elements common to the overwhelming variety of settings. The appreciation of a particular place with a particular community loses importance. Moreover, these elements and their

relationships have to be measurable, and the quantitative analysis of
mass, volume, temperature and the like replaced the qualitative interpretation of an ensemble's unity and order. Following physics, at
that time the lead science, ecologists identified energy as the common
denominator that links animals and plants with the non-living environment. Generally, the calorie became the unit of measurement, for it
permitted description of both the organic and the inorganic worlds as
two aspects of the same reality – the flow of energy.

Biology was thus reduced to energetics. But the holistic tradition of
ecology did not wither away. It reappeared in a new language: 'system'
replaced the concept of 'living community', and 'homoeostasis' the
idea of evolution towards a 'climax'. The concept of system integrates
an originally anti-modern notion, the 'whole' or the 'organism', into
scientific discourse. It allows one to insist on the priority of the whole
without vitalist overtones, while it acknowledges an autonomous role
for the parts – without, however, relinquishing the idea of a supra-
individual reality. This is accomplished by interpreting the meaning of
wholeness as 'homoeostasis' and the relations between the parts and
the whole, in the tradition of mechanical engineering, as 'self-regula-
tory feedback mechanism' steadily maintaining that homoeostasis. It
was the concept of ecosystem that thus combined the organicist
heritage with scientific reductionism, and it is this concept of ecosystem
that gave to the ecology movement a quasi-spiritual dimension and
scientific credibility at the same time.

Since the 1960s, ecology has left the biology departments of universities and migrated into every consciousness. The scientific term
has turned into a world view. And as world view, it carries the promise
of reuniting what has been fragmented, of healing what has been torn
apart – in short, of caring for the whole. The numerous wounds
inflicted by modern, goal-specific institutions have provoked a renewed
desire for wholeness, and that desire has found a suitable language in
the science of ecology. The conceptual switch that connected the
biology circuit with that of society at large was the notion of ecosystem. In retrospect, this comes as no surprise, since the concept is
well equipped to serve this function: in scope, as well as in scale, it has
an enormous power of inclusion. It unites not only plants and animals
– as the notion of 'living community' did – but also includes within its
purview the non-living world on the one hand, and the world of
humans on the other. Thus, any ontological difference between what
were once called the mineral kingdom, the plant and animal kingdoms,
and the kingdom of man vanishes: the concept's scope is universal.
Likewise, 'ecosystems' come in many sizes, big and small, nesting like

babushka dolls, each within the next, from the microscopic to the planetary level. The concept is free-ranging in scale. Omnipresent as ecosystems appear to be, they are consequently hailed as the keys to understanding order in the world. Moreover, as they appear to be essential for the continuance of the webs of life, they call for nothing less than care and reverence. A remarkable career, indeed – a technical term blown into the realms of the metaphysical. For many environmentalists now, ecology seems to reveal the moral order of being by uncovering simultaneously the *verum, bonum* and *pulchrum of* reality: it suggests not only the truth, but also a moral imperative and even aesthetic perfection.

On the other hand, however, ecosystems theory, based on cybernetics as the science of engineering feedback mechanisms, represents anything but a break with the Western tradition of increasing control over nature. How can a theory of regulation be separated from an interest in manipulation? After all, systems theory aims at control of the second order; it strives for controlling (self-)control. As is obvious, the metaphor underlying systems thinking is the self-governing machine: a machine capable of adjusting its performance to changing conditions according to pre-set rules. Whatever the object being observed, be it a factory, a family or a lake, attention focuses on the regulating mechanisms by which the system in question responds to changes in its environment. Once these are identified, the way is open to condition them so as to alter the responsiveness of the system. Today, however, the responsiveness of nature has been strained to the limit under the pressures of modern man. Looking at nature in terms of self-regulating systems, therefore, implies either the intention to gauge nature's overload capacity or the aim of adjusting its feedback mechanisms through human intervention. Both strategies amount to completing Francis Bacon's vision of dominating nature, albeit with the added pretension of manipulating its revenge. In this way, ecosystem technology turns finally against ecology as world view. A movement that bade farewell to modernity ends up welcoming it, in a new guise, through the back door.

Survival as a New *Raison d'État*

Throughout history, many reasons have been put forward to justify state power and its claim on citizens. Classical objectives like law and order or welfare through redistribution have been invoked time and again, and, more recently, development has become the goal in the name of which many Third World governments sacrifice the vital interests of half of their populations. Today, 'survival of the planet' is well on its way to becoming the wholesale justification for a new wave of state interventions in people's lives all over the world.

The World Bank, for instance, sees a gleam of hope for itself again, after its reputation has been badly shaken by devastating criticism from environmentalists: 'I anticipate', declared its senior vice-president, David Hopper, in 1988, 'that over the course of the next year, the Bank will be addressing the full range of environmental needs of its partner nations, needs that will run from the technical to the institutional, from the micro-details of project design to the macro-requirements of formulating, implementing and enforcing environmental policies' (Hopper 1988). The voices of protest, after finally penetrating the airconditioned offices in Washington, have called forth a rather self-defeating answer: the very demands to halt World Bank activities have provoked their expansion.

While environmentalists have put the spotlight on the numerous vulnerabilities of nature, governments as a result discover a new conflict-ridden area in need of political governance and regulation. This time it is not peace between persons that is at stake, but the orderly relations between man and nature. To mediate in this conflict, the state assumes the tasks of gathering evidence on the state of nature and the effects of man, of enacting norms and laws to direct behaviour, and of enforcing compliance with the new rules. On the one hand, the continuance of nature's capacity to render services, such as clean air and water or a reliable climate, has to be closely watched. On the other, society's innumerable actions have to be kept under sufficient control in order to direct the exploitation of nature into tolerable channels. To carry out these formidable objectives, the state has to install the necessary institutions like monitoring systems, regulatory mechanisms and executive agencies. A new class of professionals is required to perform these tasks, while eco-science is supposed to provide the epistemology of intervention. In short, the experts who used to look after economic growth now claim to be presiding over survival itself.

However, as is well known, many rural communities in the Third World do not need to wait until specialists from hastily founded research institutes on sustainable agriculture swarm out to deliver their recipes against, say, soil erosion. Provision for the coming generations has been part of their tribal and peasant practices since time immemorial. What is more, the new centrally designed schemes for the 'management of environmental resources' threaten to collide with their locally based knowledge about conservation.

For example, the Indian Chipko movement has made the courage and wisdom of those women who protected the trees with their bodies against the chainsaws of the loggers a symbol of local resistance acclaimed far beyond the confines of India. Yet their success has had its price: forest managers moved in and claimed responsibility for the trees. All of a sudden the conflict took on a different colour: the hard-nosed woodcutters had given way to soft-spoken experts. They brought along surveys, showed around diagrams, pointed out growth curves, and argued over optimal felling rates. Planting schemes along with wood-processing industries were proposed, and attempts made to lure the villagers into becoming small timber producers. Those who had defended the trees to protect their means of subsistence and to bear witness to the interconnectedness of life saw themselves unexpectedly bombarded with research findings and the abstract categories of resource economics. And throughout this new assault on them, the 'national interest' in 'balanced resource development' was invoked. It mattered little in the face of these alien priorities what significance the forest had for the villagers who lived there, or what species of tree would be most suitable for the people's sustenance. An ecology that aimed at the management of scarce natural resources clashed with an ecology that wished to preserve the local commons. In this way, national resource planning can lead, albeit by novel means, to a con-tinuation of the war against subsistence.

Although the resource experts arrived in the name of protecting nature, their image of nature profoundly contradicts the image of nature held by the villagers. Nature, when it becomes the object of politics and planning, turns into 'environment'. To use the two con-cepts interchangeably is misleading, for it impedes the recognition of 'environment' as a particular construction of 'nature' specific to our epoch. Contrary to the claims that we are currently being socialized into accepting, there has rarely been a concept that represented nature in a form more abstract, passive and void of qualities than 'en-vironment'. Squirrels on the ground are as much a part of the environment as water in aquifers, gases in the atmosphere, marshes along the coast or even high-rise buildings in inner cities. Sticking the label 'environment' on the natural world makes all concrete qualities fade away; even more, it makes nature appear passive and lifeless, merely waiting to be acted upon. This is obviously a far cry from, for instance, the Indian villager's conception of *Prakriti*, the active and productive power which permeates every stone or tree, fruit or animal, and sustains them along with the human world. *Prakriti* grants the blessings of nature as a gift; she has consequently to be honoured and wooed (Shiva 1989: 219).

Cultures that see nature as a living being tend to carefully circum-
scribe the range of human intervention, because a hostile response is
to be expected when a critical threshold has been passed. 'Environment'
has nothing in common with this view: through the modernist eyes of
such a concept, the limits imposed by nature appear merely as physical
constraints on human survival. To call traditional economies 'ecological' is often to neglect that basic difference in approach.

Towards a Global Ecocracy?

In the late 1980s, concern about dwindling resources and worldwide
pollution reached the commanding heights of international politics.
Multilateral agencies now distribute biomass converters and design
forestry programmes, economic summits quarrel about carbon dioxide
emissions, and scientists launch satellites into orbit in order to check
on the planet's health. But the discourse that is rising to prominence
has taken on a fundamentally biased orientation: it calls for extended
management, but disregards intelligent self-limitation. As the dangers
mount, new products, procedures and programmes are invented to
stave off the threatening effects of industrialism and keep the system
afloat. Capital, bureaucracy and science – the venerable trinity of
Western modernization – declare themselves indispensable in the new
crisis and promise to prevent the worst through better engineering,
integrated planning and more sophisticated models. However, fuel-
efficient machines, environmental risk assessment analyses, the close
monitoring of natural processes and the like, well-intended as they
may be, have two assumptions in common: first, that society will
always be driven to test nature to its limits, and second, that the
exploitation of nature should be neither maximized nor minimized,
but ought to be optimized. As the 1987 report of the World Resources
Institute states programmatically on its first page: 'The human race
relies on the environment and therefore must manage it wisely.' Clearly,
the word 'therefore' is the crux of the matter; it is relevant only if the
competitive dynamic of the industrial system is taken for granted.
Otherwise, the environment would not be in danger and could be left
without management. Calls for securing the survival of the planet are
often, upon closer inspection, nothing more than calls for the survival
of the industrial system.

Capital-, bureaucracy- and science-intensive solutions to environmental decline, in addition, are not without social costs. The herculean
task of keeping the global industrial machine running at ever increasing
speed, and at the same time safeguarding the bisophere, will require a

giant leap in surveillance and regulation. How else should the myriad decisions, from the individual to the national and the global levels, be brought into line? It is of secondary importance whether the stream-lining of industrialism will be achieved, if at all, through market incentives, strict legislation, remedial programmes, sophisticated spying or outright prohibitions. What matters is that all these strategies call for more centralism, in particular for a stronger state. Since ecocrats rarely call into question the industrial model of living in order to reduce the burden on nature, they are left with the necessity of synchronizing the innumerable activities of society with all the skill, foresight and tools of advancing technology they can muster. The real historical challenge, therefore, must be addressed in something other than ecocratic terms: how is it possible to build ecological societies with less government and less professional dominance?

The ecocratic discourse that is about to unfold in the 1990s starts from the conceptual marriage of 'environment' and 'development', finds its cognitive base in ecosystems theory, and aims at new levels of administrative monitoring and control. Unwilling to reconsider the logic of competitive productivism that is at the root of the planet's ecological plight, it reduces ecology to a set of managerial strategies aiming at resource efficiency and risk management. It treats as a tech-nical problem what in fact amounts to no less than a civilizational impasse – namely, that the level of productive performance already achieved turns out to be not viable in the North, let alone for the rest of the globe. With the rise of ecocracy, however, the fundamental debate that is needed on issues of public morality – how society should live, or what, how much and in what way it should produce and consume – falls into oblivion. Instead, Western aspirations are taken for granted, and not only in the West but worldwide, and societies that choose not to put all their energy into production and deliberately accept a lower throughput of commodities become unthinkable. What falls by the wayside are efforts to elucidate the much broader range of futures open to societies that limit their levels of material output in order to cherish whatever ideals emerge from their cultural heritages. The ecocratic perception remains blind to diversity outside the eco-nomic society of the West.

Further reading

'Environment' finally moved to the centre stage of the international debate with the report of the World Commission on Environment and Development, *Our Common Future*, Oxford: Oxford University Press,

1987. Various lines of the history leading up to that conceptual innovation are highlighted in A. Biswas and M. Biswas, 'Environment and sustainable development in the Third World: a review of the past decade', *Third World Quarterly*, vol. 4, 1982, pp. 479–91; J. McCormick, 'The origins of the world conservation strategy', *Environmental Review*, vol. 10, 1986, pp. 177–87; F. Sandbach, 'The rise and fall of the limits to growth debate', *Social Studies of Science*, vol. 8, 1978, pp. 495–520; and H. J. Harborth, *Dauerhafte Entwicklung: Zur Entstehung eines neuen ökologischen Konzepts*, Wissenschaftszentrum Berlin, 1989. M. Redclift, *Sustainable Development: Exploring the Contradictions*, London: Methuen, 1987, offers a more systematic treatment.

D. Worster, *Nature's Economy: A History of Ecological Ideas*, San Francisco: Sierra Club, 1977, is a masterly introduction to the history of ecology, the science that gave its name to the political movement. Its oscillations between Romanticism and Scientism are traced by L. Trepl, *Geschichte der Okologie*, Frankfurt: Athenäum, 1987, and P. Acot, *Histoire de l'écologie*, Paris: Presses Universitaires de France, 1988, shows its rise to an all-inclusive mode of explanation. How close the links between the hopes of social engineering and the formation of the ecosystem concept were is elaborated by P. Taylor, 'Technocratic optimism: H. T. Odum, and the partial transformation of ecological metaphor after World War II', *Journal of the History of Biology*, vol. 21, 1988, pp. 213–44, while Ch. Kwa, 'Representations of nature mediating between ecology and science policy: the case of the international biological programme', *Social Studies of Science*, vol. 17,1987, pp. 413–42, calls attention to the affinity between perceptions in the political sphere and systemic versions of biology.

For representations of nature different from environment, which motivate present-day movements, see V. Shiva, *Staying Alive: Women, Ecology and Development*, London: Zed Books, 1989. P. Richards, *Indigenous Agricultural Revolution: Ecology and Food Production in West Africa*, London: Hutchinson, 1985, points out the wisdom of traditional knowledge systems. The history of the concept of nature has been extensively reviewed by C. Glacken, *Traces on the Rhodian Shore: Nature and Culture in Western Thought*, Berkeley: University of California Press, 1967, while J. B. Callicott (ed.) has assembled a number of authors who examine the role of nature in some non-Western traditions: *Nature in Asian Traditions of Thought*, State University of New York Press, 1989.

Access to the cultural anthropology of nature can be found in the entries 'nature', 'mountains', 'trees', 'metals', etc., in M. Eliade (ed.) *The Encyclopedia of Religions*, New York: Macmillan, 1987. Y.-F. Tuan shows us systematically how many different ways the environment, across history and cultures, figured in human imagination: *Topophilia: A Study of Environmental Perceptions and Values*, Englewood Cliffs, NJ: Prentice-Hall, 1974. Regarding the discontinuities in European history, C. Merchant, *The Death of Nature: Women, Ecology and the Scientific Revolution*, San Francisco: Harper and Row, 1980, recounts the major rupture in Western attitudes, while her most recent book, *Ecological Revolutions: Nature, Gender, and Science in New England*, Chapel Hill: University of North Carolina Press, 1989, documents how the ways of knowing nature have changed from the native Indian to the colonialist and industrialist modes, focusing on the evidence from a limited geographical area.

The rising ecocratic discourse can be best examined in the special issue of the *Scientific American*, vol. 261, September 1989, with the title 'Managing Planet Earth'. For another example, in much the same vein, see M. Rambler (ed.), *Global Ecology: Towards A Science of the Biosphere*, New York: Academic Press, 1989. I have called attention in Chapter 3 to hidden assumptions in the Worldwatch Institute's yearly message (*The State of the World*, New York: Norton, 1984 and subsequent years). In contrast, I learned a lot about the deeper civilizational issues that are at stake in the present debate through J. Bandyopadbyay and V. Shiva, 'Political economy of ecology movements', in *IFDA Dossier*, no. 71, May/June 1989; and B. McKibben, *The End of Nature*, New York: Random House, 1989. As a reference tool for the literature on ethics and the environment, I found the annotated bibliography of D. E. Davis, *Ecophilosophy: A Field Guide to the Literature*, San Pedro: Miles, 1989, very helpful.

5

Sustainable Development: On the Political Anatomy of an Oxymoron

It appears as if today, near the end of the twentieth century, we are reaching the end of a cycle that was started by Columbus, as he set out for his journey across the Atlantic Ocean more than five hundred years ago. With his departure from Palos in search for a direct route to Asia, thinking of God, spices and gold, he unknowingly opened the way for the expansion of Europe to the ends of the world. First, ships discovered ever more remote coastlines, then expeditions penetrated into the innermost regions of countries and, move after move, the Europeans progressed, until barely any blank spot was left on the map. Missions and trading posts established early global interconnections, the hunger for raw materials later spurred colonial empires, and CNN and Mondovision now finally create the global experiential space. Many departures followed the departure from Palos; as a result, innumerable separate living spaces have been integrated into one single world. European civilization has circumnavigated the globe in the wake of Columbus.

At the Dawn of the Security Age

Up until recently, the burden of the unification of the world was carried almost exclusively by the peoples of the Southern hemisphere, from the plague killing millions of Aztecs and Mayas right after the white man's arrival, to the deportation of generations of blacks as slaves to America, down to the slums and *favelas* in today's mega-cities in the Third World. Those who escaped such consequences often had to struggle with political dependence, economic disadvantage and cultural degradation. Any achievements brought to the last corner of the globe by the gradual integration of the world have shrunk into insignificance in the face of the bitter consequences that have come along with it. By comparison, the countries of the North were able to corner the gains of the unification of the world on their side. Notwithstanding financial drain or humiliating retreat at times, it is sufficiently obvious that the rise of the West has in part been fuelled by the riches drained from the South through the network of global interconnections. By and large, the unification of the world seemed to have been governed by some kind of magnetic law according to which the advantages concentrate in the North and the disadvantages in the South.

But this law, after five hundred years, cannot be relied upon any longer. The bitter consequences of the unification of the world have begun to reach the North as well. Although they stand no comparison with those in the South, the tide is nevertheless turning. For the first time after Columbus' departure, the painful effects of worldwide interdependence are returning to the North. Consider, for example, the increasing economic strength of some countries in what used to be the Third World. Over the last 20 years the competitive edge of some of those countries has sharpened, putting considerable pressure on jobs and entire branches of the economy in the North, as the pupils of yesterday are about to outdistance their masters. Later, a similar constellation emerged in an entirely different area. Ever since Saddam Hussain's attack on Kuwait, if not before, the North has become aware that the many years of arming the South threaten to backfire on the North; since then governments have nervously watched the accumulation of mega-arms in several countries of the South – and of the East as well. Moreover, the population in the North feels alarmed, since a flow of immigrants and refugees legally and illegally arrive in the Northern belt of prosperity. The fear of migration and population pressure rising from the South has firmly taken root in the rich countries. And last but not least, environmental dangers are building up also in the South, dangers that threaten in the long run to engulf and to destabilize even the North. After all, the rainforests in the tropics act as 'lungs' for the global (and, by implication, the Northern) climate, the loss of biodiversity impinges upon the high hopes placed on a biotechnological future in the wealthy countries, and an unfettered motorization in China and India would finally transform the entire globe into a greenhouse.

Taking everything together, the boomerang seems to be a suitable metaphor for understanding the novel features of a rising epoch in North–South relations. The increasing integration of the world engenders consequences that threaten to rebound on the North (George

1992). Although the reasons for this reach far back into the history of
colonialism, two principal chronic conflicts have built up in the 50
years of accelerated world integration after the Second World War,
whose effects increasingly spread around the globe.

The crisis of justice　Epochs rise slowly, but the opening of the development era happened at a certain date and hour. As already mentioned,
on 20 January 1949, President Harry Truman, in his inauguration speech
before Congress, drawing the attention of his audience to the conditions
in poorer countries, for the first time defined them as 'underdeveloped
areas'. Suddenly, a concept that has since become indispensable was
established, cramming the immeasurable diversity of the globe's South
into one single category – the underdeveloped. That Truman coined a
new word was not a matter of accident but the precise expression of a
world view: for him all the peoples of the world were moving along the
same track, some faster, some slower, but all in the same direction. The
Northern countries, in particular the USA, were running ahead, while
he saw the rest of the world – with its ridiculously low per capita
income – lagging far behind. An image the economic societies of the
North had increasingly acquired about themselves was thus projected
upon the rest of the world: the degree of civilization in a country is
indicated by the level of its production. Starting from that premise,
Truman conceived of the world as an economic arena where nations
compete for a better position on the GNP scale. No matter what ideals
inspired Kikuyus, Peruvians or Filipinos, Truman recognized them only
as stragglers whose historical task it was to partake in the development
race and catch up with the lead runners. Consequently, it was the
objective of development policy to bring all nations into the arena and
to enable them to run the race.

After 40 years of development, the state of affairs is dismal. The
gap between front runners and stragglers has not been bridged; on the
contrary it has widened to the extent that it has become unimaginable
that it could ever be closed. The aspiration of catching up has ended
in a blunder of planetary proportions. Since 1960, according to the
1996 *Human Development Report*, the distance between industrial and
developing countries with regard to per capita income has tripled
(UNDP 1996). To be sure, upon closer inspection the picture is far
from homogeneous, but neither the South-East Asian showcases nor
the oil-producing countries change the result that the development
race has ended in disarray. The world might have developed – but in
two opposite directions.

This is especially true if one considers the destiny of large majorities of people within most countries: the polarization between nations repeats itself within each country. On the global as well as on the national level, there is a polarizing dynamics at work, which creates an economically ambitious middle class on the one side and large sections of socially excluded populations on the other side. The best one can say is that development has created a global middle class of those with cars, bank accounts and career aspirations. It is made up of the majority in the North and small elites in the South and its size equals roughly the 8 per cent of the world population who own an automobile. They are, beyond all national boundaries, increasingly integrated into the worldwide circuit of goods, communication and travel. An invisible border separates in all nations, in the North as well as in the South, the rich from the poor. Entire categories of people in the North – the unemployed, the elderly and the economically weak – and entire regions in the South – rural areas, tribal zones and urban settlements – find themselves increasingly excluded from the circuits of the world economy. 'North' and 'South' are therefore less and less geographical categories but rather socio-economic ones, referring to the line that divides the strong world market sectors from the competitively weak, economically superfluous sectors in society (Kothari 1993). A new bipolarism pervades the globe and reaches into every nation; it is no longer the East–West division that leaves its imprint on every society, but the North–South division.

The crisis of nature   A second result of the development era has dramatically come to the fore in recent years. It has become evident that the race-track leads in the wrong direction. While Truman could still take for granted that the North was at the head of social evolution, this premise of superiority has today been shaken – if not shattered – by the ecological predicament. For instance, much of the glorious rise in productivity is fuelled by a gigantic throughput of fossil energy, which requires mining the earth on the one side and covering it with waste on the other. By now, however, the global economy has out-grown the capacity of the earth to serve as mine and dumping ground. After all, the world economy increases every two years by about the size ($60 billion) it had reached by 1900 after centuries of growth. Although only a small part of the world's regions has experienced economic expansion on a large scale, the world economy already weighs down nature to an extent that it has in part to give in. If all countries followed the industrial example, five or six planets would be needed to serve as 'sources' for the inputs and 'sinks' for the waste of economic progress. Therefore, a situation has emerged where the certainty that ruled two centuries has been exposed as a serious illusion. Economic expansion has already come up against its bio-physical limits; recognizing the finiteness of the earth is a fatal blow to the idea of development as envisaged by Truman.

Five hundred years of protected status of the North seem to be drawing to an end. Europe's journey to the ends of the earth, initiated in the fifteenth century and completed in the twentieth century, has lifted history to new heights, but has at the same time produced a configuration of conflicts that will inevitably shape the face of the twenty-first century. A world divided and a nature ill treated is the heritage that casts its shadow forward. It is not that these conflicts as such are new, but their impact potentially spreads worldwide, as the pace of globalization is accelerating. For the unification of the world increasingly shows its seamy side; the globalization of goodies is accompanied by the globalization of nasties. What is new, in fact, is that the North is less and less protected by spatial and temporal distances from the unpleasant long-term consequences of its actions.

For several centuries the North could avoid dealing with the reality of a divided world, since the suffering occurred far away. Long distances separated the places of exploitation from the places of accumulation. However, as distances shrink, the distance between victims and winners shortens, exposing the North to the threats of a divided world. Globalization not only joins the haughty North with the South, but also the chaotic South with the North. Likewise, the bitter consequences of the ill-treatment of nature make themselves felt without delay. Many generations could afford to neglect the limits of nature as a source and as a sink; the costs of the present have been transferred to the future. The more, however, the rate of exploitation increases, the more quickly the finiteness of nature makes itself felt on a global scale. Since the distance in time, which for so long bolstered industrialism against its effects, is shrinking, the bio-physical limits of nature have forcefully emerged in the present. For these reasons, time and space, delay and distance, have ceased to provide a protective shell for the world's rich; as globalization promises the simultaneity and ubiquity of goodies, the simultaneity and ubiquity of troubles is also to be expected. The departure of Columbus, after a long cyle, is followed by the return of menace.

The Horns of the Dilemma

'Development', as a way of thinking, is on its way out. It is slowly becoming common sense that the two founding assumptions of the development promise have lost their validity. For the promise rested on the belief, first, that development could be universalized in space and, second, that it would be durable in time. In both senses, however, development has revealed itself as finite, and it is precisely this insight that constitutes the dilemma that pervades many international debates since the UN Conference on the Environment in Stockholm in 1972. The crisis of justice and the crisis of nature stand, with the received notion of development, in an inverse relationship to each other. In other words, any attempt to ease the crisis of justice threatens to aggravate the crisis of nature, and any attempt to ease the crisis of nature threatens to aggravate the crisis of justice. Anyone who demands more agricultural land, energy, housing, services or, in general, more purchasing power for the poor, finds himself in contradiction to those who would like to protect the soils, animals, forests, human health or the atmosphere. And anyone who calls for less energy or less transport and opposes clear-cutting or input-intensive agriculture for the sake of nature finds himself or herself in contradiction with those who insist on their equal right to the fruits of progress. It is easy, however, to see that the base upon which the dilemma rises is the conventional notion of development: if there were development that used less nature and included more people, a way out of the dilemma would open up. Small wonder, therefore, that in the last two decades committed minds from all corners of the world have been calling for an 'alternative model of development'.

The comet-like rise of the concept 'sustainable development' is to be understood against that background. It promises nothing less than to square the circle: to identify a type of development that promotes both ecological sustainability and international justice. Since the times of the Club of Rome study *The Limits to Growth* (Meadows et al. 1972), two camps of political discourse had emerged, one under the banner of 'environment' and the other under the banner of 'development'. The voices from the North mostly emphasized the rights of nature, while the voices from the South tended to bring the claims for justice to the fore (for an overview see McCormick 1989; Harbordt 1991; Moll 1991). In 1987, the World Commission for Environment and Development (Brundtland Commission) appeared to have succeeded in building a conceptual bridge between the two camps, offering the definition that has become canonical: sustainable development is development 'that meets the needs of the present without compromising the ability of future generations to meet their own needs' (WCED 1987: 8).

Just a quick glance, however, reveals that the formula is designed to maximize consensus rather than clarity. As with any compromise, that is no small achievement, because the definition works like an all-purpose cement that glues all parts together, friends and foes alike. The opponents of the 1970s and 1980s found themselves pinned down to a common ground, and since then everything has revolved around the notion of 'sustainable development'. Nevertheless, the price for this consensus was considerable. Dozens of definitions are being passed around among experts and politicians, because many and diverse interests and visions hide behind the common key idea. As so often happens, deep political and ethical controversies make the definition of the concept into a contested area.

The formula is based upon the notion of time. It invites readers to raise their eyes, to look at the future, and to pay due consideration to the generations of tomorrow. The definition officially confirms that the continuity of development in time has become a world problem. Under accusation is the egoism of the present, an egoism that sells off nature for short-term gain. In a way, the phrase reminds one of the words by which Gifford Pinchot, the steward of Theodore Roosevelt's conservation programme, sought to bring utilitarianism up to date: 'conservation means the greatest good for the greatest number for the longest time'. But upon closer inspection, one sees that the definition of the Brundtland Commission makes no reference to 'the greatest number', but focuses instead on the 'needs of the present' and those of 'future generations'. While the crisis of nature has been constitutive for the concept of 'sustainable development', the crisis of justice finds only a faint echo in the notions of 'development' and 'needs'. In the definition, the attention for the dimension of time is not counterbalanced by an equal attention to the dimension of space. It is therefore not an exaggeration to say that the canonical definition has resolved the 'nature versus justice' dilemma in favour of nature. For two crucial questions remain open: what needs, and whose needs? (*Ecologist* 1992). To leave these questions pending in the face of a divided world means to side-step the crisis of justice. Is sustainable development supposed to meet the needs for water, land and economic security, or the needs for air travel and bank deposits? Is it concerned with survival needs or with luxury needs? Are the needs in question those of the global consumer class or those of the enormous numbers of have-nots? The Brundtland Report remains undecided throughout and therefore avoids facing up to the crisis of justice.

Environmental action and environmental discourse, when carried on in the name of 'sustainable development', implicitly or explicitly position themselves with respect to the crisis of justice and the crisis of nature. Different actors produce different types of knowledge; they highlight certain issues and underplay others. How attention is focused, what implicit assumptions are cultivated, what hopes are entertained, and what agents are privileged depends on the way the debate on sustainability is framed. What is common to all these discourses, I submit, is the hunch that the era of infinite development hopes has passed, giving way to an era in which the finiteness of development becomes an accepted truth. What renders them deeply different, however, is the way in which they understand finiteness: either they emphasize the finiteness of development in the global space and disregard its finiteness in terms of time, or they emphasize the finiteness of development with regard to time and consider irrelevant its finiteness in terms of global space. In the following sections, I would like to sketch out three different perspectives of 'sustainable development', which differ in the way they implicitly understand finiteness. The *contest perspective* works with the silent assumption that development, unfortunately, will have to remain spatially restricted, but can be made durable for the richer parts of the world. It neglects the fact that the range of harmful effects produced by the North now covers the entire globe and limits the responsibility of the North to its own affairs. The *astronaut's perspective* takes a different view. It recognizes that development is precarious in time and seeks global adjustment to deal with the crisis of nature and the crisis of justice. As a response to the global reach of harmful effects, it favours the extension of the range of responsibility, until it covers the entire globe. The *home perspective*, in turn, accepts the finiteness of development in time and suggests delinking the question of justice from the pursuit of development. It draws a different conclusion from the fact that the range of effects produced by the North has vastly outgrown the radius of Northern responsibility, and advocates reducing the effects until they remain within the given radius of responsibility. It is possible that the relative strengths of these perspectives will shape the future of North–South relations.

The Contest Perspective

Some years ago, the French author Jean Christophe Rufin, in *The Empire and the New Barbarians*, proposed a telling metaphor for describing the changing mood in rich societies that face the globalization of threats. Dipping deep into European memory, he evoked the archetype of all frontiers, the *limes* (Latin: frontier), for describing the new perception of North–South relations. Much as the Romans erected the *limes* to separate themselves from the barbarians beyond their empire, present powers, he suggests, are busy drawing a perceptual wall between the market-integrated parts of the world and the rest. Indeed, large parts of the Southern countries now are no longer considered laboratories of the future, but seen as zones of potential turbulence. All kinds of dangers are expected: violence, hurricanes, the threat of mass migration, the population bomb ticking away. As the finiteness of development in terms of space moves into the consciousness of the North, the perception changes: the countries of the South change from places where hope resides to places where threats arise.

Having been for a long time the economic masters of the world, the Northern elites feel the pressure rising as the newly industrialized countries become players on the world market. For these reasons, the attention of economic actors is firmly focused on international competitiveness; to counter globalized threats by the weapon of 'competitive strength' is their primary concern. Given the obsession to get ahead in the race between the USA, Europe and East Asia, achieving some ecological modernization along the way is all that seems conceivable. As a consequence, concepts and strategies of sustainability cannot be allowed to interfere in the medium and long terms with the struggle for economic power; on the contrary, they are framed in such a way as to become part and parcel of that effort. How to bring the concern for the environment in line with the concern for economic efficiency and accumulation is the question squarely on the agenda of the contest perspective.

Growing for the environment First of all, in the light of the contest perspective, environmental concern emerges as a force propelling economic growth. Shifting consumer demand spurs innovation, trimming down resource usage lowers production costs, and environmental technology opens up new markets. Ecology and economics appear to be compatible, and the pursuit of both promises to be, as the magic formula goes, a positive-sum game. Growth is regarded as part of the solution, no longer as part of the problem (e.g. Reilly 1990; Fritsch et al. 1993). Indeed, it is perhaps this conceptual innovation that has done most to propel environmentalism into mainstream thought. Ever since the OECD in the early 1980s raised the prospects of an ecological modernization of industrial economies (Hajer 1995), advocating a new mix of resources, a changed structure of growth and an emphasis on prevention, a language linking business and environmental concerns has been developing. It centres around the redefinition of the environmental predicament as a problem of efficient resource allocation. Natural resources are considered grossly undervalued and therefore wastefully allocated, while human resources along with technology are under-utilized; redressing the balance would basically do the job. Thus, achieving 'eco-efficiency' (Schmidheiny 1992) is proposed as the key strategy for business, a strategy of considerable innovative power. The contest perspective goes further, however: by transferring the principle from the micro-economic to the macro-political level, it looks at society as if it were a corporation. In this view, political regulations that do not aim at efficiency are regarded as pointless or even wrongheaded. Issues such as legislation controlling multinationals, the evaluation of technologies in the public interest or a sustainable WTO (World Trade Organization) are pushed off the agenda. Through the Business Council on Sustainable Development, for instance, whose membership list reads like a 'Who's Who' of the chemical, steel and automobile industry, this perspective largely shaped the results of the UN Conference at Rio de Janeiro in 1992. Public authority in the realm of business activities remained a taboo – an outcome that, however, fits nicely in the neo-liberal Utopia of those years, which pretends that a society can be built through by-passing collective human decisions (Hobsbawm 1994: 565).

But even the contest perspective needs to look beyond the arena of competition. After all, the rich economies require more land and natural resources than are available for them within their own boundaries. Plugging into the 'syntropy islands' (Altvater 1992) of the South has for centuries fuelled accumulation in the North, a scheme that is increasingly threatened as bio-physical limits to exploitation come to the fore. As natural resources become scarce, some new regime, based either on the price mechanism or on political agreements, is mandated in order to cool down exploitation and to keep it at a manageable level. Moreover, in the 1980s the concern for nature as a resource was complemented by the concern for nature as a sink. The absorptive capacity of the biosphere for CFCs and CO_2 seemed to be exhausted, suggesting that the scarcity of sinks is even more pressing than the scarcity of sources. However, while access to sources could classically be secured bilaterally through occupation or trade, securing the access to sinks required limiting the emissions of a large number of countries. Making all utilize less can be achieved only multilaterally. For that reason, a new domain of international politics has emerged, in which international conventions are negotiated with the purpose of containing the claims to the biosphere. As a consequence, multilateral negotiations no longer centre on the redistribution of growth, as in the negotiations about the New Economic Order in the 1970s, but on the redistribution of reductions. However, given that all governments feel obliged to maximize their space for economic development, any reduction is seen as a loss. As a consequence, the ensuing conflicts are usually heated, up to a point where the environmental objectives fall by the wayside, as has happened with most of the Rio agreements.

From the conservation of nature to the conservation of growth Likewise, the concept of nature has changed. The conservation movement up until the 1970s was shaped by biocentric values; forests, waters, soils and wildlife were deemed worthy of preservation in their own right. In a way, nature was regarded as the opposite of development, embodying values of otherness and permanence to be safeguarded against the pressures of economic growth. With the 1980 World Conservation Strategy of the IUCN, WWF and UNEP, however, a shift in perception took place at the global level that had already occurred among protectionists in the USA after the turn of the century. Nature turned from a treasure to be preserved to a resource whose yield had to be sustained (Hays 1959). The emphasis thus shifted from the protection of nature to the protection of the productivity of natural resources for economic use. It was in the World Conservation Strategy that the concept of 'sustainable development' appeared for the first time. By linking 'sustainable' to 'development', however, a terrain of semantic ambiguity was created. The new concept subtly shifted the locus of sustainability from nature to development: while 'sustainable' previously referred to natural yields, it now refers to development. With that shift, the perceptual frame changes – instead of nature, development becomes the object of concern, and instead of development, nature becomes the critical factor to be watched. In short, the meaning of sustainability slides from conservation of nature to conservation of development. Moreover, since 'development' is conceptually an empty shell that may cover anything from the rate of capital accumulation to the number of latrines, it becomes eternally unclear and contestable just what exactly should be kept sustainable. This is the reason why all sorts of political actors, even fervent proponents of economic growth, are today able to couch their intentions in terms of 'sustainable development'. The term has become inherently self-referential, as a definition offered by the World Bank neatly confirms: 'What is sustainable? Sustainable development is development that lasts' (World Bank 1992: 34).

On the theoretical level, this change in perspective led to the reinterpretation of nature as capital (El Serafy 1991). With this conceptual operation, it becomes possible to compare natural capital with economic capital, to assess the costs and benefits of substituting one with the other, and to combine the two in an optimal fashion. In the light of the all-pervasive cost–benefit logic, anything – not only nature, but also human life – turns into a variable that can in principle be traded off against something else. As a consequence, supporters of this view may consider climate protection, for instance, sub-optimal in comparison to future adjustment to adverse climate effects, which appears to be a lesson more in the sustainability of money than of the environment.

The South as arena for ecological adjustment The search for competitive strength can live with the insight about the finiteness of development in space, but cannot go along with the notion of finiteness of development in time. In this view, therefore, the growth culture, and its further diffusion through 'free trade', remains unquestioned in terms of time, while its limitation in geographical space is quietly accepted. Alhough the bitter environmental effects produced in the North reach the far corners of the globe, the radius of responsibility remains restricted.

As is generally the case in the contest perspective, it is the South that emerges as the major arena for environmental adjustment. The South is urged to act responsibly, while the North is considered to be the home of reason, stability and – why not? – cleanliness. A storyline is being developed in which effects are reinterpreted as causes; one reads of environmental dangers, poverty and destabilization not as part of the global effects of the North, but as having their origins in the Third World. Responsibility thus can be repressed, with the South expected to take the initiative for urgent action. Logically, the population question figures prominently on the global agenda of the contest perspective. After all, no issue lends itself so easily to taking the South to task, no issue grants the status of innocence so clearly to the North as this one does. The exploding number of people, indeed, serves as a convenient pattern of explanation for the two most important threats facing the North: environmental insecurity and migration. The former is understood as the result of rising numbers of claimants to the biosphere, while the latter is understood as the result of rising population pressure in the countries of origin. In both cases, the reaction follows straight from the explanation: a call for strategies to contain population growth.

The inclination to define environmental problems in the Third World in such a way that their solution can come only from the North is a benign variant of the tendency to project responsibility onto the South. For example, the bulky *Agenda 21* – the plan of action resulting from the United Nations Conference on Environment and Development (UNCED) – has been largely drafted in this spirit. It divides the world ecologically into deficit countries and high-performance countries.

Environmental problems in the South are framed as the result of insufficient capital, out-dated technology, lack of expertise and slackening economic growth. And the definition of the problem already implies its solution: the North has to increase its investments in the South, to provide technology transfer, to bring in competence in eco-engineering, and to act as a locomotive of growth for the South (Hildyard 1993). It is easy to see how the conventions of development thinking shape this outlook: once again the South is pictured as the home of incompetence and the North as the stronghold of excellence.

The Astronaut's Perspective

At the foot of the Santa Catarina mountains, about forty miles northeast of Tucson in Arizona, a huge edifice of glass sends sparkles of sunlight across the plane. Noah's ark in a modern spirit. For the long, pyramid-like hall contains the world in miniature: a rainforest, grasslands, a desert, swamps, and even an ocean. Moreover, there are gardens and fields for the eight people who lived there along with a number of animals, altogether 3,800 species of plants and animals. The experiment was called Biosphere 2, and the name reveals the intention: the scientists attempted nothing less than creating a model of 'Biosphere 1' – the earth – under the glass roof. John Allen, the research director of Biosphere 2, sums his intentions up in the following words: 'Biosphere 2 presented the opportunity to develop a comprehensive biospheric monitoring and management system on a scale more approachable than Earth's. The successful development of such a model would be a large stride towards developing a more accurate model for Earth' (Allen 1991: 125).

The planet as a management object The scientists in Arizona exemplify a style of thought that often colours the discussions on 'Biosphere 1'. Environmentalism is being framed through an astronaut's perspective. Many of these environmentalists proclaim to be doing nothing less than saving the planet. For them, the blue earth, that suggestive globe, suspended in the dark universe, delicately furnished with clouds, oceans and continents, has become the reality that ultimately matters. Since the 1970s the world has been increasingly perceived as a physical body maintained by a variety of bio-geochemical processes rather than as a collection of states and cultures. The bio-physical conception of the earth as a system (e.g. Clark and Munn 1986; *Scientific American* 1989; Rambler et al. 1989; Nisbet 1991) projects a transnational space where the existence of nations, the aspirations of communities or other human realities fade into irrelevance when compared to the overwhelming presence of the natural earth. In this way, especially within an epistemic community of scientists around the globe (Haas 1990), a discourse has developed that constructs the planet as a scientific and political object. This community thinks in planetary terms; it frames 'sustainable development' through an astronaut's perspective.

Without the photographs of the earth it would scarcely have been possible to view the planet as an object of management (Sachs 1994). But there are political, scientific and technological reasons as well. Only in the course of the 1980s – with the ozone hole, acid rain and the greenhouse effect – did the border-crossing, global impact of pollution by industrial societies force itself into the foreground. Furthermore, scientists have made enormous headway in representing the biosphere as an all-embracing ecosystem, linking biota with processes in the atmosphere, oceans and the earth's crust. And finally, as happens so frequently in the history of science, a new generation of instruments and equipment has created the possibility of measuring global processes. Satellites, sensors and computers have provided the means of calibrating the biosphere and displaying it in models. In fact, research on the biosphere is rapidly becoming big science; spurred by a number of international programmes (Malone 1986), 'planetary sciences', including satellite observation, deep-sea expeditions and worldwide data processing, are being institutionalized in many countries. With this trend, sustainability is increasingly conceived as a challenge for global management. Experts set out to identify on a planetary scale the balance between human extractions/emissions on the one hand, and the regenerative capacities of nature on the other, mapping and monitoring, measuring and calculating resource flows and bio-geochemical cycles around the globe. 'This is essential', says *Agenda 21*, 'if a more accurate estimate is to be provided of the carrying capacity of the planet Earth and of its resilience under the many stresses placed upon it by human activities' (Chapter 5.1). Feeling the pulse of the earth seems to be the unstated objective of a new geo-science – the planet is put under sophisticated observation like a patient in an intensive care unit. The management of resource budgets has become a matter of world politics.

Global cooperation The image of the circular earth underscores the assumption, fundamental to this perspective, that since the effects of industrial civilization spread globally, the range of responsibility of the North should embrace the entire globe. As a consequence the entire globe is considered the proper arena for environmental adjustment –

not mainly the South, as in the contest perspective. Security against global threats is sought primarily in the rational planning of planetary conditions, not in the defence of the empires of wealth. The fragility of the biosphere under stress by human action is the storyline of this approach. It is recognized that economic development is threatened along the dimension of time. Since, however, the rational design of global conditions can never be achieved without the cooperation of many political actors, some new balance between North and South has to be found. To put it more delicately, at least some of the expectations of the less privileged parts of the global middle class have to be met if a new global order is to be achieved. In this perspective, the commitment to countering the crisis of nature does not permit the neglect of the crisis of justice.

However, the worldwide crisis of nature puts into the limelight the impotence of the world society in creating a global framework for sustainability. Has not the image of the planet shown that the unity of humankind is not just a dream of the enlightenment but a bio-physical fact? What is required, in the eyes of global ecologists, is to translate the bio-physical reality into political fact. Therefore, numerous environmentalists belong to the most outspoken promoters of global institutions and ground rules. Like US Vice-President Al Gore, at least in his earlier life:

> Merely addressing one dimension or another or trying to implement solutions only in one region of the world or another will, in the end, guarantee frustration, failure, and a weakening of the resolve needed to address the whole of the problem ... But if world government is neither feasible nor desirable, how then can we establish a successful cooperative effort to save the environment? There is only one answer: we must negotiate international agreements that establish global constraints on acceptable behaviour. (Gore 1992: 295, 302)

The strategic objective of such a plea is the establishment of multilateral regulations through common obligations across many areas of politics. Others are ready to go further: they call for new schemes of global governance, from global expert commissions to regulatory frameworks for nations and their economies, and eventually some sort of global mutilateral government. Since the inclusion of the South is imperative for such a strategy, Al Gore calls for a 'global Marshall Plan'. It would aim at concentrating all efforts on stabilizing the world population, developing environmentally sound technologies, modifying the economic rules of the game, concluding collective treaties, and launching an information campaign for the citizens of the globe. On the horizon is the noble vision of making ecology the centrepiece of a domestic world politics that would carry out the rational organization of global affairs.

The Home Perspective

'Sustainable development' in this perspective is about neither economic excellence nor biospherical stability; it is about local livelihoods. From this angle, the environment suffers in the first place from over-development and not from an inefficient allocation of resources or the proliferation of the human species. At the centre of attention is the goal and structure of development, which in the South is seen as disempowering communities, in the North as diminishing well-being, and in both as environmentally disruptive. 'Sustainable development' is therefore suspected to be an oxymoron; in one way or the other, practical and theoretical efforts aim at alternatives to economic development. What is more, it is only in that perspective that the crisis of justice figures prominently in the debate. Internationally, conserver societies in the North are expected to expand the space for Southern societies to flourish; nationally, sustainable lifestyles for the urban middle classes would give peasant and tribal communities more control over their resources. Consequently, the question of whose needs and what needs sustainable development is addressing is looming large: most inquiries in the last analysis turn around the question 'How much is enough? (Durning 1992).

In 1994 the world looked at Mexico with surprise, as hundreds of armed *indios* occupied the city of San Cristóbal de Las Casas. The Chiapas rebellion was a sudden signal. It pulled back the veil of oblivion from those indigenous and rural populations in the hinterland of the global middle classes, which are largely excluded from the fruits of the unification of the world. They are to be found everywhere, in innumerable villages and on all continents, peasants and landless workers, migrants and tribals, the periphery of the world market. Despite all their differences, they generally share the common fate of being threatened by the claims urban-industrial developers lay on their resources. The crisis of nature and the crisis of justice coincide for large parts of the world population in the experience of being marginalized by expansionist 'development'. For when water sources dry up, fields get lost, animals vanish, forests dwindle and harvests decrease, the very basis of their livelihood is undermined, pushing them onto the market, for which they have no sufficient purchasing power. Misery is frequently the result of enclosed or destroyed commons. Wherever communities base their subsistence on the renewable resources of soil, water, plant and animal life, the growth economy threatens nature and justice at the same time; the environment and people's life-support are equally degraded (Gadgil and Guha 1992). In that context, for many communities sustainability means nothing less than resistance against development (Tandon 1993). To protect both the rights of nature and the rights of people, the enclosure of extractive development, a federal state with village democracy (Agarwal and Narain 1989) and an affirmation of people's 'moral economies' are called for. Searching for sustainable livelihoods in this sense means searching for decentralized, and not accumulation-centred, forms of society.

The North as arena for ecological adjustment   Non-official NGOs, social movements and dissident intellectuals comprise most of the social base of the home perspective. What links the efforts of Southern groups with dissidents in rich countries is the fact that both expect the North to retreat from utilizing other people's nature and to reduce the amount of global environmental space it occupies. After all, most of the Northern countries leave an 'ecological footprint' (Wackernagel and Rees 1996) on the world that is considerably larger than their territories. They occupy foreign soils to provide themselves with tomatoes, rice or cattle; they carry away raw materials of all kinds; and they utilize the global commons – such as the oceans and the atmosphere – far beyond their share. The Northern use of the globally available environmental space is out of proportion; the style of affluence in the North cannot be generalized around the globe, but is oligarchic in its very structure. From the home perspective, the North is called upon to reduce the environmental burden it places on other countries and to repay the ecological debt accumulated from the excessive use of the biosphere over decades and centuries. The principal arena for ecological adjustment is thus neither the Southern hemisphere nor the entire globe, but the North itself. It is the reduction of the global effects of the North to the reach of domestic responsibility that is at the centre of attention, not the extension of Northern responsibility to coincide with the radius of the effects, as from the astronaut's perspective. The home perspective believes in making room for others by means of an orderly retreat; it proposes a new kind of rationality, which could be called 'the rationality of shortened chains of effect' for meeting the crises of justice and of nature. Good global neighbourhood, in this view, requires above all the reform of home out of a cosmopolitan spirit.

Efficiency and sufficiency   However, the reform of home is a major challenge, particularly in industrial countries. According to the current rule of thumb, only a cutback of between 70 and 90 per cent in the throughput of energy and materials over the next 40 to 50 years ahead would live up to the challenge (Schmidt-Bleek 1994). Therefore, the home perspective hesitates to over-emphasize efficient resource management and attempts to focus the social imagination on the revision of goals rather than on the revision of means. For over the longer term saving effects are invariably swallowed up by the quantity effects involved, if the overall dynamics of growth are not slowed down. Consider the example of the fuel-efficient car. Today's automobile engines are definitely more efficient than in the past, yet the relentless growth in the number of cars and miles driven has cancelled out that gain. The same logic holds across the board, from energy saving to pollution abatement and recycling. In fact, what really matters is the overall physical scale of the economy with respect to nature, not just the efficient allocation of resources (Daly and Cobb 1989). Herman Daly has offered a telling comparison: even if the cargo on a boat is distributed efficiently, the boat will inevitably sink under too much weight – even though it might sink optimally! Therefore, efficiency without sufficiency is counter-productive – the latter has to define the boundaries of the former.

A society in balance with nature, according to this view, can be approximated only through a twin-track approach: intelligent rationalization of means and prudent moderation of ends. In other words, an 'efficiency revolution' remains without direction if it is not accompanied by a 'sufficiency revolution'. Nothing is ultimately as irrational as rushing with maximum efficiency in the wrong direction. A 'sufficiency revolution', however, can neither be programmed nor engineered; it involves a mixture of subtle and rapid changes in the cultural outlook and institutional set-up of society. Therefore, this sustainablity discourse tends to focus more on values and institutional patterns, in short, on the symbolic universe of society, while both the contest and the astronaut's perspective rather highlight the energetic-material processes, in short the world of material quantities.

New models of prosperity Fortunately for the home perspective, wealth is not anymore what it used to be. Meanwhile, there are a number of indications that many industrial societies passed a threshold in the seventies, after which growth in GNP does not relate any longer to a growth in quality of life. (Cobb and Cobb 1994). This is good news for the home perspective, because it encourages these voices to assume that even a shrinking volume of production would not necessarily lead to a shrinking well-being; on the contrary, one can even imagine a growth in well-being.

Given that the negative consequences of economic growth seem to have increased faster than the positive consequences for the last 20 years, the home perspective view counts on the emergence of counter-motives to the growth philosophy of the ever 'faster, farther and more' (Sachs et al. 1998). Consider, for instance, the energy-intensive urge for acceleration. If pursued thoroughly enough, acceleration demonstrates the unfortunate tendency to cancel itself out. One arrives faster and faster at places at which one stays for ever shorter periods of time. Acceleration shows, beyond a certain level, a counter-productive tendency; it is therefore not so surprising that a renewed interest in slowness has appeared beneath the veneer of enforced acceleration. How would an advanced transportation system look like that was not shaped by the imperative of acceleration? As with time, so with space: the distance intensive lifestyle has spread widely, but a new appreciation for one's place and community is developing. What would a politics look like that centred on the regeneration of places? A similar sensibility might be growing with respect to the possession of things. The resource-intensive accumulation of goods, the thousand brands and fashions, increasingly congest everyday life. As a consequence, the ideal of lean consumption becomes more attractive, because a wealth of goods is at odds with a wealth of time. What would things look like if they were designed with a view to quality, durability and uniqueness?

Such questions are being raised, and all of them reveal a concern fundamental to the home perspective: the search for a society that is capable of remaining on an intermediary level of performance – in other words, a society that is able not to want what it would in fact be capable of providing. Self-limitation always implies a loss of power, even if it is sought in the name of a new prosperity. However, in what way a renunciation of power for the sake of the common good could be reconciled with the quest for individual liberty remains the conundrum of the home perspective. At any rate, both the crisis of justice and the crisis of nature necessitate looking for forms of prosperity that would not require permanent growth, for the problem of poverty lies not in poverty but in wealth. And equally, the problem of nature lies not in nature but in overdevelopment. It is likely that Aristotle was well aware of these interconnections, as he wrote the following: 'The greatest crimes are committed not for the sake of necessities, but for the sake of superfluities. Men do not become tyrants in order to avoid exposure to the cold' (*Politics* 1267a).

III

In the Image of
the Planet

6

One World – Many Worlds?

At present, roughly 5,100 languages are spoken around the globe. Just under 99 per cent of them are native to Asia and Africa, the Pacific and the American continents, while a mere 1 per cent find their homes in Europe. In Nigeria, for instance, more than 400 languages have been counted; in India 1,682; and even Central America, tiny as it is geographically, boasts 260 (Pörksen 1988: 15). A great number of these languages cling to remote places. They hide out in isolated mountain valleys, far-off islands and inaccessible deserts. Others govern entire continents and connect different peoples into a larger universe. Taken together, a multitude of linguistic worlds, large and small, covers the globe like a patchwork quilt. Yet many indicators suggest that, within a generation or two, not many more than a few hundred of these languages will survive.

Languages are dying out every bit as quickly as species. While, in the latter case, plants and animals disappear from the history of nature never to be seen again, with the demise of languages, entire cultures are vanishing from the history of civilization, never to be lived again. For each tongue contains its own way of perceiving man and nature, experiencing joy and sorrow, and finding meaning in the flow of events. To pray or to love, to dream or to reason, evoke different things when done in Farsi, German or Zapotec. Just as certain plants and animals are responsible for the maintenance of large ecosystems, so languages often carry subtle cultures through time. Once species disappear, ecosystems break down; once languages die out, cultures falter.

Along with languages, entire conceptions of what it means to be human have evaporated during the development decades since 1950. And yet the death of languages is only the most dramatic signal of the worldwide evaporation of cultures. Transistor radios and *Dallas*, agricultural advisers and nurses, the regime of the clock and the laws of the market have triggered an unprecedented transformation. It is, after all, scarcely an accident that Europe, the home of literacy as well as the nation-state, has only 1 per cent of all languages left. Whichever way one looks at it, the homogenization of the world is in full swing. A global monoculture spreads like an oil slick over the entire planet.

Forty years of 'development', fashioned on the model of 'one world', have gone by. The upshot of it all, if appearances do not deceive, is a looming vision of horror – modern humankind all alone for ever in the world. Ideas such as 'world society', 'unified world market' or even 'global responsibility' have in the past stimulated noble minds, and are again bandied about today, albeit with a tone of much more moral pathos than even a few years ago. But their innocence in an age of cultural evaporation is now tarnished.

One Humankind

There is a brass plate at the Fairmont Hotel on Union Square, San Francisco, to remind the passing visitor that it was here, on 4 May 1945, that a global hope was initialled. In Room 210, delegates from 46 countries agreed on the text of the United Nations Charter. Hitler's Germany was finally defeated and time was running out for Japan. The Charter promulgated those principles that were designed to usher in a new era of peace. No wars any more and no national egoisms. What counted was international understanding and the unity of humankind. After devastating conflicts, the Charter held out the prospect of universal peace, echoing the pledge of the League of Nations in 1919, but pointing far beyond a mere security system.

The Charter in fact conceptualized peace not just as the non-violent regulation of conflicts, but as the result of a global leap forward. Violence breaks out when progress is blocked. That was the conclusion the victorious powers drew from the past experience of economic depression and ensuing totalitarianism. Consequently, in the Preamble to the Charter, the United Nations solemnly announced the determination 'to promote social progress and better standards of life in larger freedom ... and to employ international machinery for the promotion of the economic and social advancement of all peoples' (UN 1968). The delegates in Room 210 were not timid in their vision. In their eyes, Austrians and Australians, Zulus as well as Zapotecos, shared in the same aspiration for 'social progress and better standards of life in larger freedom'. The histories of the world were seen as converging into one history, having one direction, and the UN was seen as a motor propelling less advanced countries to move ahead.

The project to banish violence and war from the face of the earth was clearly linked to the vision of humankind marching forward and upward along the road of progress. Humankind, progress and peace have been the conceptual cornerstones for erecting the sprawling edifice of UN organizations. The idea that both humankind and peace realize themselves through progress/development is the expectation built into their structure. The UN's mission hinges on faith in progress.

The United Nations Charter appeals to ideas that had taken shape during the European Enlightenment. At the time of Voltaire, the all-embracing, unifying power of Christianity had faded and given way to 'humanity' as the dominant collective concept. Ever since the Apostle Paul had shattered the validity of worldly distinctions in the face of God's gift of salvation, it had become thinkable to conceive of all humans as standing on the same plane. The Enlightenment secularized this heritage and turned it into a humanist creed. Neither class nor sex, neither religion nor race count before human nature, as they did not count before God. Thus the universality of the Sonship of God was recast as the universality of human dignity. From then on, 'humanity' became the common denominator uniting all peoples, causing differences in skin colour, beliefs and social customs to decline in significance.

But 'mankind', for the Enlightenment, was not just an empirical concept meaning the inhabitants of the globe; it had a time arrow built in. 'Mankind', in effect, was something yet to come, a task to be realized as man moves along the path of progress, successively shedding the ties of authority and superstition until autonomy and reason would reign. In the perspective of the Enlightenment, neither social roots nor religious commitments mattered much. The Utopian intention aimed at a world of individuals who follow only the voice of reason. In that sense, the Utopia of mankind was populated by men disembedded from their stories of the past, disconnected from the context of their places, and detached from the bonds of their communities, and united instead under the rule of science, market and the state. David Hume as well as Immanuel Kant saw humanity as something to be attained by spreading the universal values of civilisation and drawing ever more people into the course of progress. Mankind was to be the result of becoming modern. The Enlightenment's idea of unity cannot be separated from the assumption that history moves towards the rule of universal reason. It was one of those ideas, typical of that period, that were pregnant with an infinite future.

However, the rise of humanity by no means obliterated the image of the Other in European thought. Just as Christians had their heathens, philosophers of the Enlightenment had their savages. Both figures embodied the negation of what the respective societies held as their self-images. Heathens were those outside the Kingdom of God, while savages lived outside the kingdom of civilization. But there was one crucial difference. Whereas for Christendom heathens populated geographically remote areas, for the Enlightenment savages inhabited an infant stage of history. The Europe of the Enlightenment felt separated from the Other not spatially, but chronologically. As a matter of fact, the existence of strange peoples like the Iroquois, Asante or Bengali at the borders of (European) civilization contradicted the very idea of one mankind. But the contradiction was resolved by interpreting the multiplicity of cultures in space as a succession of stages in time. So the 'savage' was defined as one who would grow up and enter the stage of civilization. The 'savage', although he lived now, was assigned the status of a child in the biography of mankind, a child who was not yet fully mature, and was in need of guidance by a strong father.

In the Preamble to the UN Declaration, the quest for peace was closely linked to the hope for advancement of peoples around the globe. Towards the end of the eighteenth century the traditional notion that peace would be the fruit of justice had lost ground. It gave way to the expectation that peace would be the result of mankind reunited under the achievements of civilization. Reason and freedom would overcome prejudice and narrow-mindedness, and the age of harmony would dawn. Peace, progress and humanity were for the Enlightenment nothing less than the different faces of the future. The belief that mankind could be improved upon has driven political action from Voltaire right through to our own time.

The philosophy underlying the UN Declaration makes little sense without the view of history as the royal road to progress upon which all peoples converge. The conception of achieving 'one world' by stimulating progress everywhere betrays an evolutionary bias. It inevitably calls for absorbing the differences in the world into an ahistorical and delocalized universalism of European origin. The unity of the world is realized through its Westernization. By the mid-twentieth century the term 'underdeveloped' had taken the place of 'savages'. Economic performance had replaced reason as the measure of man. However, the arrangement of concepts remains the same – the world society has to be achieved through the improvement of the backward. And indissolubly linking the hope for peace to this world-shaking endeavour leads to a tragic dilemma – the pursuit of peace implies the annihilation of diversity, while seeking diversity implies the outburst of violence. The dilemma is unlikely to be resolved without delinking peace from progress and progress from peace.

One Market

The founding fathers of the United Nations, as well as being the architects of international development policy, were inspired by the vision that the globalization of market relationships would be the guarantee of peace in the world. Prosperity, so the argument went, derives from exchange, exchange creates mutual interests, and mutual interests inhibit aggression. Instead of violence, the spirit of commerce was to reign on all sides. Instead of firepower, productive strength would be decisive in the competition between nations. The unity of the world, it was thought, could be based only on a far-reaching and closely interconnected network of economic relations. Where goods were in circulation, weapons would fall silent.

With a naïvety hardly distinguishable from deception, the prophets of development polished up a Utopia envisioned as long ago as the eighteenth century, as if time had stopped and neither capitalism nor imperialism had ever appeared on the scene. After Montesquieu, the Enlightenment had discovered commerce as a means of refining crude manners. In this view, trade would spread rational calculation and cold self-interest, precisely those attitudes that make the passion for war or the whims of tyrants appear self-destructive. Trade creates dependence, and dependence tames. This is the logic that runs from Montesquieu through the UN down to the present-day integration of Eastern Europe and the USSR since the collapse of bureaucratic socialism there following the upheavals of 1989. And indeed, as the European Community and the Pax Americana after the Second World War suggest, economic dominions have largely replaced military dominions. The conquest of foreign territories by bellicose states has given way to the conquest of foreign markets by profitseeking industries. Global order, after the Second World War, was conceived in terms of a unified world market.

One of the most highly praised virtues of the world market is increased interdependence. The network of interests created is supposed to knit the nations together, for better or worse. From that perspective, the Pearson Report exhorted the industrialized nations in 1969:

There is also the appeal of enlightened and constructive self-interest ... The fullest possible utilisation of all the world's resources, human and physical, which can be brought about only by international cooperation, helps not only those countries now economically weak, but also those strong and wealthy. (Pearson 1969: 9)

Eleven years later, this trust in the unifying power of mutual interest was reiterated in the Brandt Report:

Whoever wants a bigger slice of an international economic cake cannot seriously want it to become smaller. Developing countries cannot ignore the economic health of industrialised countries. (Brandt 1980: 21)

But the ideology of mutual interests could not hide its major fallacy for long – the playing out of these interests takes place under unequal terms. The economists' doctrine of comparative advantage had it that the general well-being would increase if each nation specialized in doing things at which nature and history had made it most proficient – raw sugar from Costa Rica, for example, in exchange for pharmaceuticals from Holland. But the flaw in this reasoning is that, in the long run, the country that sells the more complex products will grow stronger and stronger, because it will be able to internalize the spin-off effects of sophisticated production. Pharmaceuticals stimulate research and a host of technologies, while sugar cane does not. The alleged mutual interest in free trade ends up cumulatively strengthening the one and progressively weakening the other. And when the richer country comes up with high-tech innovations that render the products of the weaker country obsolete, as with natural sugar being replaced by bio-engineered substitutes, then mutual interest withers away to the point where the weaker country becomes superfluous.

Apart from its built-in tendencies to discrimination and inequality, however, the obsession with the market as the medium of unification for the whole world is rapidly pushing all countries into a tight spot. The world market, once brandished as a weapon against despotism, has itself turned into a closet dictator under whose dominion both rich and poor countries tremble. The fear of falling behind in international competition has seized governments North and South, East and West. Not to lose ground in the economic arena has become an obsession that dominates politics down to the local level. This overruling imperative drives developing countries further into self-exploitation, for the sake of boosting exports, and industrial countries further into the wasteful and destructive mania of accelerated production, for the sake of protecting their markets.

What is overrun in this hurly-burly is the space for a policy of self-determination. The categorical imperative of world market competition repeatedly thwarts attempts to organize societies creatively and differently. Mobilizing for competition means streamlining a country; diversity becomes an obstacle to be removed. Some countries cannot keep up without sacrificing even more of their land for agricultural exports, others cannot afford to drop out of the high-tech race. There is scarcely a country left today that seems able to control its own destiny. In this respect the differences between countries are only relative: the United States enjoys more scope than India, but itself feels under intense pressure from Japan. For winners and losers alike, the constraints of the global market have become a nightmare.

One Planet

Since the late 1960s, another image of 'one world' has edged its way into contemporary consciousness – the globe in its physical finiteness. We share in 'humanity', we are connected by the 'world market', but we are condemned to one destiny because we are inhabitants of one planet. This is the message conveyed by the first photograph of the 'one world', taken from outer space, which has irresistibly emerged as the icon of our age. The photo shows the planet suspended in the vastness of the universe and impresses on everybody the fact that the earth is one body. Against the darkness of infinity, the circular earth offers itself as an abode, a bounded place. The sensation of being on and inside it strikes the onlooker instantly. The unity of the world is now documented. It can be seen everywhere. It jumps out at you from book covers, T-shirts and commercials. In the age of television, photographs are our eyewitnesses. For the first time in history, the planet is revealed in its solitude. From now on, 'one world' means physical unity; it means 'one earth'. The unity of humankind is no longer an Enlightenment fancy or a commercial act but a biophysical fact. However, this physical interconnectedness stands in relief against the background of proliferating dangers. From creeping desertification to impending climatic disaster, alarm signals multiply. The biosphere is under attack and threatens to cave in. Local acts such as driving a car or clearing a forest add up, when multiplied, to global imbalances. They turn beneficial cycles into vicious ones that undermine the reliability of nature. In the face of incalculable debacles, concerned voices call for a global political coherence that would match the biophysical interconnections. 'The Earth is one but the world is not. We all depend on one biosphere for sustaining our lives.' Having intoned this leitmotif, the Brundtland Report spells out the fateful new meaning of unity:

Today the scale of our interventions in nature is increasing and the physical effects of our decisions spill across national frontiers. The growth in economic interaction between nations amplifies the wider consequences of national decisions. Economics and ecology bind us in ever-tightening networks. Today, many regions face risks of irreversible damage to the human environment that threatens the basis for human progress. (WCED 1987: 27)

The Brundtland Report, the leading document on development policy in the late 1980s, takes unity for granted, but a unity that is now the result of a threat.

Things have come a long way since the promulgation of the UN Charter – from the moral hope of a humankind united by reason and progress to the economic notion of countries weaving themselves together through commercial ties, and, finally, to the spectre of unity in global self-destruction. What used to be conceived of as a historical endeavour – to accomplish the unity of humankind- – now reveals itself as a threat. Instead of hopeful appeals, sombre warnings provide the accompaniment. The slogan 'one world or no world' captures this experience. Seen in this light, humanity resembles a group of individuals thrown together by chance, each dependent on the others for his own survival. No one can rock the boat without causing all of us to be united – in our collective destruction. Living on earth, the ancient formula, appears to have taken on a new meaning. There are no longer any terrestrial wanderers longing for the eternal kingdom, but only passengers clinging fearfully to their vessel as it splits apart. Talk about unity has ceased to hold out promises and instead has taken on a grim connotation. As already foreshadowed by the Bomb, unity in our age has become something that may be finally consummated in catastrophe.

Amidst the wailing sirens of the rescue operations undertaken in the name of some lifeboat ethics, the pressure on peoples and countries to conform to an emergency discipline will be high. As soon as worldwide strategies are launched to prevent the boat from capsizing, things like political autonomy or cultural diversity will appear as the luxuries of yesteryear. In the face of the overriding imperative to 'secure the survival of the planet', autonomy easily becomes an anti-social value, and diversity turns into an obstacle to collective action. Can one imagine a more powerful motive for forcing the world into line than that of saving the planet? Eco-colonialism constitutes a new danger for the tapestry of cultures on the globe.

It is perfectly conceivable that, in the face of mounting pressure on land, water, forests and the atmosphere, global measures will have to be taken to trim down the intake from nature as well as the output of waste worldwide. Satellites are already prepared to monitor the consumption of resources on the planet, computer models are being devised to simulate what happens when, and a new generation of experts is in the making to survey and synchronize the manifold gestures of society. It is not the engineer, building bridges or power grids, who will be the protagonist of this new epoch, as in the old days of development, but the systems analyst.

NASA, for example, has its own ideas about the 'one earth':

> The goal of Earth system science is to obtain a scientific understanding of the entire Earth system on a global scale by describing how its component parts and their interactions have evolved, how they function and how they may be expected to continue to evolve on all timescales. The challenge is ... to develop the capability to predict those changes that will occur in the next decade to century both naturally and in response to human activity. (Finger 1989)

The oneness of the earth is understood according to this paradigm in system categories, its unity as the interaction of component parts, and the historical task as keeping the vital processes from destabilizing irretrievably. What links the peoples of the world together is no longer the rule of civilization or the interplay of demand and supply, but their shared dependence on biophysical life-support systems. The metaphor of spaceship earth captures nicely the gist of this thinking. Consequently, unity is not to be pursued through the spread of progress or the stimulation of productivity, but through securing the necessary system requirements.

But efforts to curb soil erosion, control emissions, regulate water consumption or save biodiversity, although undertaken with the best of intentions, will put people's daily activities under a new kind of scrutiny. Collecting firewood nor using spray-cans are no longer innocent activities, and how you heat your home and the food you eat become matters of global relevance. In such a perspective, the world is perceived as a single homogeneous space, this time constituted not by reason or the fluctuation of prices, but by geo-physiological macrocycles.

The consequences, however, are not likely to differ from the effects already observed in the wake of the rise of reason and the market to world dominance – namely the slow evaporation of customs and cultures. The current changes in development language from 'people' to 'populations', 'needs' to 'requirements', and 'welfare' to 'survival' are indicative of a growing negligence towards cultures in favour of mere existence. Whatever has survived the rise of industrialism is now in danger of being drawn into the maelstrom of its fall.

But recognizing the pitfalls of global eco-management does not solve the dilemma that will stay with us in the decades to come. The alternatives – to think in categories of one world as well as not to think in such categories – are equally self-destructive. On the one hand, it is sacrilege in our age of cultural evaporation to apprehend the globe as a united, highly integrated world. On the other hand, a vision of the globe as a multitude of different and only loosely connected worlds cannot dispense with the idea of ecumenism in the face of lurking violence and the devastation of nature. Not surprisingly, calls for global consciousness abound. Given that local events can affect the conditions of life in remote places, these calls aim at bringing into congruence the range of our responsibility with the range of our effects. However – and here lies the dilemma – universalism is being invoked for salvation from the present predicament, while universalism was precisely the original sin by which the predicament was provoked.

Space Against Place

For centuries, universalism has been at war with diversity. Science, state and market have dominated this campaign, while an innumerable variety of communities with their languages, customs and cosmologies, although they have sometimes struck back and reinvigorated themselves through resistance, have been the losers. It has been an unequal clash. Not only did the protagonists often fight with unequal arms when the universalist powers employed guns and dollars but, more importantly, they were unequal in their cognitive might.

Science, state and market are based on a system of knowledge about humanity, society and nature that claims validity everywhere and for everybody. As a knowledge that has successfully shed all vestiges of its particular origin, place and context, it belongs nowhere and can therefore penetrate everywhere. In a certain sense, mechanistic causality, bureaucratic rationality and the law of supply and demand are rules that are cleansed of any commitment to a particular society or culture. It is because they are disembedded from broader contexts of order and meaning that they are so powerful in remodelling any social reality according to their limited but specific logic. As a consequence, they are capable of unsettling all kinds of different cultures, each one locked in its own imagination. Since these cultures are connected to particular places with their own particular peoples, memories and cosmologies, they are vulnerable to a mental style that is not linked to any place, but rests instead on the concept of space. One way to grasp the fundamental difference between universalism and localism is to focus on the dichotomy of space and place. Universalist aspirations are generally space-centred, while localist world views are mainly place-centred. This distinction illuminates both the rise of universalism in the past, and the tension between universalism and diversity in the present.

In medieval times, when people talked about the entire 'world', they did not evoke in their listeners the image of the planet with its many inhabitants, but instead the image of an earth overarched by several spheres or heavens in permanent revolution. The tiny earth was at the centre, yet not central. Most of the attention was concentrated on the relations between the chance-governed terrestrial realm and the immutable, eternal realm of the heavens. The medieval cosmos took shape around a vertical axis that linked a hierarchy of strata of different qualities. Humanity's view was directed upwards to grasp the vaulting architecture of the cosmos, as if attracted by the soaring arches and spires of a Gothic cathedral. Although this 'world' was immense, it was nevertheless finite and had a definite shape – to look up to the heavens was like looking up to a high vault.

In early modern times, the concept of a stratified and bounded cosmos was gradually abolished in favour of a universe infinitely extended in space. The vertical axis was tilted over and laid out on a horizontal plane; what mattered now was no longer the view upwards, but the view into the distance. As the vertical dimension faltered, so the idea of qualitative differences between lower and upper layers of reality also faded away and was replaced by the conception of a homogeneous reality that could be ordered only through measurable differences in geometrical fashion. It is the horizontal plane that now dominates the imagination. The world is seen no longer as marked by boundaries and upward-rising, but as limitless and extending in circles of ever greater distance. As a result, not upward–downward movements, but geographical movements to destinations close and far, hold people's attention. 'World' now evokes the surface of the globe and not the height of the cosmos.

In other words, the abolition of the stratified cosmos has made possible the rise of 'space' to its prominent position in modern consciousness. And the rise of a space-centred perception has made it possible to conceive of 'one world'. In this perception, the world is on one level, stretching out as a two-dimensional plane where each point equals any other point; what distinguishes them is only their geometrical position. The purest case of a space-centred perception can

ously be found in cartography. On maps, the world is flattened out and places are defined by their locations in the grid of longitudinal and latitudinal lines.

However, nobody is capable of living only in 'space'; everyone lives also in 'place'. This is because being human means, all attempts to the contrary notwithstanding, to be in a physical body, and the body is necessarily tied to a place. Human experience, for that reason, evolves in specific local places. Some points in space, as a result, are always more important to people than others, since they have been the scenes of individual and collective imagination and action. Having a memory, relating to others, participating in a larger story, calls for involvement, requires presence. This presence, naturally, is lived out in particular physical settings like piazzas or streets, mountains or seashores. And these locations are in turn imbued with experience past and present. They become places of density and depth. Therefore, certain places have a special 'thickness' for certain people. It is there that the ancestors walked the earth and the relevant memories are at home. It is there that one is tied into a web of social bonds and where one recognizes and is recognized by others. And it is there that people share a particular vantage point and that language, habits and outlook combine to constitute a particular style of being in the world. Consequently, thinking in terms of places means to work on the assumption that a place is not just the intersection of two lines on a map, but a concentration of meaningful human activity that gives it a distinct quality, a distinct aura.

Ever since the temples of Tenochtitlan were destroyed in Mexico and a Spanish cathedral built out of their stones, European colonialism has been busy ravaging place-centred cultures and imposing on them space-centred values. In ever new waves and on all five continents, the colonialists have been terribly inventive in robbing peoples of their gods, their institutions and their natural treasures. The establishment of universities in New Spain, the introduction of British law in India, the blackmailing of North American Indians into the fur trade, these were all instances in the history of spreading science, state and market throughout the world.

The period of development after the Second World War fits into that history. Viewed with the space-trained eyes of the West, numerous cultures appeared as backward, deficient and meaningless. The globe looked like a vast homogeneous space, waiting to be organized by universally applicable programmes and technologies. And the developmentalists did not hesitate. They went about transferring the Western model of society to countries of a great variety of cultures.

But place-centred perceptions have not disappeared. On the contrary, the more universalism prevails, the more particularism thrives. Indeed, throughout the last centuries, the advance of space-centred perceptions has been both successful and unsuccessful. On the one side, universalism has gained the upper hand, but on the other, place-bound aspirations have affirmed themselves over and over again. Innumerable revolts against colonialism expressed the will of the particular to survive. Independence movements launched indigenous claims.

A similar picture has prevailed in recent decades during the development era. Nationalist demands, ethnic strife, tribal tensions abound. And it should not be forgotten that the failure of a universalist development is in large part due to people's tenacious adherence to the old ways proper to their respective places. To be sure, localist conceptions do not remain the same. They are reformulated, altered and newly invented in a continuous vortex of dialogue and antagonism.

Equally, universalist conceptions, though advancing powerfully, are constantly watered down, curtailed and adapted, to the perennial dismay of Western do-gooders. And repeatedly, from the Orientalist movement in the early nineteenth century to alternative travellers in our own days, dissident elites, deeply steeped in a space-intensive world view, discover place-bound traditions and turn them into weapons against the European civilization.

Cosmopolitan Localism

Today, more than ever, universalism is under siege. To be sure, the victorious march of science, state and market has not come to a stop, but the enthusiasm of the onlookers is flagging. Few still believe that order and peace will dawn at the end of the march. The centuries-old movement of carrying the torch of reason and progress to the furthest corners of the earth is tapering off. To the degree that it continues, it is carried out more from inertia than from missionary conviction.

Utopias crystallize longings that arise from frustration with the state of society. The ambition to create larger and larger unified spaces – from nation-states to regional integration and world government – has been fuelled by frustration with chauvinism and violence. Yet that concern retreats into the background as the opposite frustration spreads – the disappointment with a world that has fallen prey to homogenization. All of a sudden, the customary association of differences with violence vanishes; differences are now something to be cherished and cultivated. Indeed, the fear that modern humans will encounter nobody else but themselves on the globe is about to revolutionize contemporary perceptions. The pursuit of space-centred unity is turn-ing into the search for place-centred diversity. After all, it is only from places that variety crops up, because it is in places that people weave the present into their particular thread of history. Thus native languages are beginning to be revaluated, traditional knowledge systems re-discovered, and local economies revitalized. And, as the popularity of the prefix 're-' indicates, the unconventional is today often launched under the guise of a renaissance. The disquieting anticipation of a world fully illuminated by the neon light of modern rationality motivates the search for the darker zones, where the special, the strange, the surprising lives. A world without the Other would be a world of stagnation. For, in culture as well as in nature, diversity holds the potential for innovation and opens the way for creative, non-linear solutions. And with these misgivings growing, the tide changes. The globe is not any longer imagined as a homogeneous space where contrasts ought to be levelled out, but as a discontinuous space where differences flourish in a multiplicity of places.

Moreover, the vision of a world integrated under the rule of reason and welfare was carried by a view of history that today is rapidly becoming ripe for the museum. The unity of mankind was a project of the future, made possible by the expectation that human action would keep the course of history always on an upward road. Progress was the guarantee of unity. In the space-centred perception, the differ-ences on the globe would fall into oblivion because they were outshone by the bright light of progress; it was in relation to that promise that they didn't matter any more. But clearly enough, if our present experience shortly before the end of the twentieth century can be wrapped up in one formula, it is precisely this: that the belief in progress has crumbled, the arrow of time is broken. The future doesn't hold much promise any more; it has become a repository of fears rather than of hopes.

At this juncture, therefore, it is wide of the mark to think that the coherence of the world could be achieved by pushing ahead along a common path towards some distant promised future. Instead, co-existence has to be sought in the context of the present. Thinking unity within the horizon of the present is much more demanding for all the players involved, since the attainment of a peaceful world would then be on today's agenda and could not be postponed to a far future.

Three ideals emerge for conceiving a politics that could shoulder the responsibility of acting for a diverse but coherent world – regeneration, unilateral self-restraint and the dialogue of civilizations. Regeneration takes into account the fact that the royal road of development has vanished, since there is no longer any ideal of progress to indicate a common direction. Regeneration calls instead for actualizing the particular image of a good society which is present in each culture. As for unilateral self-restraint, this can take the place of the ideal of interdependent growth. It implies instead that each country puts its own house in order in such a way that no economic or environmental burden is pushed onto others that would constrain them in choosing their own path. And, finally, a dialogue of civilizations is imperative as the search for peaceful and sustainable coexistence puts the challenge of self-examination before each culture. A simultaneous process of confrontation and synthesis can lead to coherence, while avoiding the pitfalls of homogeneity.

Although universalism has exhausted its Utopian energies, any new localism will have a window onto the world at large. The opposite of the dominion of universal rules is not egoism, but a higher capacity for self-observation. People are seldom residents of only one mental space. They have the ability to change their point of view and to look with the other's eye at themselves. In fact, people often hold multiple localities at one and the same time. In many instances they combine rootedness in a place with affiliation to a larger community. An inhabitant of medieval Cologne knew how to be a member of the Christian Church; a villager in Rajasthan was aware of Bharat, Mother India; and Croatian peasants as well as the citizens of Cracow were part of the Habsburg empire.

In a similar vein, the one world may be thought of in terms of a meta-nation instead of in terms of a super-nation. It constitutes the horizon within which places live out their density and depth. In this perspective, 'one world' is not a design for more global planning, but an ever present regulative idea for local action. Cosmopolitan localism seeks to amplify the richness of a place while keeping in mind the rights of a multi-faceted world. It cherishes a particular place, yet at the same time knows about the relativity of all places. It results from a broken globalism as well as a broken localism. Maybe Tzvetan Todorov wanted to illustrate such an attitude when he used a phrase of the twelfth-century Hugh of St Victor: 'The man who finds his country sweet is only a raw beginner; the man for whom each country is as his own is already strong; but only the man for whom the whole world is like a foreign country is perfect (Todorov 1984: 250).

Further Reading

The idea of 'mankind' figures prominently in the Charter of the United Nations, New York: UN Office of Public Information, 1968; the notion of 'one world' in L. Pearson, *Partners in Development: Report of the Commission on International Development*, New York: Praeger, 1969, and W. Brandt, *North–South: A Programme for Survival: Report of the Independent Commission on International Development Issues*, Cambridge, MA: MIT Press, 1980; and the concept of 'one earth' in B. Ward and R. Dubos, *Only One Earth: The Care and Maintenance of A Small Planet*, New York: Norton, 1972, and WCED, *Our Common Future*, Oxford: Oxford University Press, 1987.

A very elaborate commentary on the UN Charter is offered by J. Cot and A. Pellet, *La Charte des Nations Unies, Economica*: Paris, 1985. H. Jacobson, *Networks of Interdependence: International Organizations and the Global Political System*, New York: Knopf, 1984, gives an overview of the emergence of international organizations, while P. de Senarclens, *La crise des Nations Unies*, Paris: Presses Universitaires de France, 1988, provides a conceptually oriented history of the UN.

Regarding the history of the idea of 'mankind', I found particularly useful H. C. Baldry, *The Unity of Mankind in Greek Thought*, Cambridge: Cambridge University Press, 1965, and, for the seventeenth century, W. Philipp, 'Des Bild der Menschheit im 17. Jahrhundert des Barock', in *Studium Cenerale*, 14, 1961, pp. 721–42. An excellent analysis of the semantic formation of 'peace' and 'mankind' during and after the Enlightenment is found in the articles 'Friede' and 'Menschheitt', in O. Brunner and W. Conze (ed. R. Koselleck), *Ceschichtliche Crundbegriffe: Historisches I exikon our politisch-sozialen Sprache in Deutschland*, Stuttgart: Klett-Cotta, 1975, vols 2 and 3. Very instructive on the position of the Other in different cosmologies is M. Harbsmeier, 'On travel accounts and cosmological strategies: some models in comparative xenology', in *Ethnos*, 48, 1983, pp. 273–312. For the early association of the market with peace, see A. Hirschman, *The Passions and the Interests: Political Arguments for Capitalism Before its Triumph*, Princeton, NJ: Princeton University Press, 1977, and for the secular substitution of economic for military competition, R. Rosecrance, *The Rise of the Trading State: Commerce and Conquest in the Modern World*, New York: Basic Books, 1986.

To understand the transition from 'place' to 'space', I have benefited from M. Eliade and L. Sullivan, 'Center of the world' in M. Eliade (ed.), *The Encyclopedia of Religions*, New York: Macmillan, 1987, vol. 3, pp. 166–71; from Y.-F. Tuan, *Topophilia: A Study of Environmental Per-*

ception, *Attitudes, and Values,* Englewood Cliffs, NJ: Prentice-Hall, 1974; and C. S. Lewis's article on the concept of 'world' in *Studies in Words,* Cambridge: Cambridge University Press, 1960.

Those who want to have a clearer sense about the 'internationalism' of the electronic media may look at M. Ignatieff, 'Is nothing sacred? The ethics of television', in *Daedalus,* 114, 1985, pp. 57–78; and J. Meyrowitz, *No Sense of Place: The Impact of Electronic Media on Social Behavior,* New York: Oxford University Press, 1985.

Furthermore, I found R. Panikkar, 'Is the notion of human rights a Western concept?', in *Interculture,* 17, January–March 1984, pp. 28–47, a penetrating reflection on universalism, and I liked the dense presentation of the pitfalls of Westernization in S. Latouche, *L'occidentalisation du monde,* Paris: La Découverte, 1989. T. Todorov, *La conquête de l'Amérique,* Paris: Le Seuil, 1982, and E. Morin, *Penser l'Europe,* Paris: Gallimard, 1987, have given me many insights into how to think of a world of multiple unity.

7

The Blue Planet: On the Ambiguity of a Modern Icon

Discovery of the earth took place during the journey to the moon. When in July 1969 Neil Armstrong uncoupled himself from spaceship *Apollo 11* and touched down in his landing-craft on our neighbouring planet, he found only barrenness, emptiness, and icy silence – but when he looked backwards, he went into raptures. How different the earth appeared! Shimmering blue, it floated like a spherical jewel in pitch-black space. A web of clouds enveloped it in a white vortex, beneath which continents and oceans shone with soft browns and a deep blue. Ever since those space missions transmitted the first picture of the earth rising in the moon's heavens back to our living rooms, discovery of the earth has become the essential revelation of American space flight. Amid the desolate expanses of the universe the old earth reveals itself to be the habitable, the absolutely special, star that is our home.

This image of the earth in space leads the field in the world of contemporary images. It adorns the covers of weighty environmental reports and T-shirts in all sizes, endows television news with a global touch, and leaps out of many commercials. It is to be encountered everywhere. The photograph seems to be a quality mark for all and everything. It is not going too far to say that this image of the blue planet has become an icon for our age.

Sudden awareness of the earth's uniqueness allowed an upsurge of emotion, and the first sight of the earth as a whole signified a leap forward in the history of human self-perception. Peter Sloterdijk writes:

The view from a satellite makes possible a Copernican revolution in outlook. For all earlier human beings, gazing up to the heavens was akin to a naive preliminary stage of a philosophical thinking beyond this world and a spontaneous elevation towards contemplation of infinity. Since October 1957, however, something has got under way and led to reversal of the oldest human gaze: the first satellite was put in orbit above the earth. Soon afterwards the area of space close to the earth was teeming with satellite eyes, which provide technical implementation of the ancient phantasm of God looking down from high in the heavens. Ever since the early sixties an inverted astronomy has thus come into being, looking down from space onto the earth rather than from the ground up into the skies. (Sloterdijk 1990: 57)

The Construction of the Earth through an Image

Human beings have certainly long attempted to gain a mental picture of the earth's shape and form. Two and a half thousand years ago, Pythagoras argued that the earth must be perfectly fashioned – hence a sphere. Some 500 years later Eratosthenes attempted to prove that assumption mathematically by comparing the sun's shadow in various places. Magellan finally succeeded four hundred years ago in sailing around the world. When Mercator constructed a map of the world utilizing a network of longitude and latitude, representations of the earth that were to scale and thus geometrically consistent became the norm. From the time of Martin Behaim's globe, dating from 1492, it has been possible to take a close look at models of the world, and dissemination of such globes, large and small, made the earth an everyday object at school and in the home. Nevertheless, they could not lay claim to being depictions of physical reality. Nothing could obscure their origins on the drawing-board: these were models of the world, showing nothing of the reality of the earth itself.

Visible What is fundamentally new is that the earth has now moved into the realm of visible things by way of satellite photographs. Its overall form is no longer a scientific deduction but an obvious reality, which anyone can see for themselves by looking at a piece of paper. The earth lies before our eyes just like any other object – albeit mediated through photography. Never before was the earth a reality accessible to its inhabitants' senses. The planet's existence may have been an empirical certainty but not an empirical magnitude, since the globe's gigantic mass exceeded anything that could be taken in at a single glance. Only now did the earth truly become something graspable, established as an object through the photograph from space. That photograph endows the earth with tangibility, thereby creating nothing less than a new reality.

It is important that this process involves a photograph, since only photography – among such diverse forms of representation as paintings, sculpture, maps, or models – lays claim to being both similar and to a certain extent identical to the object depicted. Elucidating the difference between a picture and a photograph, Susan Sontag writes: 'Because first of all a photograph is not only an image (as a painting is an image), and interpretation of the real; it is also a trace ... like a footprint or a death mask. While a painting ... is never more than the stating of an interpretation, a photographgraph is never less than the registering of an emanation (light waves reflected by objects) – a material vestige of its subject in a way no painting can be' (Sontag 1977: 154). Even though a photograph always selects, it claims to bear witness to a state of affairs. The photograph from space demonstrates the reality of the earth, and its reproducibility makes that reality omnipresent. That creates the basis for many contemporary variants of global consciousness.

Demarcated Nothing stands out more in the picture than the boundaries setting off the luminous earth from cold, black space.

> 'When I looked out into the blackness of space with its splendour of points of light' – reported astronaut Loren Acton – 'there I saw majesty but no hospitality. The hospitable planet was below me. There below, enclosed in the thin, moving, unbelievably vulnerable sheath of the biosphere, is everything that is dear and precious for you – the entire human drama and the entire human comedy. There is life. All good things are down there.' (Kelley 1988: 21)

The edge of the globe marks an overwhelming contrast. It separates the sphere of life from the sphere of deathly silence. Against the background of space, hostile to life, the illuminated blue earth appears a friendly, protective place. The earth's highly obvious boundaries give rise to a new feeling of inner and outer. What is demarcated there is the place where we live viewed against the nothingness of space.

Considerable disillusionment has set in with regard to the moon: no life, everywhere extreme cold, stony deserts, and an atmosphere hostile to life. Compared with that, the earth seems an oasis in the desert of the cosmos. Light and friendly, green and fertile, it stands out against the endless blackness. Is not the earth unique in the way it floats invitingly in space? The perspective from space made emphatically obvious what distinguishes Planet Earth from all other known planets: the thin layer of air and water, soil and organisms, that allows living creatures to thrive and gives them a home. No thicker than

17,000 metres (or one four-hundredth of the earth's radius), this atmospheric sheath, which bears all life, encircles the earth. That is why the view from space is accompanied by penetration of human consciousness by the idea of the earth as a biosphere. The planet literally reveals itself to be a 'ball of life'.

Small Distance diminishes. Perhaps the most astonishing outcome of the view from space, described by astronauts again and again, was the dwindling of the earth. James Irwin, who flew with *Apollo 15* in 1971, captured that experience in poetic phrases: 'The earth reminded us of a Christmas tree bauble hung in the darkness of space. With increasing distance it became smaller and smaller. Finally it shrunk to the size of a marble, the most beautiful marble you can imagine' (Kelley 1988: 38). A dramatic breach in perception: the earth, once immeasurably large, now presents itself to everyone as a little ball. Truly a reversal of perspective! Human beings previously saw themselves as being surrounded by the earth, for good or for ill. Now they themselves embrace the earth – at least with their gaze.

This reversal of perspective is obviously the outcome of the enormous distance across which the astronauts were catapulted. Rocket-impelled removal from the earth shifted the yardstick hitherto established in the limited capacities of human powers and senses. The perceptions now accessible, and the reality established, are disproportionate to human senses. The correlations between man and earth have been upturned. Astronaut Buzz Aldrin summed up that miraculous, uncanny reversal of relationships: 'The earth finally became so small that I could simply make it vanish from space by holding up my thumb in front of it' (Kelley 1988: 37).

What is involved when – disseminated by television and photography – a diminished earth, no longer bound to human dimensions, becomes the predominant idea? Two reactions are visible at present. On the one hand, people talk about the earth in a language of sentimental trivialization: Look how tiny and fragile it is! It needs our care and attention! On the other, human self-aggrandizement and claims to omnipotence become apparent: Look how easily comprehensible and manageable the earth is! It can be mastered and kept under control! Of course, the motives of 'concern' and 'control' may also coincide. Both ways of speaking seem to find accord in talking of the earth as a 'patient'.

Not all these images were taken during moon-shots. Those from satellite orbits still present the earth as an object – but a beautiful and huge one. All the same, here too the distortion of proportions shapes perception. The diminution of the planet brought about by the uncoupling of human criteria also results in human concerns becoming irrelevant. The earth depicted in that image is self-evidently and essentially a physical object with oceans, land-masses, and swirling clouds, but not a place where human beings live. What constitutes the reality of human existence vanishes in this picture of the earth. Cultures, races and nations are nowhere to be seen. That state of affairs is supported by the character of photography. A photograph always defines a particular moment and thus blocks understanding of history and the context of what is depicted. The earth thereby appears all too obviously as a physical unity, directly implying social unity because conflict-ridden human reality pales in the face of the earth's grandiose actuality. That is probably why so many astronauts have emphasized how friendly and peaceful the earth looks, time and again stressing that frontiers, differences and conflicts are as if wiped away when viewed from space. The image's strongest message is therefore a naturalistic reformulation of the idea of humanity, maintaining that human unity derives from the shared destiny of floating together on this earthly body in space – or as a poster of the blue planet succinctly states: 'All One People'.

Synoptic Height bestows an overview. The higher one climbs, the fewer obstacles block the outlook; the greater the remoteness of the ground, the further the horizon moves into the distance. The moon, however, constitutes the highest viewing-platform humanity has ever reached. From a spaceship or a satellite a picture of the entire earth (or great parts of it) is available, a synopsis of the world that could not be more comprehensive. A single glance takes in more than ever before, and the overall view across seas and continents reveals vast fields of interrelationships hitherto hidden from the human gaze. Cloud forma-tions and carpets of algae, folds in the earth and patterns of settlement, together form structures within a higher order, which emphatically suggest that apparently geographically scattered phenomena in truth often constitute aspects of larger relationships.

There is no doubt that such an overview gives a great boost to many variants of integrative thinking since superordinate patterns, in which the individual parts interact, force themselves on the observer. The synoptic power of the satellite perspective is strengthened even further by orbiting the earth. In slightly less than 90 minutes, when space shuttle *Columbia* circles the earth, the entire globe moves past far below. In addition, as the days pass, the orbit changes gradually, cover-ing the earth's entire surface. It then becomes clear that the technical programme that came into being with satellites constitutes a total view rather than just a survey. No blind spots any longer and also no unmapped areas – total observability. In their way satellite-eyes are omnipresent and omniscient.

One can hardly speak of a horizon any longer when looking down on the earth from space. At any rate, the horizon vanishes as the satellite rises and goes into orbit, becoming one with the globe's circumference. The gaze is unrestricted by borderlines and nothing remains hidden – a way of seeing that no longer knows any 'beyond', 'after' or 'behind'. The totality of the satellite's viewpoint allows such distinctions as here/there, inside/outside, and now/later to collapse. The image of the blue earth has thus left behind the limits of the perspectival and panoramic view. The classical central perspective stresses the depth of space, but here the distinction between 'in front of' and 'behind' is superseded in the macroscopic overview. While the panoramic field of vision indicates something 'beyond' the horizon, here the all-round view is no longer trapped within a single horizon but extends behind all horizons. Both perspective and panorama are ways of seeing that imply a movement, an inner dynamic, even an impulse towards transcending area, height, and time: ever onwards in terms of an ever-higher viewpoint with very much more to be seen tomorrow (Koschorke 1989). These two ways of seeing are analogous to the idea of progress, concerned with successively surmounting horizons, whereas the macroscopy of the planet demonstrates a clear-cut relationship to post-progressive thinking, whose main source of fascination is simultaneity of presence. In other words, the satellite image supports systemic perception where attention is devoted to simultaneous interactions in a network of extended relationships – and no longer progressive perception, urging ongoing discovery of new areas of possibility in the future.

Probed 'Two attitudes underlie this presumption that anything in the world is material for the camera', writes Susan Sontag. 'One finds that there is beauty or at least interest in everything, seen with an acute enough eye … The other treats everything as the object of some present or future use, as matter for estimates, decisions, and predictions. According to one attitude, there is nothing that should not be seen; according to the other, there is nothing that should not be recorded' (Sontag 1977: 176). The aestheticizing view found a grandiose object in the photograph from space. That presentation of the tranquil majesty of the earth generated astonishment among humanity. The other view, instrumental and recording, also emerges, because historically unparalleled possibilities of exploration and registration are opened up.

Here too war was the father of all things. During the Second World War attempts were made to deploy new technology for dealing with a basic problem in tracking down the enemy: how can what is hidden behind skilful camouflage be seen? Infra-red photography, which records heat radiation, was thus developed. There was hardly time for this technology to be used, but from that moment onwards the search intensified for recording instruments able to register more than the human eye could ever see. Visible light constitutes only part of the spectrum of electro-magnetic waves reflected, absorbed or transmitted by an object. All objects – whether rocks, plants or buildings – have specific radiation, which remains invisible to the eye but can be registered by appropriate sensors.

This exploration of the invisible by way of highly developed sensor technology, pursued from the early 1960s as 'remote sensing', has dominated satellite observation of the earth ever since Landsat's utilization of a multi-spectral scanner in 1972 (Mack 1990). Nevertheless, comprehensive encirclement of the earth with satellite eyes has still to be fully implemented. Only the Earth Observing System planned by NASA will lead, in the next 10 to 20 years, to a kind of reversed panopticon where the centre can be kept under continuous surveillance from the periphery (*Economist* 1991: 23).

Satellites equipped with sensors are veritable heavenly spies, scanning the earth's surface so as to gather information hidden even from people on the ground. That process links a synoptic view with probing. From a great height it becomes possible to discover far-ranging patterns of reality, lying beneath the visible surface of the world of objects. For instance, wooded areas can be surveyed in terms of more than just the species of trees located there. The trees' temperature, cholorophyll content and humidity can also be investigated – all descriptions of states of affairs beyond the concrete materiality of trees, instead involving an abstract 'biomass'. The probing character of remote surveying is obvious in the employment of magnetometers for tracking down hidden mineral deposits, or in the utilization of radar satellites that are unaffected by dark nights or thick layers of cloud. Whatever the satellite eye discovers appears as coloured areas on thematic maps or as a computer screen model of changing processes. In any case, this involves the establishment of a hitherto non-existent reality. The biogeochemical states and flows that lie behind appearances become the true, 'scientifically demonstrated' reality of the planet. What is decisive is the probed reality, not the sensed reality. These phantom images of the earth, reproduced millions of times over in photographs and on television screens, then move into everyone's awareness.

It may be advisable to speak of 'phantom images' in order to direct attention to the special iconographic status of these pictures. After all, in its progressive form remote surveying produces neither a representation nor a photograph of its object-field: it produces images of synthesized measurements. This has nothing to do with 'seeing', and nothing to do with 'sensing' either. Both words, viewed more precisely, are a metaphorical fraud. In general, sensors scanning an area supply a stream of digitalized signals, which are treated, calibrated, integrated with other data and presented in graphic terms through image processing. Mechanical data-processing plays a decisive part in all this. Remote sensing, with today's data-flow of 100 megabits a second, became possible only with the advent of high-capacity computers. Here 'observation' has long been transformed into the measurement, recording, calculation, blending, modelling and depiction of data. Indeed, these 'pictures' of the earth are nothing other than collages of the outcome of millions of electro-magnetic measurements. 'Seeing', maintains Barbara Duden, 'is no longer a criterion of reality. We have got used to attributing collages with the status of reality' (Duden 1990: 30).

The Invention of the Biosphere

In September 1970, just two years after the blue earth became a celebrated photograph-object, the *Scientific American* published an issue devoted to 'The Biosphere'. The introduction, written by the journal's editors, began with the following sentences: 'Photos of the earth show that it is blue-green in color ... The biosphere – that thin layer of air and water and soil and life, which is only ten miles thick, a four-hundredth of the earth's radius – now constitutes the background to man's uncertain history.'

The scientists writing in this issue took as the object of their research those large-scale bio-geochemical cycles that shape interactions between the living and the non-living world, even at the planetary level: the circulations of energy, water, carbon, oxygen, nitrate and minerals. Their research was particularly directed towards changes in the circulation of matter caused by human production of food, energy and materials. Only with that preoccupation – the large-scale cycles that link atmosphere, rock, water and organisms in the earth's vital sheath – and with interest in describing, analytically and quantitatively, endangerment of the stability of those cycles through human activities, does the concept of the biosphere take shape.

This term had previously turned up from time to time, but basically as a classificatory category so as to distinguish, on the global level, the sphere of living creatures from the abiotic sphere of rock and water, and also of mind. Eduard Süss, the Austrian geologist who first spoke of the 'biosphere' in 1875, and Teilhard de Chardin, the French theologian writing in the 1920s and 1930s, may have aimed at a holistic, planetary understanding of the phenomenon of life, but they limited themselves to comparing the biosphere with the lithosphere, hydrosphere and atmosphere, or in Teilhard's case the noosphere. It was Vladimir I. Vernadsky (in *La biosphère*, Paris 1929) who focused attention on relations between geochemical factors and biota, assigning life – closely related to Vitalism – a paramount place in the overall process (Grinevald 1988). However, only thanks to the influence exerted by the ecosystem theory did it become possible to represent relationships between the biotic and the abiotic as quantifiable cycles of matter, which through feedback processes strive for a balance protecting even against disturbances from outside. After the war, G. Evelyn Hutchinson linked Vernadsky's inspiration with the ecosystem theory developed by Arthur Tansley and Raymond Lindemann. He comprehended nature in terms of the metaphor of a self-regulating machine, and stimulated investigation of the regulatory mechanisms responsible for a system's self-maintenance when subject to adverse external influences (Sachs 1991/92: 83–97). The systems approach gained the upper hand in ecology – mainly within the International Biological Program (1964–74) – because in public perception it accorded well with ideas about social engineering prevalent at the time. This process of clarification achieved a degree of agreement towards the end of the 1960s, as can be seen from *Nature*'s publication in 1969 of a terminological notice, stating that 'the biosphere consists of living and non-living components. It is the total complex of soil, water, air and living organisms that forms a complete ecosystem' (*Nature* 1969, 500–1). It was also Hutchinson who wrote the opening essay ('The biosphere') for the *Scientific American*, allowing the conclusion that within the concept of the biosphere the planetary totality is comprehended as the largest possible ecosystem, which, through cybernetic mechanisms, tends towards a state of stability but is increasingly endangered by human activities.

During the past two decades the concept of the biosphere has been further developed, particularly under the influence of what is known as the Gaia hypothesis (Lovelock 1979). This says that living organisms as a whole play the predominant part among the components that comprise the global ecosystem. Traditionally, geo-physical and geo-chemical aspects (land, oceans, atmosphere) constitute limiting factors for the world of organisms, which are at most modified by their activity, whereas the Gaia hypothesis insists that the overall activity of organisms – from plankton to poplars, from viruses to whales – regulates decisive characteristics of the lithosphere, the oceans and the atmosphere. To the extent that living creatures control such factors as temperature on earth, oxygen in the atmosphere or the salinity of seas, they created (during the course of evolution), and continue to create, an environment for themselves in which life can flourish. Consequently it is the unflagging effectiveness of the earth's organic sheath that makes it hospitable to life. The earth thus does not simply *have* a biosphere: it *is* a biosphere. Without the planetary interaction of living creatures neither individual forms of life nor the earth as we know it would exist. Our world would be desolate and empty like other planets.

It is hardly by chance that James Lovelock was working for NASA in the 1960s when he picked up the scent of what was later to become the Gaia hypothesis. He was confronted with the question of how to discover life on other planets – its forms and techniques of detection. Investigation of the conditions that make life possible on other planets logically led to the consideration of conditions for life on earth. Only through space flight did viewing various planets within a unified comparative context become inescapable, entailing an observation point (or even just a probe) external to the planets as the basis for such comparisons. The space programme, with flights beyond the earth's gravity, achieved the extra-terrestrial perspective. Space probe, satellite and spaceship opened up zones completely different from the earth. From that distance, attention then turned back to our planet, sparking off an avalanche of questions about the specific differences entailed in Planet Earth and the basis for its existence.

Lovelock was involved in that search during the 1960s and in 1969 he formulated a preliminary version of the Gaia hypothesis. Many times since he has confirmed the context of his discovery:

> It is often difficult to recognize the larger entity of which we are part
> ... So it was with the Earth itself before we shared with the astronauts
> vicariously that stunning and awesome vision ... This gift, this ability
> to see the Earth from afar, was so revealing that it forced the novel top-
> down approach to planetary biology. (Lovelock 1988)

Lovelock's thesis of the globality of life and its priority over non-organic cycles are the two cornerstones of modern understanding of the biosphere. Both theses derive from a space perspective of earth.

To my mind the outstanding spin-off from space research is not new technology. The real bonus has been that for the first time in human history we have had a chance to look at the Earth from space, and the information gained from seeing from the outside an azure-green planet in all its global beauty has given rise to a whole new set of questions and answers. (Lovelock 1979: 8)

These 'questions and answers' really did condense into no less than a reorganization of a whole series of sciences around a new research paradigm and a new research methodology.

Lovelock's 'Gaia' hypothesis remains disputed. However, whatever fate its details may meet, 'Gaia' offers a comprehensive concept, which unites an entire series of exciting interdisciplinary research by chemists, biologists, geo-physicists, oceanographers, and others. (Clark and Munn 1986: 6)

The picture of the blue planet constituted the earth as a scientific object compelling a reordering of specialized disciplines, inviting the integration of new methods such as remote surveying and computer systems and opening up an extensive arena for large-scale inter-disciplinary research. Since the biosphere is conceived as a system of interactive components where no single part – oceans, atmosphere, rock, vegetation, animal world, human beings – can be adequately understood in isolation from the others, the sciences – and particularly the bio-sciences on one side and the geo-sciences on the other – are challenged to undertake greater integration. At the same time, satellite technology offers a new generation of instruments of exploration, producing a vast amount of new data, which make up a technical infrastructure serving as the basis for institutionalization of new scientific activities. Finally, there was also no lack of social demand for a science devoted to the biosphere – quite the contrary. 'There can be no doubt that the new science of the biosphere is necessary for our survival … Without a solid scientific foundation we can understand neither the individual nor the cumulative global effects of our local, regional, and global actions' (Botkin 1985). It is therefore not surprising that for some years now, emanating from the USA, there has been a veritable frenzy of establishing global geo-research. The National Science Foundation, for instance, has set up a Global Geosciences programme in order to induce academic disciplines to dismantle some of their delimitations of specialization. The International Council of Scientific Unions, always active on the threshhold of space travel since the memorable 1957/58 International Geophysical Year, is advocating an International Geosphere–Biosphere Programme. UNESCO is reorienting its Man and the Biosphere Programme, and NASA, that long-troubled big set-up to which we owe icons of the blue planet, also sees its chance, and is developing an Earth System Science programme (Malone 1986).

The Image and Sentimental Ecology

While Lovelock's hypothesis was still encountering deaf ears among the scientific community, the sudden flash of insight involved in naming his earth 'Gaia' already touched the feelings of a broad public. When taking a walk with Lovelock, William Golding, the writer and Nobel prizewinner, hit on the idea of viewing the scientist's living earth as an incorporation of Gaia, the Greek goddess and Earth Mother. That turned out to be a choice with the power of shaping consciousness, leading to the rare instance of a scientific theorem being forced on scientists by the public rather than slowly making its way from the laboratory into general consciousness. When Lovelock's *Gaia* appeared in 1979, there came to pass a modern epiphany for Gaia within history. For parts of the ecology movement, the profound reason for and the elevated objective of their concern was made manifest in Gaia. The excrescences of industrial society were seen as ultimately threatening not just people living near Lake Erie or asthmatics in smog-ridden areas, but nothing less than the whole of the planetary organism on which all life ultimately depends. 'Save the Earth' would previously have been an absurdly comical battle-cry, but ever since the earth's essence was identified as involving its thin protective sheath, the planet seems vulnerable to human assaults. The picture of the blue planet became a symbol of life-giving nature. From a poster incorporating a photograph of the earth it calls out: 'Love Your Mother'.

That photograph from space was also charged right from the start with the premonitions and hopes of an ecological *Zeitgeist*. Carl Sagan, as a space author not unconcerned about his own interests, remarked just a few years after the moon landing that 'many leaders of the environmental movement in America were originally influenced by the space photographs of earth, by those pictures showing a tiny, delicate, fragile world, which is exceptionally susceptible to human predators – a meadow amid the universe' (Sagan 1975: 60). It can be asked whether Earth Day 1970, the first national manifestation of the environmental movement in the USA, would have been given that name without the satellite photograph. What is certain is that for Earth Day 1990 (the second such occasion) the country was flooded with devotional motifs of the earth on pennants, posters and postcards. The earth has become an object of post-modern popular piety.

Obviously that image displays a number of characteristics that resonate with ecological sensibility. Above all, the photograph reveals the earth as a physical body viewed as a whole. The earth, it becomes directly apparent, represents that all-embracing totality within which everything takes place. Is it not inevitable that such an image becomes a powerful triumph for a movement that does not tire of insisting, time and time again, on the whole taking precedence over perfecting the parts? After all, on many fronts the main issue is to track down the repressed consequences for the whole of individual decisions. The photograph showing the earth as the largest totality, thus depicts the ultimate and fundamental reference point for ecological commitment. The planet, shimmering in space, impresses itself on contemporary consciousness as a yearned-for expression of collective rationality. Such a way of viewing things is intensified by the striking fact that nothing on this image is to be seen as clearly as the boundaries dividing the luminous earth from the cold blackness of space. This provides visual demonstration that the earth is finite. Such evidence of spherical finiteness endows with photographic credibility the message of environmentalists that nature cannot be exploited indefinitely. Human arrogance must obviously come to grief at the planetary limits, if not earlier.

Moreover, the globe carves a cosy inner space out of the hostile universe, which makes our earth stand out as the place where we live, indeed as our home. The boundaries create a place, and that place creates belongingness. The image constitutes a 'We' involving all human beings. 'Home' is the succinct message printed on many postcards depicting the blue planet. To be sure, the unity of the human race is thus determined as a bio-physical fact, and no longer as an achievement of cultural comprehension, but such a naturalization endows the idea of humanity with the consecration of facticity. The photograph thereby creates a new idea of global interdependence. Worldwide interconnection may also entail money flows and television news, but it is primarily and inescapably brought about by the shared life-giving sheath. Beyond that, the sphere of interdependence has been radically enlarged. It is no longer restricted to humanity but now comprises all living creatures. In earlier times nature provided the background against which humanity stood out in terms of its common features, but now the universe comprises the backdrop against which the unity of nature – inclusive, of course, of humankind – imperiously imposes itself. Humanity primarily appears as a natural being whose fate and challenge it is to be closely interlinked with the planetary web of life. That is why the environmentalists' call for ecological responsibility becomes something akin to an ontological justification. The demand that we should live in peace with nature is not arbitrarily plucked out of thin air, but is presented as being rooted in the order of being.

However 'Gaia', that genial name, evokes considerably more than rationality. It appeals to a search for ultimate validity and holiness. Lovelock himself opened the way:

> When I first saw Gaia in my mind I felt as an astronaut must have done as he stood on the moon, gazing back at our home, the Earth. The feeling strengthens as theory and evidence come in to confirm the thought that the Earth may be a living organism. Thinking of the Earth as alive makes it seem, on happy days, in the right places, as if the whole planet were celebrating a sacred ceremony. (Lovelock 1988: 205)

Astonishment, awe and a feeling of incomprehensibility are awoken by the picture of the blue planet; an outsized reality becomes visible, upholding and incorporating everything that happens on earth. 'This is why, for me, Gaia is a religious as well as a scientific concept.' Lovelock expresses profound satisfaction about the fact that his religious intuition was confirmed in his scientific work, leading to a language making possible communication of this personal experience in a secularized world. That satisfaction is shared by many people, particularly among an Anglo-Saxon public. Ecological commitment thus stands for radical change in comprehension of the world and life, which places its hopes in a holistic perspective uniting empiricism and ethics, science and religion. The central element in this ecological view of the world is that human beings can no longer lay claim to a privileged place within the universe. The crown of creation has become a particularly complex manifestation of the global life process. The origin of humankind can be told in terms of the history of the planetary evolution of life. Humanity's present existence is upheld by being embedded in the global web of all life, and its future will depend on incorporation in Gaia's process. A prevalent ecological mood thus finds expression in a religious concept that is earth-centred rather than man- or god-centred. The earth, or more precisely the biosphere, becomes an object of veneration. The image of the blue planet can thus also be more strictly viewed as an icon. It is not simply a depiction, but is seen by some people as a symbol of Gaia's life-giving power. Where there is worship, prayer and invocation follow as a matter of course. This invocation is to be found in a New Age publication devoted to practices for meditation on Gaia:

We ask for the presence of the spirit of Gaia and pray that the breath of life continues to caress this planet home. May we grow into true understanding – a deep understanding that inspires us to protect the tree on which we bloom, and the water, soil and atmosphere without which we have no existence ... We ask for the presence of the spirit of Gaia to be with us here. To reveal to us all that we need to see, for our own highest good and for the highest good of all. (Seed et al. 1988: 2)

The Image and Technocratic Ecology

Almost twenty years after the *Scientific American* proclaimed the biosphere to be a new object of scientific research, the journal once again pointed the way to new shores. The cover of the September 1989 special issue shows America and Europe as seen from a satellite with the imperative 'Managing Planet Earth' set above the outlines of continents and seas. A synthesis of the new perspective is to be found right at the start of the title essay:

Our ability to look back on ourselves from outer space symbolizes the unique perspective we have on our environment and on where we are headed as a species. With this knowledge comes a responsibility ... the responsibility to manage the human use of planet earth. It is as a global species that we are transforming the planet. It is only as a global species – pooling our knowledge, coordinating our actions and sharing what the planet has to offer – that we may have any prospect for managing the planet's transformation along the pathways of sustainable development. Self-conscious, intelligent management of the earth is one of the great challenges facing humanity as it approaches the 21st century.

High-flying words, to be sure, and also considerable overestimation of humanity, yet such rhetoric, no matter what its prospects for realization may be, creates a new reality that enters people's minds. This is obvious in an epoch where environmental themes have attained the commanding heights of international politics and become an object of worldwide campaigns. This new perception is beginning to colour the language of international debate. With such large-scale events as the Rio UN Conference on Environment and Development its echo will also be heard ever more clearly beyond academic deliberations.

Without the photograph of the earth it would scarcely be possible to view the planet as an object of management. On the other hand, a number of further conditions were necessary for global expansion of the horizon of ecological management strategies towards the end of the 1980s. At the start of the previous decade talk of global responsibility was still mainly a moral appeal aimed at urging local, or at most national, action in the name of the environment. 'Think globally, act locally' was the slogan of those years. Environmental policy involved regional planning of resources, or was concerned with more quality of life at the local level. Only in the course of the 1980s – with the ozone hole, acid rain and the greenhouse effect – did the border-crossing, global impact of pollution by industrial societies force itself into the foreground. The planet revealed itself to be an all-encompassing refuse dump. At the same time scientific ecology turned its attention to studying the global biosphere, where two decades previously researchers had mainly been concerned with individual spheres of nature, such as deserts, tropical forests and tidal shallows. In recent years scientists have increasingly discovered the biosphere as an all-embracing ecosystem, which links biota with processes in the atmosphere, oceans and the earth's crust. And finally, as so frequently in the history of science, a new generation of instruments and equipment created the possibility of measuring global processes. During the past decade, satellites, sensors and computers have provided the means for calibrating the biosphere and representing it in models. While the environmental crisis took care of the relevance of planetary surveying, ecology promises to provide the cognitive foundations, and technology to come up with the necessary means. Since these factors took effect at the same time, Planet Earth has moved into a managerial perspective in recent years.

After the heroic phase of voyaging to the moon and other manned missions, space-flight technology seems to be consolidating itself with services for managing the earth. Hope of future expansion is directed towards observation of the earth alongside communications technology. For some years now NASA's development work in that area has been coordinated in the Mission to Planet Earth programme, while France's SPOT satellite venture, the European ERS-1 mission and anticipated Japanese activity in space largely place their hopes in demand for earth observation. Satellites serve there as environmental spies in space that register far-reaching changes in the planet's life-giving sheath. Damage to nature can be mapped from a great height. Extensive felling of trees and desertification, clouds of poison and oil slicks, and even army manoeuvre areas cannot be hidden from satellite surveys. For instance, since early summer 1991 ERS-1 has been in an 800 km-high orbit over the North and South Poles, which takes the satellite around the globe six times a day with the earth turning away beneath, gradually offering its entire surface for scrutiny. Sensor technology provides a synoptic, probing viewpoint, enabling recording of the state of vegetation, movements of the seas and layering within the atmosphere. Apart from such analyses, satellites linked with high-powered computers also supply an ongoing flow of data with which scientists hope to produce models of, and validate, complex natural phenomena such as changes in climate. The purpose of establishing models is the simulation on a screen of the course taken by extensive and highly complex natural processes with a diversity of starting points. For example, researchers used oil spillage in the Persian Gulf for producing a model to predict the course and impact of this catastrophe. The repercussions of a variety of protective measures along the river systems that feed the North Sea can be predicted with regard to overall pollution in this marine area. Even though what will in fact come to pass remains in the lap of the gods, it is nevertheless becoming apparent that coupling space travel, sensor technology and data-processing brings a drastic increase in power for ongoing observation of natural developments on a continental and planetary scale, recognizing human influences and making forecasts. As with a patient under intensive care, this programme's underlying intention is that the earth should be kept under continuous observation so that therapies can be rapidly deployed before the planet collapses.

The projected long-term objective over the next 10–20 years is development of a Global Resource Information Database accessible from everywhere, which will allow so-called decision-makers to appraise the environmental impact of their actions from the local to the planetary level (Gwynne and Mooneyhan 1989: 243–56).

All the data fed in locally are to be labelled in terms of location on the earth's surface (and in some cases time dimension), a procedure that at least in principle opens up the prospect of being able to call up the natural profile of any place on earth from any other location. Just as states have established sophisticated economic statistics since the Second World War, intended to reflect the economic and social situation within that society, so too is a databank – but worldwide in extent - now being established for keeping the biosphere's condition under observation.

The viewpoint of a satellite on an ecological mission is both all-embracing and all-penetrating. The planet's natural covering stretches out beneath it and any region can be called up on a screen, utilizing three-dimensional computer graphics, and be subjected to test assessments. The potential for knowledge and comparative simulation gives rise to expectations of future capacity to shape changes within nature on our planet as a form of rational planning. In fact, an urgent need for these services seems to exist. Does not the environmental crisis demonstrate that human dominance over nature still leaves much to be desired? Science and technology, it is said, may have changed nature enormously, but – to date at least – in an uncontrolled fashion. What is on the agenda for a technocratic ecology is therefore rationalization of intervention in nature. Viewed from that perspective, the challenge of the current phase of development in industrial societies involves moving on from an epoch of blindness to one of enlightenment in humanity's dominance over nature. In fact, only achievement of conscious control of the unwanted consequences of the exploitation of nature would permit us to talk of a successful dominance of nature. Far from wanting to reduce industrial society's overall consumption of nature, such a policy seeks salvation in optimal regulation of the remodelling of nature. The picture of the blue planet – small and easily comprehensible – suggests the 'planability' of a process that was hitherto the precondition for human existence. Only under the influence of that image could the *Scientific American* in September 1989 raise crucial questions with regard to these key themes:

> Two central questions must be addressed: What kind of planet do we want? What kind of planet can we get? ... How much species diversity should be maintained in the world? Should the size or the growth rate of the human population be curtailed ...? How much climate change is acceptable?

The pictures from space provide documentation of a kind of knowledge based on distance. However, this form of knowledge has a rather fateful history, since our domination over nature is based upon it. A space-rocket taking off provides a vivid illustration of what dominating nature has always involved: detaching the human observer from lived nature and confronting what was previously humankind's own world as a separate and neutral realm, open to intervention. Viewing the earth from space clearly continues this tradition of domination-prone knowledge, which is why the demand for expanded dominance links up so tightly with planetary sciences. For shooting a satellite into space is perhaps the most radical way of implementing that distance from our world. On the basis of their visual characteristics alone, the satellite pictures thus invite fantasies of large-scale planning.

This furtive invitation is underlined by the fact that in the pictures all trace of human reality is dissolved into nothingness and only natural actualities remain to be seen. No traditions, no institutions, no history – the world has vanished into the earth. The way is thus free for covering up humanity's conflict-ridden reality, resolving the social into the biological. A planner's secret dream of not being disturbed in his proposals for intervention by the contradictory and contrary ideas of the people affected achieves fulfilment in the planet as object. It is thus anything but chance when in the international debate there are more and more biologizing expressions. Human beings become 'populations', citizens 'species'. Quality of life degenerates into 'survival', 'sustainability' replaces general well-being and 'evolution' history. Those terms in the ascendant instead indicate a form of perception that could be called biospheric utilitarianism. New words such as 'biomass', 'biodiversity' and 'bioreservations' betray the same inclination towards declaring the planet and its dynamics to be politics' prime point of reference (Beney 1993).

However, that seems to be precisely the perspective the WCED in the Brundtland Report puts forward for global environmental policy in the 1990s. In its first sentences, the report celebrates the image of the blue planet twinkling as it floats amid the darkness of space, small and vulnerable. Then it states that 'humanity's inability to fit its doings into that pattern is changing planetary systems fundamentally', and concludes the paragraph with a programmatic declaration: 'This new reality, from which there is no escape, must be recognized – and managed' (WCED 1987: 1).

8

Globalization and Sustainability

Symbols are the more powerful the more meanings they are able to admit. They actually live on ambivalence. The Cross, for instance, counted both as a token of victory for conquerors and as a token of hope for the vanquished. That ambivalence raised it above the fray; a single clear message would have meant that it divided rather than united. The same may be said of the image of the blue planet, now a symbol unchallenged by either Left or Right, conservative or liberal. Whatever their differences, they are all fond of adorning themselves with this symbol of our epoch. To fall in with it is to announce that one is abreast of the times, in tune with the world, focused on the future, truly prepared to set off into the new century. In this picture are condensed the opposing ambitions of our age. It is hoisted like a flag by troops from enemy camps, and its prominence results from this plurality of meaning. The photograph of the globe contains the contradictions of globalization. That is why it could become an all-weather icon.

No sooner had it become available, in the late 1960s, than the international environmental movement recognized itself in it. For nothing stands out from the picture as clearly as the round margin that sets it off from the dark cosmos. Clouds, oceans and land masses gleam in the wan light; the earth appears to the observer as a cosy island in a universe unfriendly to life, holding all the continents, seas and living species. For the environmental movement the picture's message was plain: it revealed the earth in its finitude. That circular object made it obvious that the ecological costs of industrial progress could not be shifted forever to Noplace, that they were slowly building up into a threat to all within a closed system. In the end, the externalization of costs belonged to the realm of the impossible. In a finite world, where everyone was affected by everyone else, there was an urgent need for

129

mutual care and attention, for more thought about the consequences of one's actions. Such was the holistic message – and, certainly, it was not without some effect. Since the days when a few minorities launched their appeal so full of foreboding, the image of the planet as a closed system has steadily gained currency and even recognition in international law. The conventions on ozone, world climate and biodiversity prove that the perception of the earth's bio-physical limits has attained the supreme political consecration.

For some time, however, ecologists have no longer had a monopoly on the image. At various airports, in the endless passageways between check-in and exit, a well-lit publicity board has been visible in recent years that strikingly expresses a different view of globalization. It shows the blue planet pushing itself on the observer from its blue–black background, with a laconic text: 'MasterCard. The World in Your Hands.' The hurrying passengers are being told that, wherever they fly in this big wide world, they can count on the services of their cards and slot themselves into a global credit and debit network. The credit-card empire stretches out across all frontiers, with purchasing power in any location and accounting in real time, and its electronic money transfers ensure that the traveller is always provided for. In these and numerous other variations, the image of the planet has turned since the 1980s into an emblem of transnational business; hardly any company in telecommunications or tourism – not to speak of the news industry – seems able to manage without it.

This has been possible because the picture also contains quite a different message. In its detachment from the pitch-black cosmos, the terrestrial sphere stands out as a unified area whose continuous physical reality causes the frontiers between nations and polities to disappear – hence the visual message that what counts is the boundaries of the earth. Only oceans, continents and islands can be seen, with no trace of nations, cultures or states.

In the picture of the globe, distances are measured exclusively in geographical units of miles or kilometres, not in social units of closeness and foreignness. The satellite photographss generally look like renaturalized maps, seeming to confirm the old cartographical postulate that places are nothing more than intersections of two lines – the lines of longitude and latitude. In marked contrast to the globes of the nineteenth century, which sharply delineate political frontiers and often use different colours for different territories, any social reality is here dissipated into morphology. The earth is depicted as a homogeneous area offering no resistance to transit – or only resistance caused by geographical features, not to human communities and their laws, customs or purposes. Every point of the hemisphere turned towards the observer can be seen at the same moment, and this simultaneous access of the human gaze suggests the idea of unobstructed access on the ground too. The image of the planet offers the world up for unrestricted movement, promises access in every direction, and seems to present no obstacle to expansionism other than the limits of the globe itself. Open, continuous and controllable – there is an imperial message too in the photographs of the earth.

The image symbolizes limitation in the physical sense and expansion in the political sense. Little wonder, then, that it can serve as a banner for both environmental groups and transnational corporations. It has become the symbol of our times across all the rival world views, because it brings to life both sides of the basic conflict that runs through our epoch. On the one hand, the ecological limits of the earth stand out more clearly than ever before; on the other hand, the dynamic of economic globalization pushes for the removal of all boundaries associated with political and cultural space (Altvater and Mahnkopf 1996). The two narratives of globalization – limitation and expansion – have acquired a clearer form over the past three decades and fight it out in both the arena of theory and the arena of politics. The outcome of this struggle will decide the shape of the new century.

The Rise of the Transnational Economy

Since the mid-1970s, when the Bretton Woods system of fixed exchange rates gave way to floating parities determined by the market, the world economy has witnessed the collapse of boundaries in a process that started slowly but has gradually speeded up. Of course, the quest for raw materials and markets had for centuries been impelling capitalist companies beyond their national frontiers, but only in the last few decades has an international order been created that works programmatically towards a transnational economy with open borders. Whereas all the first eight GATT rounds since the war dismantled more and more tariff obstacles to the exchange of goods, in line with the traditional ideal of free trade, the last of these, the Uruguay Round, and the newly constructed World Trade Organization have laid the legal foundations for politically unregulated movement of goods, services, money capital and investment right across the globe. The Uruguay Round, concluded in 1993, drew more widely the circle of freely tradeable commodities and also deregulated 'software products' such as planning contracts, copyrights, patents and insurance. Controls on the movement of capital, allowing easier inward and outward financial flows, have been progressively removed over the past 20 years, first in the USA and Germany, then in the mid-1980s in Japan, and finally in the countries of the South. In order to make foreign investors feel more at home everywhere, the WTO (and the OECD with its provisionally stalled multilateral investment agreement) have imposed on each state an obligation to accord at least the same rights to foreign as to domestic investors.

A Utopian energy is at work in all these initiatives. This can be seen in the ever more frequently declared intention to create a 'level playing field', a global arena for economic competition in which only efficiency counts, unfettered and undistorted by any special local traditions or structures. All economic players are supposed to have the right – at any place and any time – to offer, produce and acquire whatever they want. Up to now, this free play of the market has been hindered by the dizzying diversity of the world's social and legal orders, which have grown out of each country's history and social structure. The aim now, therefore, is to wrench economic activities from their embeddedness in local or national conditions and to bring them under the same rules (if any) everywhere in the world. There should be no blocking, weakening or interfering with market forces, because that leads to efficiency losses and suboptimal welfare.

This Utopian model of economic globalization also features the earth as a homogeneous area, to be crossed at will by circulating goods and capital. Only supply and demand, and in no case political priorities, are supposed to speed up or slow down these flows and to point them in the right direction. The world is conceived as a single huge marketplace, where factors of production are bought at their cheapest ('global sourcing') and commodities are sold at their highest obtainable price ('global marketing'). Just as in satellite pictures of the planet, no role is played by states and their particular laws; places where people live are foreshortened to mere locations of economic activity. And yet, to the continual annoyance of the neo-liberal heaven-stormers, societies everywhere prove sluggish and resistant. The globalizers thus have the onerous task of adapting base reality to ideal model; their mission is tirelessly to overcome obstacles to the free flow of commodities and thus to make the world comprehensively accessible. That is precisely the programme of the WTO's multilateral economic regime.

In the last few decades, of course, a material infrastructure has also been created for transnational integration. Without the global network of telephone lines, glass fibre cables, microwave channels, relay stations and communications satellites, there would be no open-border world – or at least not as a routine part of everyday life. For electronic data flows – which can be converted into commands and information, sounds and images – eat up kilometres at the press of a key or the click of a mouse. Geographical distance ceases to be of any significance, and since the costs of the transfer and processing of data have dramatically fallen, worldwide interaction has become the daily bread of globally oriented middle classes. Thus, electronic impulses translate what the external view of the planet already suggested: the unity of space and time for any action in the world. In principle, all events can now be brought into relation with one another in real time for all parts of the earth. Whereas the picture of the globe conveyed the absence of boundaries as a visual experience, electronic networking converts it into a communications (and air transport into a travel) experience. The constant high-volume, lightning-fast flow of bits of information around the globe achieves the abolition of distance as well as the compression of time; electronic space produces a spatio-temporally compact globe (Altvater and Mahnkopf 1996).

The information highways may be compared to the railways: the digital network is to the rise of a global economy what the railway network was in the nineteenth century to the rise of a national economy (Lash and Urry 1994). Just as the railway infrastructure became the backbone of the national economy (because falling transport costs enabled regional markets to fuse into a national market), so the digital infrastructure is the backbone of the global economy, because falling transmission costs enable national markets to fuse into a global market. Distance is not, of course, truncated in the same way everywhere in the world. This results in a new hierarchy of space: the 'global cities' stand at the top of the pyramid, closely bound together across frontiers by high-speed air and land links and by glass fibre cables, while at the bottom whole regions or even continents – Africa or Central Asia, for example – constitute 'black holes' in the informational universe (Castells 1998: 162), not connected to one another in any significant degree.

On closer examination, then, the networks of transnational interaction rarely assume configurations that stretch across the whole planet; they are not global but transnational, because they bind together only shifting segments of the earth. They are deterritorialized rather than globalized. Unlike earlier types of internationalization, this is particularly the case for the characteristic economic forms of the global age – geographically extended chains of value creation and global finance markets. Basing themselves upon an infrastructure of electronic and physical traffic, companies are now in a position to split up their value-creation process and locate individual parts in areas of the world with the most advantageous wage, skill or market environment. Thus, for a product taken at random, the early stages may take place in Russia, the further processing in Malaysia, the marketing in Hong Kong, the research in Switzerland, and the design in England. Instead of the traditional factory where products were largely manufactured from beginning to end, a network of partial locations makes it possible for previously unheard-of efficiency gains to be achieved. The textbook case of collapsing frontiers, however, is provided by the operations of finance markets. Shares, loans and currency stocks have long left 'paper' behind and become digitalized; their owners can be switched at the press of a key, quite regardless of borders or geographical distance. Nor is it an accident that the most extensively globalized market is the one that deals in the least physical of all commodities: money. Dependent only on an electronic impulse, it can move angel-like in real time anywhere within a homogeneous space. It seems as if the narrative of collapsing frontiers can best be translated into reality when it takes place within the incorporeality of cyberspace.

How Economic Globalization Reduces the Use of Resources

For the protagonists of economic globalization, there is no greater thorn in the side than closed economic areas. Import restrictions and export regulations, product standards and social legislation, investment guidance and laws on the sharing of profits – in short, political pro-visions of any kind that establish a difference between one country's economic system and those of others – are perceived by the globalizers as so many obstacles to the free movement of the factors of pro-duction. They therefore seek to undermine, and gradually to break up altogether, the state-defined 'containers' of national markets, and to replace them with a transnational arena where economic actors are no longer prevented by special rules and regulations from carrying through the dynamic of competition. The multinational economic regimes – whether geared continentally to ASEAN, NAFTA or the EU, or globally to GATT and the WTO – come down to the construction of homo-geneous competitive areas stretching across nations.

The promise held out in these initiatives is one of a world that gets the utmost out of its limited means. A way has to be found of satisfying more and more people around the world, with more and more claims, and it is from this challenge that the friends of globalization derive their task – indeed, their mission – to subject the world's economic apparatuses to a course of efficiency-raising treatment. For the point of market liberalization is to ensure, through the selective power of competition, that capital, labour, intelligence and even natural resources are everywhere deployed in the most efficient manner. Only such treatment continually renewed, argue the globalizers, can lay the basis for the wealth of nations. True, companies do not act out of lofty motives but simply take advantage of opportunities for profits and competitive triumphs; nevertheless, the 'invisible hand' of the market is expected in the end to produce greater prosperity for all, even at a world level. A dynamic must therefore be set in train that exposes every protected zone of low productivity to the bracing wind of international competition.

The main targets for such a strategy are the state-run economic complexes in the former Soviet Union and in many countries of the South. In fact, external protectionism and internal sclerosis often go hand in hand, for parasitical structures arise most easily where power elites can use their possession of the state to appropriate a country's wealth. Insulated from competition, whether internal or external, the power elite can get away with deploying capital and other resources in short-term operations that produce a maximum surplus – a considerable part of which is then stashed away in foreign bank accounts. Along with the state monopoly of economic activity, the pressure on workers and the underprovision of consumers, it is especially the frenzied exploitation of natural resources that here rakes in a quick profit. Growth soon becomes synonymous with expanded extraction from nature: oil in the Soviet Union, Nigeria or Mexico, coal in India and China, wood in the Ivory Coast and Indonesia, minerals in Zaire. Of course, it was no accident that the use of resources in the former communist countries was much higher than in the West, for natural treasures were seen as a cost-free (because state-owned) means of fuelling industrial development – especially as growth pressures were directed to extensive rather than intensive ways of increasing production. The opening up of bureaucratically ossified economies to competition was thus to the benefit of resource efficiency. Almost as soon as the wall of restrictions and subsidies crumbled, new suppliers from outside appeared on the scene and placed the old wasteful economy in question. Globalization razes strongholds of mismanagement to the ground, and in such cases cuts down on the use of natural resources by enforcing at least economic rationality.

This efficiency effect does not operate only through expanded entry to the market. Trade and investment also increase access to technologies that, in comparison with domestic ones, often bring considerable gains in efficiency. This applies in particular to such sectors as mining, energy, transport and industry. Examples range from the export of more

economical cars from Japan to the United States, through the introduction of new power station technology in Pakistan, to the savings in
material and energy that came with new blast-furnaces in the Brazilian
steel industry. There is strong evidence that more open national economies deploy more resource-efficient technologies at an earlier date,
simply because they have better access to the most modern – which
usually means more efficient – technological investment. Moreover,
transnational corporations tend to standardize technologies between
countries at a more advanced level, rather than expose themselves to all
kinds of coordination costs. The connection is by no means necessary,
of course, but it is probable – and it may be said that more flexible
investment rules generally favour entry to a higher technological trajec-
tory (Johnstone 1997). The efficiency effect of more open markets is
visible not only in supply-side technology transfers but also on the
demand side: commodity exports from the fast-developing countries to
the post-industrial regions of the North have to stand the test of
consumer preferences in the North, and since the market demand there
often displays greater environmental awareness, production structures
in the exporting country may have to adapt to those standards.

The justification for economic globalization, then, is supposed to be
that it establishes an empire of economic efficiency, and that this effect
often extends to the use of energy and raw materials (OECD 1998).
This is understood as a growth in micro-economic rationality, as a
striving to deploy the factors of production in an optimal manner
everywhere. Of course, the promoters of globalization have to play
down the fact that this can equally well go together with a decline in
macro-rationality as regards both political–social relations and the environment. For market rationalization may lower the use of particular
resources – that is, input per unit of output – but the total use of
resources will nevertheless grow if the volume of economic activity
expands. Growth effects may all too easily eat up efficiency effects. In
fact, so far in the history of industrial society, efficiency gains have quite
consistently been converted into new opportunities for expansion. This,
from an ecological point of view, is the Achilles' heel of globalization.

How Economic Globalization Expands and Accelerates the Use of Resources

In recent years globalization has been hailed, often with the full red-
carpet treatment, as opening a new era for humanity. Yet its goals are
surprisingly conventional: it serves on its own admission to spur world
economic growth, and it involves – under changed historical conditions

– such long-standing strategies as intensive development and growth through expansion. On the one hand, there is the shifting distribution of the value-creation chain across far-flung regions of the world, which enables companies – in their choice of the best location for each stage of production – to enjoy to the full rationalization benefits that were simply not available before. The advancing digitalization of economic processes has also created new scope for productivity gains – for example, through flexible automation in manufacturing, simulation techniques in research, or perfectly timed logistics in networks of cooperation. With the restructuring of large parts of the world economy, it has thus become possible to wring further growth from long drawn-out productivity competition in OECD markets that were largely saturated at the end of the 1970s. On the other hand, growth has occurred through expansion – and, in particular, through the quest for new markets abroad. Many companies that might not have been able to make much further progress on local markets decided instead to tap demand in other OECD and fast-developing countries. The combined result of these two strategies may be seen in the fact that the world economy is well on its way to doubling between 1975 and the year 2000. Even if all GNP growth does not involve a parallel rise in the flow of resources, there can be no doubt that the biosphere is under ever greater pressure from the anthroposphere.

Direct foreign investment and the expansion effect The Utopian horizon of globalization is a permeable borderless world in which goods and capital can move around freely. Whereas the various GATT agreements expanded the exchange of goods over a period of decades, the further elimination of national barriers has in the last 15 years mainly affected the mobility of private capital. Between 1980 and 1996 the cross-border exchange of goods increased by an annual average of 4.7 per cent, but foreign investment rose by 8.8 per cent per annum, international bank loans by 10 per cent, and the trade in currency and shares by 25 per cent (*Economist* 1997a). If one looks at the geographical distribution of these flows it becomes clear that, although the lion's share of the capital traffic remains as before within the USA–EU–Japan triad, transfers of private capital have sky-rocketed mainly in the ten 'emerging markets' of East Asia and South America. They rose from an annual $44 billion at the beginning of the 1990s to $244 billion in 1996, before settling down at some $170 billion after the 1997 financial crisis in Asia (French 1998: 7). An important sub-category – accounting for one-half in the case of manufacturing, more than one-third in services, and 20 per cent in the primary sector – has been foreign investment to buy up existing firms or to found new ones. For the investing company, the point of this has been to control the further extraction of natural resources, to erect a platform within a transnational chain of production, or to gain access to export markets. For the host state, on the other hand, the aim has been to draw in investment capital and know-how, as part of a fervent desire to take off economically and to catch up with the rich countries at some point in the future.

With the migration of investment capital from the OECD countries, the fossil model of development has spread to the newly industrializing countries and even well beyond them. Whether it is a question of factories in China, chemical plants in Mexico or industrial agriculture in the Philippines, the countries of the South are entering on a broad front the resource-intensive fossil stage of economic development. That fateful style of economics that consolidated itself in Europe in the late nineteenth century, resting to a large degree upon the transformation of unpaid natural values into commodity values, is now expanding to more parts of the world in the wake of foreign investment. Certainly, a good part of this development is also being driven by locally accumulated capital, but the gigantic influx of foreign investment has deepened and accelerated the spread of – environmentally speaking – robber economies. Everywhere prevails an industrial–social mimetism, a copying of modes of production and consumption that, in view of the crisis of nature, may already be regarded as obsolete. For in the conventional path of development, monetary growth always goes together with material growth; a certain uncoupling of the two appears only in the transition to a post-industrial economy. The favoured targets for investment are thus precisely raw materials extraction or energy and transport infrastructure, which all push the use of natural resources up and up. Even if input per unit of output is lower than at a corresponding stage in the development of the rich countries, the absolute volume of the flow of resources has been increasing prodigiously.

The removal of national obstacles to investment activity stands in an increasingly tense relationship with the earth's bio-physical limitations. Thus the fast-industrializing countries recorded a steep rise in their CO_2 emissions (varying between 20 and 40 per cent in the 1990–95 period), while the industrialized countries – at a higher level, of course – increased theirs only slightly (Brown et al. 1998: 58). All in all, fossil fuel use will double in China and East Asia between 1990 and 2005, to reach a volume almost comparable to that of the United States (WRI 1998: 121). The motor car may serve as a symbol in this respect. In South Korea (before the crisis broke), car ownership was expanding by 20 per cent a year (Carley and Spapens 1998: 35). On the streets of India, virtually the only car to be seen in 1980 was the venerable old Ambassador limousine – a real petrol-guzzler, of course, but limited in numbers and therefore discharging far less gas than the huge fleet of more efficient vehicles turned out by the nine automobile corporations now operating there. Thus, in countries where transport has until now been mainly a question of bicycles and public services, further development of their eco-friendly systems will be blocked and replaced by a structure dependent upon high fuel use. It is altogether consistent with the logic of fossil expansion that the World Bank, for all its lip-service to 'sustainable development', allocates two-thirds of its expenditure in the energy sector to the mobilization of fossil energy sources (Wysham 1997).

Another symbol of a lifestyle widely regarded as modern, the Big Mac, may serve to illustrate the mounting pressure on biological resources. In little more than five years between 1990 and 1996, the number of McDonald's restaurants in Asia and Latin America quadrupled (UNDP 1998: 56), against a background of tripled meat consumption over the past 25 years. Such trends mean more and more water, cereals and grazing land for cattle, so it is hardly surprising that, in the 1980s alone, the countries of South-East and South Asia lost between 10 per cent and 30 per cent of their forests (Brown et al. 1998). The forest fires in Indonesia, whose dense clouds of smoke covered half of South-East Asia in 1997–98, originated in massive slash-and-burn clearances and were widely interpreted as a warning of the destructive power of the Asian economic miracle.

Deregulation and the competitive effect   The creation of a global competitive arena requires efforts not only a quantitative expansion but also a qualitative restructuring. Alongside the geographical extension of the transnational economy, its internal reordering has also appeared on the agenda of the day, for new rules of economic competition are indispensable if there is to be a homogeneous space no longer riven by national economic idiosyncrasies. There is no other way for would-be globalizers than to dismantle the national regulatory apparatuses that have previously encompassed economic activity. These apparatuses, which generally reflect a country's historical experiences, social sets of interests and political ideals, combine the logic of economics with other social priorities, in both fragile compromises and institutions built to last. At a later stage of the secular process that Karl Polanyi called 'disembedding', the dynamic of economic globalization is intended to release market relations from the web of national norms and standards and to bring them under the law of worldwide competition.

Whatever these norms cover – labour conditions, regional planning or environmental policy – they are neither wrong nor right but are seen as obstructing entry into the global competitive arena. In this view of things, norms might be acceptable at a global level – although the question does not really apply, of course, in the absence of a political authority. Deregulation is thus a catch-all term for attempts to further global competition by dissolving the links between economic actors and a particular place or a particular community.

Like any regulation of economic activity in the name of the public interest, protection of the environment is also coming under pressure in many countries. As the number of economic actors on the global market continues to grow, so too does the competition between them – which is why governments everywhere tend to attach a higher value to competitive strength than to protection of the environment or of natural resources. New ecological norms, often imposed by democratic public opinion after years of struggle and controversy, are perceived by companies as a hindrance to competition and in many cases fiercely resisted. As competitive interests gain the upper hand over protective interests, it becomes many times more difficult to halt deforestation in Canada or overmining in the Philippines, to stop the building of more motorways in Germany, to introduce eco-taxes in the European Union, or to maintain ecological product standards in Sweden. However, although governments are often enough determined to make their country a more attractive site for footloose capital, it is doubtless an exaggeration to speak of a 'race to the bottom' in matters concerning environmental standards (Esty and Gerardin 1998). Sometimes the protective interests are too strong, or it may be that environmental factors are not all that significant in a siting decision. It would be more accurate to say that environmental regulation has tended to get 'stuck in the mud' as a result of increased competition (Zarsky 1997). True, world market integration has brought a certain convergence among national regulatory systems, but this has been happening too slowly and at too low a level. In many countries, the process of economic globalization has blocked any real progress in national environmental policy.

Not surprisingly, the ambition to standardize competitive conditions throughout the world – especially in the case of cross-border trade – clashes with the right of individual countries to shape economic processes. Now that tariff barriers for industrial goods have been largely dismantled through the successive GATT rounds, should environmental reasons be allowed to put certain categories of import at a disadvantage? This question has been much disputed ever since the Uruguay Round, and it continues to give rise to controversy within the WTO and

OECD over deregulation and protection interests. Under the trade rules currently in force, individual states are entitled to lay down environmental and health standards, so long as the same kinds of goods are subject to the same regulation regardless of whether they are imported or locally produced. Of course, this applies only to the composition of a product: a government might decide, for instance, to slap a special tax on all cars above a certain power threshold. Here, it seems, the principle of national sovereignty contradicts only the principle of the unregulated circulation of goods. What is forbidden in international trade, however, is to discriminate against goods whose production process does not conform to certain environmental standards. Which chemicals are used to produce an item of clothing, whether wooden products come from forest clearance areas, whether genetic engineering methods have been used to produce a plant – on none of these questions is a government allowed by WTO rules to express a collective preference. Thus, in the well-known tuna affair, the ban on dolphin fishing could not be maintained under NAFTA rules, and one of the present disputes between the USA and the EU is over whether governments have the right to keep hormone-intensive beef out of their markets. Moreover, since local production standards are also put under strain when importers are able to gain a competitive advantage by externalizing environmental costs, individual states lose the power to insist that production processes in their own country should be environmentally sustainable. The deregulation interest nullifies the protection interest. Through the competitive effect of free trade, even gentle course corrections towards a sustainable economy are soon brought to a standstill.

All the deregulation efforts are also meant to cleanse the economy of extraneous influences, thereby ensuring optimal deployment of the factors of production. Consumers are ostensibly the main ones to benefit, since deregulated operations encourage a more varied supply through easier market entry as well as lower prices through greater competition. Nevertheless, a regime of ruthless efficiency in environmentally significant sectors may lead to greater overall use of resources. If the price of heating oil, petrol, coal or water falls, then normally demand for them will rise and it will be even less worth introducing conservation technologies. Deregulation of the electricity market in the OECD countries, for example, certainly helped promoters of energy-efficient power stations to enter the market, but it also showed that lower prices may hinder a changeover to cleaner energy sources such as natural gas and, more important still, actually encourage higher electricity consumption (Jones and Youngman 1997). Anyway, it is fairly easy to see that falling prices within a price system that does not accurately reflect environmental costs will accelerate the quarrying of resources. So long as prices do not tell the ecological truth, deregulation will only take the market further down the ecologically slippery slope – and it is not exactly rational to keep running more efficiently in the wrong direction. But the purer competition becomes as a result of deregulation, the less will ecological rationality be able to assert itself against economic rationality. Under the given price system, global competition will deepen the crisis of nature (Daly 1996).

Currency crises and the sell-out effect Nowhere has a global competitive space been raised so clear of national boundaries as in the case of the finance markets. Goods take time to be carried from one place to another, foreign investment requires factories to be built or dismantled, and even services such as insurance cannot be traded overseas without a network of branches and representatives. Only financial transfers in the form of shares, loans or currencies are scarcely subject any longer to restrictions of time and space. Every day, billions of dollars change hands online in virtual space through mere touches on VDU keyboards, irrespective of physical distance. Only on these electronic markets does capital finally attain its secret ideal of completely unfettered mobility. For the money markets have very largely shaken off the inertia not only of temporal duration and geographical distance, but also of material goods; less than 2 per cent of the currency trade is now covered by actual commodity flows (Zukunftskommission 1998: 73). This virtual economy has been made possible technologically by electronic networking, and politically by the deregulation of international capital traffic in the industrialized countries in the 1970s and 1980s, as well as in major developing countries in the 1990s.

As we have seen, it was the collapse of the Bretton Woods system in 1971 that gave the impetus to this development. Currencies could become commodities, their price set by the laws of supply and demand on the capital markets. But the value of a currency is a matter of fateful significance for a country: it determines the purchasing power of the national economy in relation to other national economies around the world. In fact, the ups and downs of freely convertible currencies reflect the expectations of future growth and competitiveness that investors entertain about the respective economies. In a way, a country's whole economy thus becomes a commodity, whose relative value crystallizes through the return envisaged by investment fund managers. This gives the finance markets great power *vis-à-vis* economically weak countries, so great that fluctuations in the exchange rate can decide the fate of whole nations. Governments, whether democratic or authoritarian, often find themselves compelled to gear their economic, social and fiscal policies to the interests of investors, with the result that the interest of their own people in social and economic security all too easily goes by the board. It is as if investors cast a daily ballot by transferring huge sums of money from one country to another (Sassen 1996); the global electorate of investors lines up, as it were, against a country's local electorate, and not infrequently the government allies itself with the investors against its own electors. At the same time, however, the currency crashes in Mexico in late 1994, in several East Asian countries in 1997, and in Russian and Brazil in 1998 made it plain that investors are as jumpy as a herd of wild horses that stampedes off now in one direction, now in another as danger threatens. The collective optimism with which investors forget about risks during an upturn is matched by the collective panic with which they flee out of loans and currencies during a downturn. Investment-seeking capital storms into countries and back out again. On its way in, it gives rise to false dreams; on its way out, it leaves behind ruined human lives and ravaged ecosystems (Cavanagh 1998).

Currency crises are quite likely to threaten nature in the affected countries, for those that are rich in exportable natural resources come under intense pressure to exploit them more extensively and at a faster tempo. The falling value of the currency means that they have to throw larger quantities onto the world market in order to stop their export earnings falling through the floor. An exchange-rate crisis thus intensifies the already chronic hunger of indebted states for foreign currency, so that they will be able to repay loans and to import at least the minimum of food, goods and capital. But often the only option left is to use freely available nature as a currency-earner – as one can see from the current boom in the export of oil, gas, metals, wood, animal feed and agricultural produce from countries in the South hit by the financial crisis. Fishing rights are being sold by Senegal, for example, to fleets of vessels from Asia, Canada and Europe; tree-felling rights by Chile to US timber corporations; and exploration rights by Nigeria to the oil multinationals (French 1998: 23). In times of need, desperate countries have to flog off even their 'family silver'. So it is that valuable forest land is sold off stretch by stretch under the pressure of the debt burden. Mexico, for instance, after the peso collapse of 1994, rescinded its laws protecting national forests – and the people living in them – in order to promote a stronger export orientation. Brazil launched an action plan to make the export of wood, minerals and energy financially more attractive through massive infrastructural investment in Amazonia. Indonesia, after another currency crash, was

compelled in talks with the International Monetary Fund to change its
land ownership legislation so that foreign cellulose and paper corporations could move in on the forest (Menotti 1998b). One might
even, as Menotti acerbically suggests, speak of a causal link between
falling currencies and falling trees.

Measures to rectify the economy after a currency and debt crisis –
measures imposed under the often blackmailing care of the IMF structural adjustment programmes – also usually lead to forced selling of
natural assets on the world market, for the aim of the numerous
structural adjustment programmes in both the South and the East is
to bring the balance of payments back into equilibrium through an
increase in exports, and thus to entice investors back into the country.
A glance at the history of these programmes shows, however, that –
alongside the weaker sections of society – the environment is supposed
to make all the sacrifices for an export upturn. True, the removal of
environmentally damaging subsidies and the liberalization of markets
do generally promote a more efficient use of resources. But the rate
of exploitation soon increases with the mobilization of raw materials
and agricultural produce for export; land demand and pesticide use
rise together with the switch over to cash crops; and tourism and
transport also experience major growth (Reed 1996). Furthermore, the
new exporters' rights to natural resources collide with the hereditary
rights of less endowed sections of the population to use forests, water
and land; the poor are pushed to the sidelines, and compelled by rising
prices to plunder marginal ecosystems for their survival. In this connection, a number of studies have concluded that the negative environmental effects of structural adjustment programmes far outweigh the
positive benefits (Kessler and Van Dorp 1998).

It is not uncommon, however, for the law of supply and demand to
cancel out the fruits of the export drive. Prices often fall as demand
increases on the commodity markets, and once more the lower earnings have to be offset by greater export volumes. Should the recipient
countries also be hit by a financial crisis, both demand and commodity
prices come under renewed pressure. This is precisely what happened
after the Asian financial crisis of 1997. Commodity prices on the world
market slid lower and lower – by more than 25 per cent within a year
(*Die Zeit*, 24 September 1998). And since the crisis also depressed
demand in countries such as Japan, South Korea and Malaysia, the
price spiral kept moving downward and forcing dependent countries
to intensify the exploitation of raw materials for export. Thus money
flows overshadow commodity flows in quite a special way during
periods of economic downturn.

Vanishing distance and the transport effect The sudden awareness of living in a shrinking world may well be the fundamental human experience in the age of globalization. The satellite image of the blue planet visually presents what things are tending towards in reality: all places appear present at the same time. While distance between places becomes insignificant, the same time comes to prevail everywhere: space vanishes, time standardizes. For currency traders and news editors, company buyers and tourists, managers and scientists, less and less importance attaches to distance and, of course, more and more to time. It hardly matters any longer where on the globe something happens; what counts is when it happens – at the right time, too late, or not at all. Globalization, in all its facets, rests upon the rapid overcoming of space, rendering the present ubiquitous without delay. Computers, after all, count seconds, but not kilometres. How the earth is shrinking under the sway of time, how near everything is and how fast everything goes – it is in such experiences that the growing spatio-temporal compactness of the globe becomes discernible (Altvater and Mahnkopf 1996).

Spatial compression requires transport, whether along physical or electronic channels. Electronic networking is the first constitutive element in the process of globalization; without online data transfers there would not be the nervous system of signal communication that, in lightning-quick reactions, binds together events on the globe without consideration of space. If one thinks, however, that in 1995 there were 43.6 computers and 4.8 Internet users per thousand of the world's population (UNDP 1998: 167), four-fifths of whom lived in the industrialized countries, then it is all too clear that one can speak of globalization only in a geographical, and certainly not a social, sense. No more than 1 to 4 per cent of the world's population are electronically linked to one another, and no more than 5 per cent have even sat in an aeroplane. From an ecological point of view, electronic communication is assuredly less wasteful of resources than is physical transport. Yet one should not underestimate the additional strain that the construction and maintenance of a digital infrastructure place upon the earth's resources. High-quality materials used in hardware and peripherals are obtained through numerous refining processes that impose a large (and often toxic) extra burden on the environment, cables of all kinds use a lot of material, and satellites and relay stations also cannot be had without a drain on the environment. Finally, whatever the many prophets of the information age merrily predict, electronic networking will in the long term probably generate more physical travel than it replaces. Anyone who has established close contact with distant places via electronic media will sooner or later want to seal the contact face to face. In any event, the main effect is a positive feedback between electronic and physical transport systems: globalization itself means transport and still more transport.

All forms of economic globalization, outside the international finance markets, rely heavily upon physical transport. Everywhere distances are springing up – on both the consumption and factor markets, they are growing longer and more numerous. T-shirts come from China to Germany and tomatoes from Ecuador to the United States; machinery from Europe stands in Shanghai harbour; the global class of 'symbol analysts' (Castells 1996) keep bumping into one another in the airports of OECD countries. After all, the value of world trade has been rising by more than 6 per cent a year, roughly twice as fast as the world economy itself. Foreign products – from meat to precision machines – play a more prominent role in many countries, and even small firms seek their fortune on overseas markets. And yet the word 'international trade' has a number of false associations. It no longer means that nations exchange goods that they themselves do not produce – as in the classical exchange of raw materials for industrial goods – but that foreign suppliers appear alongside local ones in largely OECD-centred trade. They no longer make up for gaps in the local supply, but try to oust the local supply either through undercutting or through the use of different symbols (Pastowski 1997). Korean cars for Carland America, Mexican beer for Beerland Germany: roughly a half of world trade takes place *within* industrial branches; that is, the same commodities are being imported and exported at the same time (Daly 1996: 5). The main purpose of international goods transport is thus to ensure the competitive presence of many suppliers in as many places as possible.

Distance-chopping and rapid transport for high-quality goods and people are mainly provided by the international air system. Passenger transport, if it continues growing at its present annual rate of 5 per cent, will double every 15 years, and although by now roughly a half of air travel is for leisure purposes, the geography of economic globalization is reflected in the increased flow. Between 1985 and 1996, the income of airline companies grew sevenfold on routes within China and threefold within South-East Asia and between Europe or North America and North-East Asia, whereas on other routes there was at most a twofold increase or sometimes, as in the case of Africa, stagnation (Boeing 1998). Air freight has been rising still faster: after annual growth of 7 to 12 per cent in the mid-1990s (ibid.), the assumption is that it will now average 6.6 per cent and add up to a tripling of revenue by the year 2015 – figures naturally surpassed by the anticipated growth rate for international express services, where DHL and similar firms reckon on an annual increase of 18 per cent.

Without rapidly declining freight costs, the expansion of global markets would not have been possible. For such costs must not be a decisive factor, if the dynamic of supply and demand is to develop independently of geographical location. The more freight costs weigh in the balance, the less worthwhile it becomes to use price and innovation to gain an advantage over far-flung competitors; lower marginal costs in production would soon be eaten up by greater outlays on transport. Only if the costs of overcoming space tend towards insignificance can corporate strategies alone determine the choice of location. A number of reasons have been given for the relative cheapening of freight. First, it is precisely on global markets that transport volume is being constantly reduced in relation to a given value of trade. For a computer producer in Texas, for example, it matters little whether his hard disks come from Singapore or California, as transport costs become less significant, the more the economic value of a transported good is independent of its size or weight. In fact, those branches of the economy that go in most for 'global sourcing' – computers, motor vehicles, consumer electronics, textiles – are often not the largest-volume traders (Sprenger 1997: 344). Second, containerization and easier transfers between modes of transport have greatly increased efficiency (*Economist* 1997b). But the third and main reason why distance has been losing its resistance is that the price of fuel oil, used in nearly all forms of transport, has fallen dramatically since 1980. As a matter of fact, that price is far from reflecting the full ecological costs of the production and consumption of oil. For all the efficiency gains, transport in the OECD countries is the only sector in which CO_2 emissions have continued to increase in recent years. Transport also requires various facilities: vehicles, highways, harbours and airports, a whole infrastructure, which uses a considerable amount of materials and land. Yet most of these costs are passed on to society and do not show up in the freight bills. It becomes easy to overlook the extent to which the overcoming of geographical distance and temporal duration is paid for through the spoliation of nature.

How Economic Globalization Fosters a New Colonization of Nature

The results of the GATT Uruguay Round, which ended in 1993 with a package of trade agreements and the founding of the WTO, included an accord on intellectual property rights. In contrast to the main preoccupation, which had been to dismantle national controls on cross-border trade, it was here a question of introducing a new level of regulation. Yet both strategies – deregulation as well as re-regulation – were pursued in the name of freedom of trade. The contradiction disappears as soon as one realizes that the aim in both cases was to create uniform legal foundations for a global economic space. While a plethora of national obstacles to the circulation of goods and capital had to be dismantled, it was also necessary to establish an international legal framework that would give such circulation a powerful helping hand. Factor mobility can be obstructed by a mass of laws, but it can also be left hanging in mid-air if there are no laws at all. Especially relevant in this respect was the case of property rights in goods based on genetic engineering – a case in which legal security had been defective in most countries around the world. This was the gap that the agreement on 'trade-related intellectual property rights' (TRIPS) was designed to close, for without it the exploitation of newly available raw materials – the genetic material of forms of life – would not have much of a commercial future.

Under the TRIPS agreement, all countries are required to provide legal protection for patented inventions of both products and processes, in all fields of technology. Industrial patents, of course, have long assured their owners an exclusive income from inventions for a certain length of time, but a similar system has only slowly come to apply to biological products and processes. The protection of a patent is nevertheless indispensable for the commercialization of research-intensive products, since only proprietary rights give them a commodity status – otherwise they would just be useful objects freely available in the public domain. For this reason, a guaranteed property system is the legal–social corset of a market economy, just as the more or less forcible enclosure and appropriation of common territory (fields, pasture, forest, fishing grounds) was the historical prerequisite for the lift-off of agrarian capitalism. If the research-intensive products are organisms such as seeds or plants, this raises the additional marketing problem that they easily reproduce themselves (Flitner 1998). Seeds, for example, bring forth plants, which in turn bear the seeds for the next sowing. The commodity character of a living organism does not last long, therefore; the second generation no longer needs to be bought. But this is bad news for any investor, since if commodities can reproduce themselves, it means that the reproduction of capital is on shaky ground. That leaves just two possibilities. Either their reproducibility is curtailed (for example, through the insertion of 'terminator genes'), or patents allow fees to be charged for the use of a technologically modified living process.

Patents to genetic innovations ensure the economic control of 'life industries' over modified organisms and their offspring. Only through the establishment of proprietary rights over cells, micro-organisms and organisms does the genetic material of the living world become available to be marketed. Patents empower firms to take ownership of parts of the natural realm, to turn it into an economic resource, and as far as possible to monopolize it so that no one can use it unless they pay for an approved purpose. Life patents thus play for 'life industries' the same role that land deeds played for emergent agrarian capitalism. They define ownership, keep other users away, and establish to whom the benefits of use should accrue. Activities such as planting, animal-raising or curative treatment, which used to be part of the public domain, thus come increasingly under the control of corporations. Whereas colonialists used to appropriate mineral or land resources by physically controlling a territory, the genetic engineering firms exploit genetic resources through world-recognized patents over DNA sequences.

The consequences for plant diversity, however, are likely to be similar. There is no need to consider the numerous dangers bound up with an uncontrollable spread of transgenic species; even the accident-free introduction of genetic technology into the agriculture of the South would cause a whole range of plants to disappear from the evolutionary picture. Whereas agrarian capitalism led in many places to monoculture of natural plant varieties, the life industries might force specialization in a few genetically optimized, and economically useful, plants (rather along the lines of the 'Green Revolution' of the 1960s and 1970s) (Lappé and Bailey 1998). In the fierce competition for markets that is likely to ensue, non-industrial and local strains would fall by the wayside – which would undermine food security, especially for poorer people without the means to purchase industrial produce. All plants other than a few strains capable of large-scale cultivation would be lost. A global system of legal patents for genetic inventions, which incorporated and irrevocably modified parts of the human biological heritage for commercial ends, would threaten to result in nothing less than a simplification of the biosphere.

How Economic Globalization Changes the Geography of Environmental Stress

In recent years, more and more salmon dishes – fresh, smoked or grilled – have been appearing on German menus, almost as if it were a fish from local waters. By now Germans consume nearly 70 million kilos a year of the favoured fish, which is brought from farms in Norway or Scotland to supermarket displays (Oppel 1999). But as in the mass farming of any other creature, large quantities of feed have to be supplied – to be precise, five kilos of wild deep-water fish have to be processed into one kilo of fishmeal, which is then used to feed salmon for consumption. This raw material is mostly caught off the Pacific coast of South America, where catches are declining because of overfishing, and it is then turned into meal in Peruvian harbour towns that are in danger of suffocating in the gaseous, liquid and solid waste matter that results from the process. While German consumers can feast themselves on fresh low-calorie (and rather expensive) fish, people in Peru are left with pillaged seas and filthy dirty towns.

This example shows how a lengthening of the supply chain can shift the ecological division of labour between countries of the South (and East) and those of the North. For economic globalization does not mean that the costs and benefits of economic activity are globalized. On the contrary, it is more likely that extension of the value-creation chain to different locations around the world will bring a new allocation of advantage and disadvantage. When a production process is divided up among different countries and regions, a tendency soon appears to separate costs and benefits by redistributing them up and down the chain. Anyway it would be wrong to imagine that the worldwide networking of offices, factories, farms and banks is accompanied by a decentralization of all functions from production and planning to finance, not to speak of the collection of profits (Sassen 1996). Despite many attempts to increase the autonomy of sub-units, the opposite is generally the case: that is, the diversification of economic activities leads to a concentration of control and profit at the nodal points of the network economy (Castells 1996). The flux of investment into distant countries is offset by a reflux of power and profits to the originating country, or, more precisely, to the 'global cities' of the North. As special export zones multiply in Bangladesh, Egypt or Mexico, where cheap labour, tax breaks and lax environmental norms considerably reduce production costs, the sky is the limit for the towers of banks and company offices in Hong Kong, Frankfurt or London.

The changed distribution of economic power goes together with a change in how the pressure on the environment is distributed across geographical space. If power, in an ecological sense, is defined as the capacity to internalize environmental advantages while externalizing environmental costs, then it may be supposed that the lengthening of economic chains will start a process that concentrates advantages at the upper end and disadvantages at the lower end. In other words, the environmental costs incurred within the transnational value-creation chains will become especially high in the countries of the South and East, while the post-industrial economies will become ever more environmentally friendly. Or to use an analogy (with the salmon example in mind), the rich countries will increasingly occupy the upper positions in the food chain (where larger volumes of low-value inputs have step-by-step been converted into smaller volumes of high-value food), while the developing or poorer countries will occupy the middle and lower positions. In fact, along with numerous individual examples, a series of highly aggregated data on international flows of materials lend credence to this interpretation. Thus, 35 per cent of total resource consumption is incurred abroad in the case of Germany, 50 per cent in Japan, 70 per cent in the Netherlands, and so on (Adriaanse et al. 1997: 13). The smaller the area of an industrialized country, the greater seems to be the geographical separation between the sites of pressure on the environment and the sites of consumption benefit. In all these countries, there has been a tendency over the past 15 years for a growing proportion of environmental consumption to take place abroad (involving not so much raw materials as semi-finished products).

In agriculture, Southern regions of the world no longer supply only agrarian mass produce as in the days of colonialism, but also supply goods with a high dollar value per unit of weight for affluent consumers in the North. Highly perishable items such as tomatoes, lettuce, fruit, vegetables and flowers come as air freight to Europe from Senegal or Morocco, to Japan from the Philippines, or to the United States from Colombia or Costa Rica (Thrupp 1995). As in the case of salmon, health-conscious shoppers with an average to high income are only too pleased to have a supply that does not depend on the season, while plantations and glasshouses in the areas of origin impose irrigation, pesticide use and the repression of local farmers. Nor are things much different with shrimp or meat production. The breeding of shrimps and prawns in Thailand or India for the Japanese and European markets means that people have to wade through toxic residue to catch them and that many a mangrove forest has to disappear from the scene. More refined consumption in the North at the price of the environment and subsistence economics in the South: this pattern has rooted itself deeply in the food-produce market since the 1970s. The raising of cattle and pigs in Europe draws in manioc or soya both from the United States and from countries such as Brazil, Paraguay, Argentina, Indonesia, Malaysia or Thailand. The old law that the market puts

purchasing power before human need asserts itself still more powerfully in a world economy beyond frontiers.

Of course, the expansion of the fossil development model into one
or two dozen aspiring economies in the South and East has done most
to change the geography of environmental stress. As the newly industrialized nations entered the age fuelled by fossil resources, the
possibility presented itself of stretching the industrial production chains
beyond the OECD countries. The South's share of world output has
thus been growing (and the OECD's slowly declining) in primary
industry, metalworking and chemicals (Sprenger 1997: 337; Mason
1997), rising in the last of these from 17 per cent in 1990 to 25 per cent
in 1996 (French 1998: 27). What is happening is not so much migration
for environmental reasons as a redistribution of functions within the
world economy. The stages of an international production chain that
put most pressure on the environment are usually in less-developed
regions, while the cleaner and less material stages tend to be in the G-
7 countries. In the aluminium industry, for instance, the quarrying of
bauxite takes place in Guyana, Brazil, Jamaica and Guinea (along with
Australia). The actual smelting of the aluminium, which is the next
stage along, moved more and more in the 1980s from the North to
countries such as Brazil, Venezuela, Indonesia or Bahrain, while the
research and development stage remained chiefly located in the OECD
area (Heerings and Zeldenrust 1995: 33). Despite higher use overall,
the production of aluminium grew strongly in Japan and weakly in
Europe; imports from the South filled the gap (Mason 1997).

A look at the computer branch further along shows just how much
high-tech industry lives off the new ecological division of labour. In
the case of 22 computer companies in the industrialized countries,
more than half of their (mostly toxic) microchip production is located
in developing countries (French 1998: 28). Does this not show in outline
the future restructuring of the world economy? The software economies of the North will pride themselves on their plans for a cleaner
environment, while the newly industrialized economies will do the
manufacturing and contend with classical forms of water, air and soil
pollution, and the poorer primary economies will do the extracting
and undermine the subsistence basis of the third of humanity that
lives directly from nature.

Which and Whose Globalization?

Globalization is not a monopoly of the neo-liberals: the most varied
actors, with the most varied philosophies, are also caught up in the

transnationalization of social relations; indeed the ecological movement is one of the most important agents of global thinking. Accordingly, the image of the blue planet – that symbol of globalization – conveys more than just one message. The imperial message of collapsing frontiers always found itself confronted with the holistic message of the planet's finite unity. A clear line can be drawn from Earth Day 1970 (often seen as the beginning of the American ecological movement) to the United Nations conference on world climate held in Kyoto in 1997. In the squares where people assembled on that first Earth Day, speakers and demonstrators underpinned their demands for comprehensive environmental protection with photographs of the earth taken less than a year before from the surface of the moon. And nearly thirty years later, the emblem of the planet was prominently displayed on the front of the conference hall where, for the first time, the world's governments entered into legally binding commitments to limit pollution levels. That picture shows the earth as a single natural body binding human beings and other forms of life to a common destiny; it globalizes our perception both of nature and of the human story. Only with that image did it become possible to speak of 'one earth' or 'one world' in the true sense of the term. For neither the name of Friends of the Earth, nor the title of the Brundtland Report, *Our Common Future* (WCED 1987), would have meant much without that photo of the planet.

But the 'blue planet effect' and its message of finitude go deeper still: they produce a way of seeing that places local action within a global framework. The picture shows the outer limits of the living space of everyone who looks at it. Does not everyone know that, if only the image were sufficiently enlarged, he or she would be able to find himself or herself on it? For the observing subject cannot be separated there from the observed object; in scarcely any other example is self-reference so inextricably woven into the image. This visual superimposition of global and individual existence has shifted the cognitive and moral coordinates of our perception of ourselves. The consequences of an action, it suggests, may extend to the edges of the earth – and everyone is responsible for them. All of a sudden, car drivers and meat buyers are linked to the greenhouse effect, and even a hairspray or an air ticket is seen as having overstepped the global boundaries. 'Think globally, act locally': this electoral slogan of the ecological movement has played its part in creating a 'global citizen' who internalizes the earth's limits within his or her own thinking and action. The narrative of limitation derives its moral force from this association of planet and subject in a common drama. The ecological experience is thus undoubtedly one dimension of the experience of globalization, because it overturns people's conventional notion that they live and act in national political and social spaces that are clearly demarcated and separated from one another (Beck 1997: 44).

Yet the ecological movement cannot escape the fact that, however provisionally, the imperial message has won through. One sign of this is the way in which multinational corporations have almost completely seized for themselves the image of the blue planet. The perception of the world as a homogeneous space, visible and accessible all the way across, has everywhere become hegemonic. This vision is imperial, because it claims the right to roam the world unhindered and to grab whatever it fancies – exactly as if there were no places, no communities, no nations. The mechanisms of GATT, NAFTA and the WTO were born in the spirit of frontier demolition. They codify the world as a freely accessible economic arena, in which economics enjoys the right of way. The newly established rules are designed to proclaim trans-national corporations as sovereign subjects within global space, exempt from any obligation to regions or national governments. State pro-tectionism is thereby abolished, only to be replaced by a new pro-tectionism that favours corporations. Transnational partnerships are entitled to claim all sorts of freedoms and rights, while territorial states – not to mention citizens or civic associations – have to take second place.

When people look back on the last century of this millennium, they will be forced to conclude that Rio de Janeiro was pretty good on rhetoric, but Marrakesh was taken in real earnest. Here the UN con-ference on the environment held in Rio in 1992 stands for a long series of international agreements – notably the conventions on climate and biodiversity – that were supposed to steer the world economy in less ecologically harmful directions. Marrakesh stands for the founding of the World Trade Organization after the end of the GATT Uruguay Round, and for the growing importance of the IMF as a shadow government in many countries. There the basis was laid for an economic regime in which the investment activity of transnational actors would be free of regulation anywhere on the globe. These transnational regimes – the environmental and the economic – are attempts to give a political–legal foundation to transnational economic society, but the two stand in marked contradiction to each other. The environmental regime is concerned with protection of the natural heritage, the economic regime with equal rights to exploit it; the environmental agreements are based on respect for natural limits, the economic agreements on the right to carry through economic expansion successfully. Paradoxically, moreover, they wager on different systems of responsibility and accountability. On the one hand, the environmental agreements appeal to sovereign states as responsible entities that are supposed to uphold the public good in their territory. On the other hand, the economic agreements assume sovereign, transnationally active corporations that belong to no territory and are therefore responsible to no state. Already today the world's hundred largest economies comprise 49 countries and 51 corporations (Anderson and Cavanagh 1997: 37).

It is therefore not clear how the conflicting messages that appropriate the image of the blue planet can be reconciled with each other. Even transnational civil society has succeeded only on specific occasions in confronting corporations with their responsibility towards nature and the overwhelming majority of the world's citizens. If the holistic message stands for 'sustainability' and the imperial message for 'economic globalization', then it would seem necessary to suppose that, however great the synergies at a micro-level, the chasm between the two is continuing to widen. But that is the greatness of a symbol: it can hold together divergent truths within a single visual form.

IV

Ecology and Equity in a Post-development Era

9

Ecology, Justice and the End of Development

For global environmentalists, 1997 was a year of anniversaries. Ten years had passed since the World Commission on Environment and Development, chaired by Gro Harlem Brundtland, offered its famous formula of how nature could be preserved and development nevertheless continued: sustainable development is development 'that meets the needs of the present without compromising the ability of future generations to meet their own needs' (WCED 1987: 8). After the golden post-war decades with their explosion of world economic output, the bitter insight that conventional development burns off resources that are essential for the generations to come had thus received an official blessing. All of a sudden the future changed its tone: it was no longer a bright period when the fruits of development could be harvested, but appeared as a potentially gloomy period when the bill for the party would finally have to be paid. Against this background, the Brundtland Commission pleaded with governments to consider the time dimension in all their decisions and to weigh benefits in the present against losses in the future. For politicians are not just accountable to their contemporaries, but also bear responsibility for generations to come. They are consequently supposed to consider the effects of action taken today upon the conditions of life in the future. The commission called for justice between generations or inter-generational equity, a concept that had gradually come to the fore since the 1972 UN Conference on the Environment in Stockholm. In the light of this concept, the essence of sustainablility is to be found in a particular relationship between people and people rather than between people and nature. In fact, the concept can serve as the cornerstone for a new ethical framework; it extends the principle of equity among the human community along the axis of time.

However, in highlighting justice in time the canonical formula underemphasizes justice in social space. Constraints imposed by the present generation on future generations are given prominence over constraints imposed by powerful groups on less powerful groups within one generation. The Brundtland definition puts the spotlight on 'needs' and 'generations', terms that are socially neutral, comprising both rich and poor, powerful and powerless classes. Yet such distinctions are crucial when it comes to intra-generational equity. Whose needs and what needs are supposed to be met? In a divided world, these are core questions that decide whether sustainable development will be part and parcel of a democratic project or eventually deepen social polarization. Is sustainable development supposed to meet the needs for water, food and minimal purchasing power or the needs for air-conditioning and university studies abroad? Are the needs in question those of the global consumer class or those of the enormous masses of have-nots? Is sustainable development concerned with the survival needs of the majority world or with the luxury needs of the minority world? The Brundlandt Commission left these questions in the air; the report remained evasive throughout about the effects of power and over-consumption. This fuzziness certainly facilitated the acceptance of 'sustainable development' in circles of privilege and power, but obscured the point that there will be no sustainability without restraint on wealth. In other words: that more intra-generational equity is a condition for achieving inter-generational equity.

The other anniversary is equally unlikely to shed more light on the issue of justice, at least not in an environmentally reasonable sense. In 1992 the UN Conference on Environment and Development in Rio de Janeiro was as ambiguous about equity within generations as the Brundtland Commission five years before. It is true that the conference would probably not even have taken place if the demands of the Southern countries that inequality should be addressed had not been accommodated. But the concern for equity was couched in the language of 'development', circumventing again the question: whose development and of what? In fact, the Rio Declaration first reiterates the 'right to development' before it proceeds to state the need for environmental protection – which was the motive for convening the conference in the first place. Although during the conference Southern governments countered demands for environmental restrictions with calls for a better balance in North–South relations, they entered an unholy alliance with the North in their praise of development. Both South and North continued to perceive themselves as moving along one single track, each country hoping for redemption in economic growth, albeit starting from different levels. Feeling compelled to mobilize the ever scarce resources to that end, they converged in assigning sustainability a back seat in the vehicle called economic development. While the South thus entertained its desire to follow the well-to-do nations, the North could feel free to indulge in its competitive compulsion to keep on rushing ahead. This way, overdevelopment was scarcely an issue, and the fact that it produces both poverty and biospherical risk was off the agenda. As the quest for justice was firmly wedded to the idea of development, nobody had to change profoundly and all parties could turn to business as usual – a result amply borne out in the following years.

Point of Departure

The expectation that justice will be brought about through development is deeply ingrained in the post-war political discourse. To be sure, its roots reach back to the European Enlightenment, when the people of the globe were recognized as mankind, unified by common dignity and destined to move towards the reign of reason and progress. But it was only after the war that the perception of the world as a site where in a few decades equality could be engineered took hold. For instance, the United Nations solemnly announced their determination in the Preamble to the UN Charter 'to promote social progress and better standards of life in larger freeedom ... and to employ international machinery for the promotion of the economic and social advancement of all people'.

Politically, two historical shifts converged in creating a global consensus around this idea. On the one hand, the United States, after the terrors of war, were in search of a new world order that would guarantee peace. In their view, the outbreak of war in Europe had been caused by the economic upheaval following the Great Depression. Remembering their own successful management of economic crisis during the New Deal, when John Maynard Keynes had advised stabilizing the economy through state action, they projected the need for economic growth – steered along through public intervention – upon the globe. The Point Four Program of technical assistance, according to President Truman in his *Memoirs*, 'aimed at enabling millions of people in underdeveloped areas to raise themselves from the level of colonialism to self-support and ultimate prosperity' (Truman 1956: 252). Economic development had to be launched globally in order to lay the base for peace. On the other hand, with the demise of England and France as colonial powers, decolonization set in and new nation-states emerged. With independence achieved, most of these states saw their

être in economic development. They secured the support of
~~~izens~~ by holding out the promise of greater economic output.
After extended periods of humiliation during colonialism, they longed
for recognition and rushed to join the modern world. For that purpose,
they were even ready to turn their societies upside down in order to
remake them in the image of the West. Rising income levels and
increasing export earnings seemed to be the obvious road to attain a
standing equal to that of the industrial countries. As a result of both
historical shifts a global consensus emerged around 'development'
(Sachs 1992b; Lummis 1992) as the supreme aspiration that bound
North and South together. Social justice, on the level of international
politics, was therefore recast as catching up with the rich. Both the
hegemonial needs of the North and the emancipatory needs of the
South were nicely taken care of in this perspective.

Landslide

The twentieth century, claims British historian Eric Hobsbawm, came
to an end ten years before its calendary demise. The Short Twentieth
Century, he argues, lasted from 1914 util 1991, spanning the breakdown
of nineteenth-century civilization in the First World War and the
collapse of the Soviet Union after the end of the Cold War. During
most of this period governments felt entitled to intervene in economic
affairs for reasons of social welfare. Particularly in the decades after the
Second World War, with the disastrous consequences of massive unemployment in Europe in the early 1930s still evident and communist
destabilization looming, nation-states claimed an active role in guiding
their economies for, as they saw it, the benefit of all citizens. However,
the rapport between territory, wealth creation and governance, which
provided the basis for the welfare state, began to disintegrate in the
1980s and 1990s. Hobsbawm calls it a landslide. 'As the transnational
economy established its grip over the world, it undermined a major,
and since 1945, virtually universal, institution: the territorial nation-
state, since such a state could no longer control more than a diminishing
part of its affairs' (Hobsbawm 1994: 424).

Before this landslide, states had been the centres of gravity, nationally and internationally. They were therefore in the position to forge a
social contract between the wealthy and the poor and to redistribute
resources accordingly. In the North, the welfare pact was based on an
economy producing jobs, on a state redistributing surplus, and on
workers purchasing goods and paying taxes. In the South, the developmentalist state mobilized productive resources of all kinds, claiming to

cater to the needs of its population. And internationally, the development consensus was in effect a social contract that promoted a system of bilateral and multilateral cooperation that was supposed to close the gulf between the haves and the have-nots. But the social contract was in all of these cases made possible by a certain congruence between the polity and the economy, as both were to a large extent bounded by territory. Inasmuch, however, as the power of territories diminishes in the age of globalization, such social contracts are bound to unravel.

Indeed, the power of territories is on the decline, and not just in the economic arena. Satellite television, jobs abroad, cyberspace and air travel converge in delinking place from community. A transnational sphere of reality has taken shape, oblivious of boundaries and cutting across national territories. Nevertheless, the emergence of the globe as an economic arena where capital, goods and services are able to move without much consideration for local and national communities has delivered the most serious blow to the idea of a polity built on reciprocal rights and duties among citizens. As corporations attempt to reach out to gain foreign markets, they feel held back by the weight of domestic responsibilities. The same holds true for the elites. As they aspire to catch up with the vanguards of the international consumer class, their sense of responsibility for the disadvantaged sections of their own society withers away because, instead of feeling superior with respect to their compatriots, they now feels themselves to be inferior with respect to their global reference groups. Globalization thus undercuts social solidarity. Through transnationalization, capital is in the position to escape any links of loyalty to a particular society. It prefers not to be bothered by things like paying taxes, creating jobs, reinvesting surplus, keeping to collective rules or educating the young, because it considers them mere obstacles to global competition. As the transnational arena becomes the frame of reference, the national community loses relevance. As a result, in many societies a split opens up between the globally oriented middle class on the one side and – in terms of the world market – superfluous populations on the other. While globalization removes barriers between nations, it thus erects new barriers within nations.

Under the impact of that shift, the basis of the developmentalist state is cracking. More often than not, the states ally themselves with the globalizing forces and increasingly show disregard for the majority of their citizens who live outside the global circuit (Kothari 1993). They are ever more committed to promoting the insertion of their industries and middle classes into global markets, and consider the non-competitive social majority a liability rather than a boon. While 'development' still contained the hope of redistribution of wealth and power in favour of the poor, 'globalization' redirects state action to providing better opportunities for the well-to-do in their scramble for international standing. As a consequence, the promise of development for all, which was once the glue keeping states together across social and ethnic groups, crumbles and leaves the state with less legitimacy. In the wake of this shift, not the needs of people but the rights of corporations are the focus of politics in the era of globalization. Governments, therefore, are backing out from the development consensus as they increasingly consider the quest for justice outside their competence.

Furthermore, the landslide undermined not just the domestic but the international development consensus. For decades it was taken for granted that governments of the North, either directly or indirectly, would extend assistance to Southern countries in order to steer them along the path of development. With the rise of the neo-liberal world view this understanding has withered away, and the claims of the South for more equity remain largely without echo. In particular the notion – upon which the UN was built – that 'the social advancement of peoples' would be a matter of international public responsibility has lost acceptance; private investors are hailed as benefactors of human-kind instead. Whereas in the development discourse the state was supposed to be the engine of transformation, this role is taken over by transnational corporations in the globalization discourse. Therefore, international agencies focus their attention on creating a worldwide 'level playing field' for companies, while redistributive action between governments falls by the wayside. In the neo-liberal view, greater equity – if it matters at all – is seen as expanding the reign of the law of demand and supply across the globe. Not more development co-operation but more investment opportunities seem to offer the prospect of catching up with the North. Whenever, therefore, the 'right to development' is invoked today, it is likely to be a call of national elites to be more fully admitted to the global circuit of capital and goods, and not a call for greater solidarity with the majority world beyond the hustle and bustle of the world market.

Impasse

However, the more serious blow to the post-war idea of merging justice and development comes not from changing political but from changing environmental conditions, because the future, in the image of 'development', is constructed as an infinite process of continuous improvement. Tomorrow's conditions, so the story goes, will always surpass today's conditions, if society is put in motion and managed in a rational way. 'Development', during the decades after the Second World War, was nothing other than a reincarnation of the late eighteenth-century idea of material progress, only now projected world-wide and considered attainable within a few decades through planning and engineering. Like progress, development is open-ended: it knows no point of arrival. Within such a framework it became possible, domestically as well as internationally, to conceive of justice as an ever increasing participation of ever more people in an ever growing surplus. The famous metaphor of the growing cake that offers larger pieces for everyone without imposing smaller pieces on anybody illustrates nicely how justice is understood when humankind is perceived as a net-gain community. The quest for justice, in this view, is best satisfied by the incorporation of ever more people in an open-ended global growth process. Given that the overall size of the cake is growing, everybody will be absolutely better off, even if the relative size of the pieces remains the same. It is easy to see that this notion of justice has prevailed for at least half a century, not only on the international level but also on the level of national welfare politics. And it is equally easy to see that it derives its attraction from the promise to achieve justice without redistribution. In other words, the dedication to growth has always been fuelled by the desire to sidestep the hard questions of justice.

Such an open-ended conception of justice and growth rests on a fundamental assumption – an assumption, however, that has become increasingly shaky in the last quarter of this century. For the long march to greater justice through expanding growth can continue without getting stuck only as long as growth generates more advantages than costs. Indeed, this expectation about the benign nature of growth has dominated Western thought ever since around 1800. It was largely taken for granted that the economic process will turn out to be a positive-sum game – that the benefits will by far outweigh all the burdens accumulated in the process. If this had not been the case, society would have been foolish to opt for an unfettered pursuit of growth. What is looming behind this expectation, of course, is modernity's notorious optimism about the consequences of human action. After all, the moderns believe that the consequences of their actions will on balance always be positive, while non-modern cultures tend to have a greater awareness of the fragility of human action, judging the outcome of such action as fundamentally uncertain. Such scepticism has been left behind by the moderns, and the belief that economic growth, all things considered, will eventually result in a higher state of welfare for everybody follows from this rose-tinted outlook.

But this optimism about the future – already shaken by the catastrophic events of the twentieth century in the heartlands of Europe – has been finally shattered by what is somewhat euphemistically called the ecological crisis. Far from being just a transitory phenomenon, the emergence of bio-physical limits to economic growth redefines the conditions of wealth creation for the twenty-first century. The open-ended nature of growth cannot be taken for granted any longer – on the contrary, it appears that growth itself is undercutting its own prospects to a point where its finite nature becomes obvious. From the local up to the global level, it has become evident in many instances that resources (water, timber, oil, minerals, etc.), sites (land for mines, settlements, infrastructure), and sinks (soils, oceans, atmosphere) for the natural inputs of economic growth are becoming scarce. From now on, material progress has to operate under multi-layered constraints. Even though economic growth has lasted for only a few generations and has been limited to a minority of the world's population, its finiteness has already become apparent.

The principal ecological constraints are by now well known (e.g. UNDP 1998: 65–8). On the side of fossil inputs for economic growth it is less the availability of resources in the earth that is currently threatened than the availability of biospherical sinks for absorbing the gases released when these resources are burned. As the greenhouse effect gathers momentum, climatic turbulences are likely to appear that, among other things, will cause crop failures, flooding, hurricanes, droughts and an increased rate of losses in biodiversity. On the side of biological resources for growth it is rather the long-range availability that is at stake. In the course of the last 50 years, for example, one-third of arable land has been seriously degraded worldwide, and one-third of tropical forests, one-quarter of the available fresh water and one-quarter of the fish reserves have disappeared, not to mention the extinction of plant and animal species. At present there is no evidence of a change in these trends – on the contrary, in most areas the pressures on nature are bound to increase.

However, ecological constraints represent only half the story. They are exacerbated by the fact that the rule of the thumb according to which 20 per cent of the world population consume 80 per cent of the world's resources still holds true. In the global context, the industrialized countries have already overshot their limit: they are living well beyond their means. The 'ecological footprint' (Wackernagel and Rees 1996) they produce is larger – in some cases much larger – than their own territories, and they have to tap into the resources available for other countries. In fact, the OECD countries surpass the permissible average size of such a footprint by a magnitude of about 75–85 per cent, while only 9 out of 52 analysed countries remain below this permissible average altogether. As matters stand today, the wealthy 25 per cent of humanity occupy a footprint as large as the entire biologically productive surface area of the earth (Wackernagel and Rees 1997). Of course, such a level of resource consumption cannot be imitated by the rest of the world and any emerging country would be well advised to remain considerably below that level in its industrial development.

Consider, for instance, the greenhouse effect. Oceans and terrestrial biomass are capable of absorbing 13–14 billion tons of carbon dioxide each year, a volume that the world could therefore afford to release without harmful consequences through the burning of wood and fossil energies. If one divided this admissible budget by today's world population of 5.8 billion, everybody would be allowed to emit 2.3 tons of CO_2. However, the average German citizen at present accumulates nearly 12 tons (and the average US citizen 20 tons) of carbon dioxide emissions every year. It follows that a country like Germany under present circumstances has overdrawn its carbon budget by a factor of five. Still, this rough calculation is favourable for developed countries, as it considers only present greenhouse gas emissions and not their increase over the past two hundred years, over which time more than 80 per cent has been produced by industrial countries (Sachs et al. 1998: 72). In any case, the German level of 12 tons, short of major climate disruptions, will not be attainable by developing countries. If all countries followed the German pattern of production and consumption, the world would annually release 67 billion tons into the atmosphere. Given that only 13–14 billion tons are tolerable, we would need five planets to have sufficient sinks for CO_2 – but we have only one. A similar argument holds true for living resources, such as fish. Despite the fact that fish is essential for the food supply in poorer countries, Japan, Europe, USA and Russia account for more than 40 per cent of the catch, although they comprise just a little over 20 per cent of the world population (ibid.: 75). Thus a global commons, ocean fishing grounds – a quarter of which are already exhausted and nearly half of which are already exploited to the biological limit – is excessively appropriated by the rich, and patterns of fish consumption (including animal feed) are sustained that could spread to the rest of the world only at the price of eliminating fish from the seas altogether.

Climate change is the most obvious example, and other emerging limits tell a similar story: global equality on the level of the highly industrialized countries would seriously undermine the biosphere's hospitality for humans. Given these historically new circumstances, the metaphor of the growing cake has become dangerously misleading. The prospect of greater equity can no longer lie in the perspective of ongoing growth. True, there is no eternally fixed relationship between the monetary and the physical size of an economy, but up to the arrival of the post-industrial society economic growth has always implied correspondingly higher inputs of energy and materials, while this connection weakens under post-industrialism, albeit on very high absolute levels of resource consumption. Assuming for the time being a close link between monetary and physical growth, it is therefore not an exaggeration to say that, beyond a certain threshold, conventional economic wealth is intrinsically oligarchic; it could be acquired across the globe only at the price of biospherical disruption. Moreover, in a closed space with finite resources the underconsumption of one party is the necessary condition for the overconsumption of the other party. From this angle, it is wrong to assume that economic growth evolves like a positive-sum game – on the contrary, growth is accumulating adverse side-effects at such a scale that it is heuristically useful to regard it rather as a zero-sum game. The rising tide, before lifting all the boats, is likely to burst through the banks.

The illusion that growth can be relied on as a positive-sum game could be sustained because the costs associated with it remained invisible for a long time. What rendered them largely invisible is the fact that they had been successfully shifted elsewhere. Indeed, the novelty brought home by the environmental crisis is the recognition not that growth injures nature but that unpleasant consequences can no longer be kept at a distance. After all, the creation of economic value has always been the art of internalizing benefits and externalizing costs. How benefits and costs are separated out, and who is able to retain the first while shifting the latter elsewhere is obviously a matter of power; it is for this reason that power has always been an essential ingredient of value creation. Reaping value is made much easier when – mediated through power – a gradient can be established that makes the benefits acrue to the centre and the costs slide off to the periphery. Above all during the industrial age, fossil materials and energies could increase the power of money only insofar as the social and environmental costs involved did not have to be accounted for by the economic actors. What appeared as value in official accounts showed up, so to speak, as disvalue in the imaginary accounts of future generations, distant countries or poor people.

In the history of progress, time, space and social class have been the major dimensions along which costs have been shifted out of sight and out of mind. As to the dimension of time, it was unrecognized practice for more than a century to move some of the bitter effects of economic progress along the axis of time to future generations. As a consequence, there is by now little doubt that the depletion of fossil reserves, the degradation of soils, the loss in biodiversity and the change in climate will in all likelihood diminish the chances of future generations to lead flourishing lives, at least in the sense of today's aspirations. As to the dimension of space, the rise of Western nations was greatly facilitated by their power to concentrate the social and environmental costs of resource mobilization in geographically remote areas. Large distances protected the centres from feeling the bitter effects of mining, monoculture and deforestation, effects that were experienced mainly by colonized peoples around the world. And finally with regard to social class, the consumer classes often succeeded in passing on environmental burdens to less advantaged groups, leaving the noise, the dirt and the ugliness of the industrial hinterland on their doorsteps. Particularily hit are those groups – as can be observed in many Southern countries today – that derive their livelihood directly from the free access to land, water and forests. Building dams and extracting ore, drilling groundwater wells and capitalizing agriculture for the benefit of the urban classes often degrade the ecosystems such people depend on. More often than not, small peasants, artisans and tribals are displaced and subsequently marginalized in order to step up the resource provision for the dominating middle class (Gadgil and Guha 1995).

However, the distances that once safely separated places of accumulation from places of exploitation, and winners from victims, have shrunk. Costs shifted to the future spill into the present, geographically there are few frontiers of exploitation left, and socially the powerless come closer, be it through television or migration. As with globalization in general, the world has become a smaller place, not only for goodies but also for troubles. It is as if the latency period of industrial affliction is finally over, making the illness break out in many places and instances simultaneously. The old thermodynamic truth that production generates both wealth and waste is looming large; as with the globalization of wealth production, the waste production is closing in upon the planet. For that reason, the notion of the 'world risk society' (Beck 1985) adequately captures the present historical constellation. For with economic growth the manufactured risks seem to grow at a faster rate than the riches produced. Justice at the beginning of the twenty-first century, therefore, will be concerned more with the reduction of risks than with the redistribution of riches.

The New Colour of Justice

In a world risk society it has become obsolete to turn the desire for justice into a demand for more and accelerated economic development. As the environmental space available for humanity is finite and in some respects already overstretched, conventional growth of enormous physical scale is bound to heighten the various threats. And there is no doubt that these threats will make everybody, but particularly the poorer countries, worse off. This shift towards a world risk society profoundly modifies the background conditions for the relationship between rich and poor, between Northern and Southern countries. At the time of President Truman, the worldwide development project could still appear as a global positive-sum game in which all could be expected to gain eventually; there was no suspicion that the journey towards modernization could at some point be overtaken by a rising flood of risks. Under the new historical constellation this certainty has vanished, turning the unfettered pursuit of conventional development into a doomed adventure. As a consequence, the demand for justice and dignity on behalf of Southern countries threatens to accelerate the rush towards biospherical disruption, as long as the idea of justice is firmly linked to the idea of development. Delinking the aspiration for justice from the pursuit of conventional development therefore becomes vital, both for rescuing the ideal of justice as 'development' falters and for inventing paths of social improvement that do not systematically overstep the limits of nature.

Certainly, 'development' contains a noble hope whose roots reach back to the first half of the nineteenth century, the founding period of socialist thinking. The rapid advances of technology led to the socialist belief that there was a floor of minimal technological progress below which equity could never be achieved. With all the advances in agriculture and industrial technology before their eyes, progressives of all shades believed that this floor had been reached, and that from now on nobody would have to go hungry. As a consequence, they worked towards rationalizing society and spreading technical progress in order to uplift the poor, first in Europe and then in the rest of the world. However, although there is more than a kernel of truth in the assumption that a certain level of technology is indispensable for overcoming chronic scarcity, it is about to reveal itself as dangerously one-sided. The emerging bio-physical limits suggest that there is also a ceiling to nature-intensive development beyond which equity can no longer be achieved. Chemical agriculture, the automobile society or meat-based nutrition are cases in point. These levels of development are structurally oligarchic: they cannot be generalized across the world without putting the life chances of everybody in jeopardy. Given the fact that the 20 per cent who enjoy the highest income of the world population lay claim to 85 per cent of the world's timber, 75 per cent of its metals and 70 per cent of its energy (UNRISD 1995), there is no way – even taking a considerable saving potential into account – that their lifestyle can serve as the imagined standard of equity. For this reason, the socialist intuition of the nineteenth century has to be complemented by the environmentalist insight of the late twentieth century that justice calls for an upper limit to material-intensive development. It appears that this insight is making some headway into official circles, given that the 1998 *Human Development Report* affirms that 'the poor countries have to accelerate their consumption growth, but they must not follow the road taken by the rich and rapidly growing economies in the past half a century' (UNDP 1998: 8).

It is, however, often overlooked that environmental consumption on the part of the rich, globally and nationally, has an enormous bearing on the possibilities for achieving greater social justice. One reason for that is the common confusion between cleanliness and sustainability. True, for 25 years environmental policy has largely focused on cleaning and protecting air, water and soils. Regulators have concentrated on reducing the flow of harmful substances into nature, and filter technologies have been mounted at the ends of pipes in order to control emissions at the tail end of production. If the environmental crisis is defined in terms of too much pollution, the issue of justice enters only when the social distribution of harmful impacts – who gets polluted more than others? is considered. The environmental justice movement in the USA, for instance, has mobilized protest around the frequent siting of polluting industries in non-white areas. But the issue of justice acquires a different and probably more fundamental relevance if the environmental crisis is defined in terms of excessive resource use. Such a shift in attention from the tail end to the front end of the economic cycle, however, is overdue for ecological reasons. For even a clean economy could cheerfully continue eroding soils, cutting down forests, degrading biodiversity and heating the atmosphere. What really matters is the sheer volume of material input, not so much the pollutants in the output (Schmidt-Bleek 1994). After all, the average German consumes about 80 tons of energy and materials annually and the average Dutch or US-American perhaps 3–

7 tons more (Adriaanse et al. 1997: 12). These megatons of materials and energy have to be mobilized, at home or in distant countries, for keeping the entire volume of goods and services on offer. It is this voracity of the industrial system that puts pressure on biospherical sources and sinks, including the people connected to them. For this reason, not a clean but a lean economy is the implicit Utopia of sustainability. It aims to make the systems of wealth creation less dependent on resource use. Seen in this light, the issue of justice does not in the first place concern the social distribution of pollution but rather involves the social distribution of resource consumption.

The resource perspective, of course, becomes particularly significant when the overall availability of sources and sinks is limited. Under such circumstances the question of 'Who takes how much?' acquires the utmost political importance. This question, however, does not arise in a pollution perspective that moves developing areas into the focus of attention, since pollution tends to be more intense in such areas. It is only in a resource perspective where overconsumption is defined as the critical problem that industrialized countries are put on the spot. For rich countries may be relatively clean, but they remain, in the present state of affairs, always omnivores. One way to conceptualize the resource perspective in a context of finiteness is the notion of environmental space. It signifies the total amount of energy and materials that can be utilized by a given society without hurting the principle of ecology or the principle of equity (FOE 1995: Carley and Spapens 1998; Sachs et al. 1998). According to the principle of ecology this amount is limited by the earth's carrying capacity, like the avail-ability and renewability of resources or the absorptive capacity of natural systems. And the principle of equity confines this amount to a size that can be reconciled with the equal claims of other countries on the resources in the world. In this sense, a society can be called sustain-able when its demands on nature do not exceed the environmental space it is entitled to use. Fusing an ecological and a social notion of space, the concept of environmental space therefore captures the two central concerns of sustainablility at once: the concern for ecology and the concern for equity. It allows us to rephrase the crucial question of environmental justice as follows: are the rich countries capable of living without the surplus of environmental space they appropriate today?

However, conventional development thinking continues implicitly to define equity as a problem of the poor. Facing the gap that separates the rich from the poor, developmentalists perceive this gap in the first place as a deficit of the powerless and not as a fault of the powerful.

They see a lack of credit, education or tools and advocate remedies for bringing the poor up to the task. They launch themselves into raising the living standards of the poor towards the level of the rich. In short, it was the poor who had to be developed in order to achieve greater equity. But in designing strategies for the poor, developmentalists work towards lifting the bottom, rather than lowering the top (Haavelmo and Hansen 1991; Goodland and Daly 1993). The wealthy and their way of producing and consuming remain entirely outside the spotlight, as always in the development discourse where the burden of change is solely heaped upon the poor. However, with the emergence of bio-physical limits to growth the classical notions of justice, which were devised in a perspective of finitude and not in a perspective of infinity, acquire new relevance: justice is about changing the rich and not about changing the poor. It was only after the Enlightenment, as optimism in progress had firmly settled in, that justice was discussed in terms of promoting the poor rather than converting the rich. In a world of environmental finitude this tradition of thought is bound to surface again. Today, any debate on equity will have to focus first on lowering or at least transforming the top instead of lifting the bottom. Against the backdrop of drastic global inequality in resource use, it is the North (along with its outlets in the South) that needs structural adjustment. Over and above redistributing riches, the North is called upon to shape its patterns of production and consumption in such a way that Southern countries are not deprived of what they are entitled to use.

Given that the Northern consumer class occupies the available environmental space to an excessive extent, a systematic retreat from using other people's land and share of the global commons, like the atmosphere and the oceans, is the most important step to take in the spirit of global resonsibility. The environmental space (Opschoor 1992; FOE 1993; Spangenberg et al. 1995) that can be legitimately claimed by a society is delimited by environmental constraints on the one side and by the rights of other societies on the other. In a way, these criteria can be seen as expressing different dimensions of justice. The first speaks about equity between generations, and the second about equity within one generation. While the first criterion has been widely celebrated since the Brundtland Report, the second remains the object of hot debate. Some argue that rights to resources are to be distributed according to historical achievement, others point to varying degrees of responsibility for resource consumption in the past, while others invoke different resource needs in different climate zones. Yet the only morally defensible rule is that all citizens of the globe should have an equal right to the world's natural resources. However, such a rule should not be mistaken as a planning objective for planetary redistribution; it is rather a moral principle guiding one's own behaviour. Loosely improvising the Kantian imperative, it makes sense to say that a society can be called sustainable only if the maxim of its action is such that this maxim can be the maxim of every other society. Justice above all requires circumspection and self-critical conduct; the principle of the equal right of all people to the world's resources is a yardstick to make one's own society a fair global player.

Industrialized countries, as recent research has shown (Factor 10 Club 1995; McLaren et al. 1997; Sachs et al. 1998), if they aspire to become good global neighbours, will have to bring down their throughput of energy and materials by a factor of 10 within the next 50 years. In other words, if they intend to take sustainability seriously, they will have to reduce their resource weight by 80–90 per cent with respect to the year 1990. No doubt this enormous challenge will amount to a civilizational transition of sorts, bringing both technological talents and new public virtues to bear. It will amount to both an efficiency revolution giving a new shape to technical progress and a sufficiency revolution giving rise to a certain lack of interest in monetary and material growth. Sufficiency was the hallmark of justice before the dreams of infinity took over; sufficiency in resource consumption is now bound to become the axis around which any post-developmentalist notion of justice will revolve. In future, for industrialized countries and classes, justice will be about learning how to take less rather than how to give more. Whoever calls for equity will have to speak about sufficiency. The anniversaries of both the Brundtland Report and the Earth Summit will remain lukewarm events if this continues to be kept in diplomatic disregard.

10

The Two Meanings of
Resource Productivity

A major shift in environmental policy-making is increasingly becoming commonplace. Over the last 25 years environmentalists have been busy fighting pollution; now they set out to innovate production. Following the Clean Air and Clean Water Act in the USA, environmental policy was shaped by the perception that nature – air, water, soils and organic life – had to be shielded against myriad harmful substances emanating from the industrial system. Consequently, legislation aimed at curbing excessive contamination, technologies were mounted to filter the waste stream, and success was measured in terms of decrasing pollution levels. This perception is now obsolete. It has come to be realized that the hunt for harmful substances will always lag behind new forms of pollution, while clean-up technologies in any case just transform waste from a diffuse into a concentrated state. Moreover, surrounding the industrial system with pollution control technologies is an enormously costly enterprise, and not even rich countries will be able to shoulder such an expense in the long run. Finally, as common sense suggests, prevention is always superior to therapy. In this sense, it is undoubtedly more intelligent to avoid pollution right from the beginning, at the planning stage, rather than cleaning up at the end of the pipe. Environmentalism thus drops the posture of defence and moves into advocating broad-range structural change in technology and ways of living (Weizsäcker et al. 1997). Direct protection of nature matters less within this framework, since emphasis is instead placed on redesigning the ways of society from scratch.

At the core of this search for sustainable ways lies the concept of resource productivity. Its rise to the status of key idea in environmental thought results from the view that the total consumption of megatons of energy and materials (and, in a different dimension, also of land) deserves decidedly more attention than the nanograms of pollutants present in the environment (Ayres and Simonis 1994; Schmidt-Bleek 1994; Factor 10 Club 1995). Since all industrial processes involve extracting natural resources from the earth, transforming them into goods and services, and leaving behind wastes of all kind, it is the materials cycle – the flow of materials from nature to the economy and back – that is fundamental to both the economy and ecology. It is of particular importance that the major part of the material flow never enters the economy in the form of objects, but remains degraded or wasted somewhere alongside the life-cycle of a given product. For instance, getting access to mineral ores may involve cutting open mountains and deviating water courses, while cultivating crops may cause the erosion and eventual dissipation of fertile soil. What therefore counts is the overall volume of the material cycle that flows through the economy. Indeed, the volume of materials on earth mobilized through human activity is larger than the volume mobilized through natural forces, like wind, weather and erosion (Schmidt-Bleek 1998: 39), a fact that highlights the stress placed on the earth by industrial man.

It is in this light that the objective of sustainability, so far as industrialized countries are concerned, can be reformulated as the capability of creating human welfare with an ever diminishing amount of natural resources. As the framework of economic activities is still anchored in the concept of a throughput economy where enormous quantities of natural inputs are finally transformed into enormous quantities of solid, liquid or gaseous waste, such a reduction will amount to reinventing basic structures of production and consumption. In other words, making wealth creation less dependent on resources requires a broad-range and long-term de-materialization of the economy. It is a lean and not a clean economy that lies on the Utopian horizon of the sustainability idea. Before this, enhancing resource productivity emerged as the strategic imperative for a transition to a lighter economy. The notion of *resource productivity* merges the two ambitions contained in the sustainability idea into one formula: it calls for a considerable reduction in resource use while suggesting an accomplished economic life at the same time. Small wonder that environmentalists across the world have embraced the concept of resource productivity; they value it as a compass guiding voracious economies towards both greater compatibility with nature and adequate levels of wealth. However, most elaborations do not do sufficient justice to the broad scope of the concept. Instead, they get trapped into a narrow economistic understanding of *productivity*, obscuring the richness of its meaning in history and in present parlance. It is time to explore the ambiguity of the concept and to indicate the way towards a non-reductionist vision of sustainability.

Productivity as Abundance

Analogies sometimes illuminate. To highlight the connection between limits and creativity, Paul Hawken, in *The Ecology of Commerce*, hit upon analogies that open the eyes for a surprising sense of productivity: 'If our economy is "limited" because it is part of the greater closed system of nature, those limits are no more constricting than a blank canvas before Cézanne, a flute before Jean-Pierre Rampal, a tree trunk before a pileated woodpecker' (Hawken 1993). No doubt Cézanne as well as Rampal can be called extraordinarily productive artists, yet their productivity is of a particular kind – it has nothing to do with the optimal allocation of tools. Indeed, for many writers of the Romantic period, an artist like Cézanne would have been a model of productivity. In particular, Kant and Goethe saw art as the outcome of the imaginative powers of a genius; they called this capacity *productive* (Hentschel 1984; König 1989). They were by no means alone; the word *productivity* had entered wider circulation in the decades before 1800. Locating productivity in the powers of man, Kant and Goethe broke with an ancient tradition that acclaimed nature as the subject of production. Prior to the Romantic period, nature's power to generate life had been seen as the essence of productivity, a view that culminated with the physiocrats, who considered nature to be the only source of value. For centuries God was thought to be the creator, nature the producer, and man the manufacturer (Robert 1992). However, this 'division of labour' collapsed towards 1800 and man emerged as the source of production. While the philosophers extolled man's creative capabilities, the early classical economists, writing during this period, centred on man's manufacturing capacity. Disregarding nature and reducing God to the built-in providence of the 'invisible hand', they enthroned man-the-labourer as the producer of all wealth. However, all these conflicting views about the source of productivity – nature, the labourer or the artist – were grounded in the common understanding that productivity is to be assessed by the quality of outcomes. They shared what could be called a substantive notion of productivity.

This notion of productivity stems from an admiration for what is being produced. A force is called 'productive' because the result of its action is held in high esteem – nature brings forth life, labourers wealth, and artists works of the imagination. In short, as the *Merriam-Webster Dictionary* defines it, a force is called productive when it has 'the quality or power of producing in abundance'. In one way or another, some outcomes of nature, work or art are judged to enhance the world and are called *productive*, while other outcomes fail to enhance the world sufficiently and are therefore called *unproductive*. What is productive adds to the richness of the world; it expands the range of possibilities and brings forth abundance. It is in this sense that today we colloquially speak about the productivity of a certain person, a certain piece of land or a particular fishing ground. The substantive meaning of productivity thus connotes fertility, plenty and usefulness, highlighting the power to create something new.

Productivity as Efficiency

However, at the end of the nineteenth century the abundance meaning of productivity was superseded by what can be called the formal or efficiency notion of productivity. This distinction is borrowed from Karl Polanyi, who distinguished a formal and a substantive definition of *economic*:

> The first meaning, the formal, springs from the logical character of the means–ends relationship, as in *economizing* or *economical*; from this meaning springs the scarcity definition of economic. The second, the substantive meaning, points to the elemental fact that human beings, like all other living things, cannot exist for any length of time without a physical environment that sustains them; this is the origin of the substantive definition of *economic*.' (Polanyi 1977: 19)

The concept of *productivity* can be analysed in much the same way. In its formal sense the concept disregards any quality of results, but instead focuses on the relationship between means and ends. Particularly in economic contexts, the concept has been designed to assess the effective use of labour, materials, and equipment for producing a defined output. Allowing organization analysts to express mathematically the ratio between the various sets of inputs and outputs, the concept serves as a powerful instrument in business and elsewhere to optimize the allocation of resources. Although this formal meaning prevails in present-day language, it was only around 1900 that it gained the upper hand over the substantive meaning. Up to this date, the notion of *productivity* had implied a value judgement about the results of an activity, but now it was stripped of any qualitative dimension and reduced to expressing the ratio between input and output (Hentschel 1984: 24). This shift was not an accident but part of a larger transition in economic thought, which made economics into a mere science of means.

Can Limits be Productive?

However, as Polanyi has argued with respect to the formal notion of *economic*, the formal notion of productivity, contrary to the allegations of most economists, is by no means void of normative content. Wherever applied, the notion suggests striving for maximum results at minimum expense. But this rule is not a matter of course. It postulates, in other words, efficiency (reaching a goal with the least costly means) and not just effectiveness (reaching a goal with adequate means). Such a norm, though, makes sense only under the assumption that means are chronically scarce and have to be economized upon as much as possible. However, means appear to be chronically scarce only because of the expectation that ends will always progress infinitely and never be satisfied. If ends were limited and the means therefore satisfactory, the optimization urge would lose its hold. Coming back to Paul Hawkens' remark quoted above, it would make no sense at all to call Cézanne productive in the formal meaning of the word; his means – canvas and brush – were not scarce and waiting for improvement, but few and sufficient. In other words, the efficiency notion of productivity implies that there will never be enough to go around; it is shaped by the founding assumption of economics that ends are infinite. In contrast to the substantive meaning of productivity, the formal notion has nothing to say about the results of an activity and remains silent about the quality of outcomes. It aims instead at permanently streamlining resources in order to meet undefined, but none the less ever expanding, ends.

In the framework of the substantive or abundance definition of productivity, means can be limited, but none the less sufficient. In the example above, the canvas of Cézanne or the flute of Rampal are definitely limited in surface and size, yet this limitation does not strangulate the creativity of either Cézanne or Rampal. On the contrary, the limits these tools pose emerge as the precondition for the artistic achievement of both. Limits have a double nature, being both restraining and facilitating: they act as constraints only with respect to one particular order of things, but open up possibilities with respect to another order of things. On the one hand, the confines of the canvas restrict the surface available to the painter. On the other, however, they determine the base upon which a sophisticated creation can rise. No Cézanne with an unlimited canvas, no art without making much out of little. Creation, it appears, is always the sublimation of constraints. The example of Cézanne illustrates what at first seems to be a paradox. Limits may set free action, because they foreclose options. As they concentrate attention, they help to mobilize energies and stimulate excellence. Herein lies the power of limits. It is only in the light of the abundance definition of productivity that the power of limits can be appreciated.

The Full Sense of Resource Productivity

When environmentalists speak about *resource productivity*, they often oscillate between these two meanings. On the one hand, resource productivity can be read in the substantive sense, referring to the type of satisfaction gained from a given amount of materials and energy. On the other hand, it can be used in the formal sense, indicating the ratio between a given output and the amount of materials and energy utilized. It is immediately obvious that the formal meaning prevails in the discourse on sustainability, as it does in the rhetoric of economics in general. In its common usage it is synonymous with *efficiency*, a term that arose at the end of the nineteenth century in the context of thermodynamics, comparing the quantities of different fuels required for producing a given amount of heat. Whenever the discussion on sustainability is dominated by the formal meaning of productivity, the environmental predicament becomes redefined as a problem of efficient resource allocation. Framed in this way, resource productivity serves as a conceptual instrument for analysing the relationship of natural inputs to other factors of production such as labour, technology or capital, and calls for rebalancing this relationship to minimize the amount of nature used. However, by focusing all attention on the means–ends relationship this approach provides no conceptual tools for assessing the outputs produced – it addresses the 'how', but not the 'what'. Unequipped as it is to consider the quality of outputs, the formal notion of resource productivity tends to leave the outcomes of production unquestioned – it takes the goals and desires of society for granted and confines itself to better managing the means to achieve them.

However, even some proponents of the efficiency approach feel compelled to move closer towards a substantive notion of resource productivity. They can not quite avoid wondering how necessary, useful or desirable are the various outputs of resource-efficient action. For instance, a number of authors (Weizsäcker et al. 1997; Schmidt-Bleek 1998) emphasize strategies such as durable products, high-quality objects, shared use, regional sourcing, rail-based transport, and a shift to services. Advancing these proposals, however, they tacitly assume, or simply claim, that the new structures and services will generate benefits similar to the previous wasteful practices. Confident that the restructured means will also somehow make people happy, they implicitly postulate that satisfaction will remain unaltered or even flourish in a new way. In other words, they convey a message about resource productivity in the substantive sense. It is interesting to note in this context that in recent years some authors who used to advocate resource efficiency have shifted their emphasis towards promoting resource productivity. By exploiting the ambivalence of the word productivity, they can imply that they are speaking about technology and well-being at the same time.

However, a full appreciation of resource productivity in the substantive sense calls for a debate on civilization, rather than a debate on technology. It requires us to wonder how productive society's economic output is in terms of welfare, use value, beauty and meaning. What is all this effort worth? And what do we want? This is the direction in which the questions must be asked. If one assumes that the real benefit an economy generates is the overall satisfaction of consumers, it even becomes possible to reformulate these questions in more technical terms: such inquiries examine the ratio of satisfaction to output instead of examining only the ratio of output to natural resources (Nørgård 1995). What is at stake in these inquiries is the efficiency of the economy as a whole, which can be expressed as the satisfaction achieved per unit of monetary value. After all, if the aim of a sustainable economy is to make people satisfied with the least throughput of resources, consumption has to be regarded not as a straightforward benefit, but as a cost of living that should be kept low.

Satisfaction of people in society, however, is part of a larger picture – it depends on society's aspirations, shared narratives and institutional values. It is at this point that – next to sciences and engineering – the humanities must join in the research on resource productivity. History and anthropology, philosophy and psychology focus, as Wilhelm Dilthey once said, on understanding relations of meaning rather than on explaining relations of cause and effect. There is no objectivist way to deal with issues such as needs and desires, habits and rules, perceptions and paradigms, fears and hopes, yet this is the stuff out of which a civilizational change is made. With the overall agenda one of leaving the fossil age, such a humanities-based research will address the multiple limits of a civilization based on fossil materials. In the perspective of this research, limits are both restraining and facilitating, and have to be explored in their productivity for satisfaction. Following this path, one can once again learn by reflecting on the productivity of Cézanne. Just as Cézanne produced art out of few but sufficient means, a post-fossil society is called upon to cultivate forms of satisfaction for which fewer means turn out to be sufficient. From this point of view, the productivity of a sustainable society will be measured not by the eco-efficiency of an ever expanding number of technologies, but by the quality of the civilization it creates out of limited means.

The Blind Spot of Efficiency

In the last 15 years, some of the best and the brightest environmentalists have tried to reformulate environmental policy as the modernization of economic growth. Striving to leave the legacy of 'Limits to Growth' behind, they concentrated on devising concepts and strategies to enlist market forces in the battle against environmental decline. From this perspective, ecology and economics appear to be compatible, and the pursuit of both is expected to be a positive-sum game. In fact, it has been this innovation that has done the most to propel environmentalism into mainstream thought. At the core of this approach lies the aspiration to find, on the level of companies, an overlap between economic efficiency and ecological efficiency; this overlap will then create circumstances where it will pay to bring down resource use (e.g. Schmidheiny 1992; Fussler 1997). This represents nothing less than a call for a new management philosophy aimed at steering the course of a company in a direction that will reduce the overall input of nature per unit of output. Following the imperative of higher eco-efficiency, business strategies usually centre on product design to enhance durability and recyclability; on production processes to reduce resource flows; and on strategic orientations to replace some output with services. Furthermore, new business strategies are expected to be supported by new generations of resource-saving technologies. It is hoped that if technological progress shifts direction from increasing labour productivity to increasing resource productivity, then all will be in place to inaugurate an age of sustainable capitalism.

The fascination with eco-efficiency springs from the many examples, proven or anticipated, that demonstrate what is often possible when inertia and the power of conventions give way to reinvention and the power of imagination. However, the fallacy of eco-efficiency stems from this same source, because the many examples of greater eco-efficiency, big and small, do not necessarily add up to a drastically reduced overall volume of resource consumption – the stated objective of the 'Factor 10' approach. Eco-efficiency sometimes raises the prospects of enormous efficiency gains, but fails to account for the long-term effects of economic change. Confusing the macro level with the micro level, efficiency enthusiasts often infer from impressive business examples a decreasing resource intensity of the economy on the whole. However, numerous cases of less resource use on the micro level do not automatically translate into less resource use on the macro level – at least not along the axis of time, if the economy is ruled by a dynamics of expansion.

Three effects – rebound, volume and growth – can be distinguished. All of them counteract the specific resource reductions achieved on the level of products or companies. Rebound effects are those that arise directly from efficiency gains stimulating new expansion. For example, a more fuel- and cost-efficient heating system may induce people to utilize more heat, since it can be had at the same price. The mobile phone, decreasing time and effort involved in calling, causes telephone contacts to increase. And the amount of paper consumed has grown in tandem with the ease of printing out and copying documents; there has never been so much paper used as in the much-hyped 'paperless office'. In all these cases, technological efficiency has lead to increased net consumption of resources. Particularly under competitive conditions, any efficiency gain – no matter whether economic, ecological or timewise – invites actors to convert the capital, resources or time saved into an expansion of output. Lower prices invite customers to buy more things, higher recycling rates in materials facilitate more output, and faster transport leads to people travelling longer distances. Paradoxically, it is often precisely the economic gains from improved technical efficiency that increase the rate of resource throughput (Wackernagel and Rees 1997: 19). In fact, for decades, efficiency has been the driving force behind competition and growth – per unit gains have fuelled new rounds of expansion. Efficiency gains can in principle be converted into more quality or less overall inputs, but under competitive conditions there is always a strong incentive to follow the road of expansion.

Volume effects arise from expanding demand for an eco-efficient product. All rebound effects are volume effects, but not all volume effects derive from rebound effects. Demand may grow independently of higher per unit efficiency, but the consequence is the same as with rebound effects: when more is asked of less, the net saving effect is reduced or completely cancelled out. Cars, as mentioned earlier, are considerably more fuel-efficient today than they were 20 years ago, but the increase in the numbers of cars, in their size and power, and the number of kilometres driven has long swallowed up that gain. Similar processes are at work in a variety of circumstances. Paper production has become much more water-efficient, but the overall output of paper has grown to an extent that the absolute level of water consumption has not diminished. Personal computers require considerably fewer resources than the old mainframe computers, but this gain has been rendered irrelevant by the fact that the number of computers has grown by a factor of 10,000. Efficiency gains on the micro level are therefore – over time – likely to be eaten up by growth in volume on the macro level. While they save time in the face of ecological limits in the short term, they are bound to be insufficient over the long term.

Finally, growth effects arise from the expansive tendencies of the economy as a whole. Independent of per unit efficiency, the dynamics of expansion abroad and intensification at home lead to continuously higher volumes of output. Take as an easy example the spread of small appliances in households. Houses might be better insulated and refrigerators might use less electricity, but energy consumption rises largely because of the 'stand-by' functions of devices such as television sets, video-recorders, cordless telephones and hand-held vacuum cleaners Large-scale trends like economic globalization exhibit conflicting tendencies of a similar kind. On the one hand, free trade stimulates the diffusion of more efficient technologies such as state-of-the-art power plants or digital equipment into the most distant corners of the world. On the other hand, however, free trade is meant to boost economic growth worldwide, which will make global resource use for all kinds of public and private consumption sky-rocket. In sum, the weight with which an expansive economy presses upon the resources of the earth can be mitigated by higher specific resource efficiencies, but if expansion continues unabated, the overall weight will nevertheless continue to grow.

However, it is overwhelmingly clear that the search for sustainability implies a drastic reduction in absolute levels of resource consumption, be it for fossil fuel, for sweet water or for timber. For this reason, any statement about relative efficiency on the micro level remains of little relevance as long as it is not linked to assumptions about the development of absolute volumes on the macro level. There is no logical connection between statements of relative efficiency and statements of absolute scale, but it is in the end the absolute scale of resource consumption that matters (Daly 1991). From this point of view, for example, 100 efficient Indian Maruti cars are not better than 30 old and wasteful Ambassador cars. Indeed, the paradoxical situation in which resource efficiency rises while the ecological efficiency of the economy as a whole diminishes seems to be a recurrent pattern of development. When relative improvement in resource use goes hand in hand with an absolute rise in resource use, not much is gained in ecological terms.

Efficiency and Sufficiency

It is for this reason that the efficiency perspective, if it is to become meaningful, must be embedded in a broader sufficiency perspective. The question 'how much is enough?' cannot be avoided. The transition towards sustainability can be achieved only through a twin-track strategy: an intelligent reinvention of means as well as a prudent moderation of ends. If this dual approach is not taken, the expansive dynamics, remaining unexamined and eventually unchecked, will undermine all successes achieved from boosting resource efficiency. Moreover, the twin-track approach makes the transition to sustainability easier because the pressure for higher efficiency of means is softened when certain levels of sufficiency in goals are socially accepted

Such a conclusion is not astonishing if one sees history moving in a co-evolutionary manner (Norgaard 1994). From the co-evolutionary perspective, socio-cultural forms evolve in interaction with technical forms, just as technical forms evolve in interaction with socio-cultural forms. Therefore, as 'Factor 10' envisages a technical infrastructure of the economy that works at a drastically lower scale of physical throughput, the institutional rules and cultural forms that prevail in society will also change accordingly. 'Factor 10' philosophy, like all environmental economics, recognizes that the economic system is subordinate to the natural system; it thereby assumes the existence of a proper physical scale for the economy beyond which the natural system – and in consequence the economic system that depends on it would slide into turbulence. Eventually, however, the social scale of the economy will also have to correspond to the economy's physical scale: the balance to be struck between the economic system and the natural world has to be matched by some balance between the economic system and the social world. Unless social thresholds for the expansion of the economic system are taken into consideration, it is difficult to imagine how the physical thresholds of the economy can be maintained.

As it is not plausible to seek limits to economic expansion only in one dimension – the physical one – research on sufficiency must also explore limits in the social and cultural dimensions. Such a focus, however, implies a move from the formal notion to the substantive notion of resource productivity. Since social and cultural limits cannot take hold without being integrated into people's perceptions and desires, any debate on sufficiency is bound to be a debate about the productivity of limits. Can the appreciation of limits lead to a more flourishing society? Can even self-limitation be part and parcel of self-liberation? These are the kind of questions around which the inquiry about sufficiency revolves. In other words, this inquiry aims to explore the ultimate efficiency of the economic system as a whole, its satisfaction efficiency. As this is obviously not an evaluation that can be done in an objectivist manner, its discussion proceeds by looking into the history of needs, examining consumption patterns, exposing institutional habits, delineating technological styles, probing world views, and highlighting emerging desires. The challenge of the sufficiency debate is to contribute to society's reflexion about its own well-being and to determine whether a reduced emphasis on economic expansion can enhance the quality of civilization. The question 'How much is enough?' leads without much detour to the question 'What do we want?' Sustainability in the last instance springs from a fresh inquiry into the meaning of the good life.

11

Speed Limits

It was the German aristocrat Friedrich von Raumer who, while travelling in England in 1835, mailed back home the first eye-witness report on what amounted to a revolution in the history of mobility: the railway between Liverpool and London:

> The fiery dragon in front, snorting, groaning, and roaring, until the twenty cars are fixed to its tail and it moves them, light as a child, over the level tracks at an extreme rate of speed. A path has been broken through mountains, valleys have been raised; the dragon throws sparks and flames into the night of the arched tunnel. But despite all the violence and despite all the roars, a human being turns the monster to his will with the touch of a finger. (Riedel 1961: 111)

Body and Machine

Raumer's account betrays the excitement and bewilderment he must have felt watching the train running across valleys and mountains. Comparing the locomotive with the horse, he and his contemporaries were immediately struck by the effortlessness and apparent tirelessness of the railway. After all, horses as well as humans, when moving quickly, are threatened by exhaustion and weakness. It is their bodies that set a limit – they become tired, get hurt, need a rest. Living beings can be fast only in proportion to their organic powers. Not so the railroad. It bursts the bounds of organic nature, appears to race tirelessly over mountains and through valleys, hindered by neither its metabolism nor the landscape. Energy stored in fuel by far outstrips bodily powers, just as rails made out of steel remove most of the resistance offered by the countryside. In the machine age, neither the body nor the topography defines a natural measure for speed. As a consequence, the modern idea that human motion was set on an infinite path towards ever increasing acceleration was able to take hold.

Like a projectile, as the the nineteenth-century perception saw it, the train shoots through space (Schivelbusch 1987); the passenger, however, sits calmly as forests and villages are flying by outside, blurring into a stream of fuzzy images. What happens outside is of no concern. For the traveller, the space between departure and destination fades into a mere distance to be covered as quickly as possible. The railroad fostered enthusiasm because it brought distant goals within easy reach; it established in people's minds a map of accessibility that lay over and above that of the muscle-powered world. In 1843, the German poet Heinrich Heine captured that new experience in his famous remark: 'I feel the mountains and forests of all countries advancing towards Paris. Already, I smell the scent of German lime-trees; the North Sea breaks on my doorstep.' He thus put in a nutshell a sensation of giddiness that exists today: speed makes distant places rush towards you. It abolishes distance and finally annihilates space.

In effect, a new layer of reality, a new perceptual space emerged with the railroad. Consider the famous painting *Rain, Steam and Speed – the Great Western Railway*, by William Turner. The railway engine comes towards the viewer like an iron projectile cutting through space. But the surrounding landscape has lost all contours, evaporated into cloudy spots, vanished into flurries of brownish colour. Only those aspects that serve to overcome distance – the rails, the locomotive and a bridge – appear to deserve figurative reality (Burckhardt 1994: 274). In fact, the painting depicts two different orders of space, the static one of the fading landscape and the dynamic one of rails and engines, designed to overcome the first. It suggests what indeed happened with the arrival of the railroad: the speed of engines supplanted the speed of bodies, a vehicular space gradually settled upon the natural space.

This was the radical break that inaugurated the age of acceleration. Between Caesar and Napoleon there had not been – except perhaps through harness and sail – much progress in speed. Only since the fossil reserves deep under the surface of the earth were tapped in order to obtain fuel for the propulsion of vehicles have the gates to the new age been thrown open. The combustion engine allowed the transformation of the earth's treasures into vehicle speed. In subsequent decades, innumerable railways, automobiles and aeroplanes, along with huge infrastructures of rails, highways and airports, have been lined up against the resistance offered by time and space. While in the natural space, movement is constrained by fixed duration and fixed distance, in the vehicular space duration and distance turn into variables that can be manipulated. In that sense, the mission of successive armies of transport technologies has been nothing else than the reduction and gradual abolition of duration and distance. However, it was the mobilization of carbon, iron and then oil that made the mobilization of time and space possible. The vehicular space is based on a robber economy.

Colliding Timescales

For the modern mind, as the philosopher Günter Anders once suggested in ironic allusion to Kant's 'forms of apperception', space and time are the basic forms of hindrance (Anders 1980: 338). Anything that is away is too far away. The fact that places are separated by distances is seen as a bother. And anything that lasts, lasts simply too long. The fact that activities require time is seen as a waste. As a consequence, a continuous battle is waged against the constraints of space and time; acceleration is therefore the imperative that rules technological innovation as well as the little gestures of everyday life.

However, any social system can be likened to a body sustained by a metabolism that makes it dependent on the environment. No living body can exist without consumption of nature and the elimination of residues. Neither a body nor a social system is isolated from nature; both are linked into the biosphere and the geosphere. Modern society, as everybody knows, weighs very heavily on nature; its metabolism has reached a volume and a velocity that threatens to throw into disorder the very ecosystems it depends upon. In that secular predicament, what matters is less the fact that nature is utilized, but how much is used in what way and – above all – at what speed. Generally speaking, the ecological crisis can be read as a clash of different timescales: the timescale of modernity collides with the timescales that govern life and the earth.

Consider, for instance, a rather simple example: the depletion of non-renewable resources. Every year, the industrial system burns as much fossil fuel as the earth has stored up in a period of nearly a million years. Within a second, in terms of geological time, the planet's reserves are about to vanish in the fireworks of the industrial age. It is obvious that the rate of exploitation of non-renewable resources is infinitely faster than the processes of sedimentation and melting in the earth's crust. Industrial time is squarely at odds with geological time. It is probably not an exaggeration to say that the time gained through fuel-driven acceleration is in reality time transferred from the time stock accumulated in fossil reserves to the engines of our vehicles.

Global warming is another example. The transport of CO_2 from the surface of the earth up into the atmosphere and back is part of the global carbon cycle. Under natural conditions, the absorption of CO_2 through vegetation and the oceans is about in equilibrium with the release of CO_2 through respiration and decomposition. But with additional production of CO_2 through the burning of fossil fuels, the absorption capacity is overstressed. Too much CO_2 remains in the atmosphere, threatening global warming. In other words, the faster speed of industrial emissions outstrips the slower speed of assimilation.

Should the greenhouse effect occur, nature will become a further victim of acceleration. For instance, certain types of trees along the US–Canadian border – although they slowly migrated for millennia as they followed the shifting temperature zones after the most recent ice-age – will be outrun by the speed of global warming. While the trees are capable of moving at a speed of about half a kilometre a year, a rise in atmospheric temperature of 1–2 degrees within 30 years would require them to run at a speed of 5 km a year in order to follow the advancing climatic zone. Not having enough time for adaptation, they will perish. Outdistanced, exhausted and finally defeated, they are condemned to become victims in the unequal race between industrial and biological time.

The collision between industrial and biological time is most tangible in animal raising and plant cultivation. It is often the same story over and over again: the natural rhythms of growth and maturation are considered much too slow by the industrial (and post-industrial) mind (Schneider et al. 1995). Enormous resources and ingenuity are brought to bear against the time inherent to organic beings in order to squeeze out more output in shorter periods. Cows and chickens or rice and wheat are selected, bred, chemically treated and genetically modified in order to accelerate their yield. However, the imposition of industrial time on natural rhythms cannot be achieved without a staggering price. Animals are kept in appalling conditions, disease spreads, pollution advances, soils degenerate, the diversity of species is narrowed down, and evolution is not given enough time to adapt. A host of ecological problems in the area of agriculture derive from the fact that the rhythms of nature are kept hostage for the high-speed economy of our time.

These examples are sufficient to suggest that speed is a critical factor in environmental destruction. The speed regime of modern society drives up the rate by which nature is being used as a mine and as a dumping ground. The throughput of energy and materials occurs at a speed that often leaves no breathing space for nature's ability to react to the recurrent attacks. Natural systems change according to inherent timescales. Processes such as growth and decay, formation and erosion,

assimilation and regeneration, selection and adaptation follow rhythms
of their own. Pushed along under the fast beat of industrial time, they
are driven into turbulence or destabilized. The speed of capital accumulating is at variance with the speed of nature regenerating.

Double Power

Speed is fascinating because it confers power. The pleasure of feeling
like a master over time and space – driving a fast car or sending
electronic impulses around the globe – is one way in which Descartes'
affirmation of man as the master and possessor of nature has been
turned into reality. This power, however, is deeply ambiguous. The
writer C. S. Lewis, in his 1947 work ominously titled *The Abolition of
Man*, called attention to the seamy side of this power. Speaking about
the bomb and the radio, he writes that man is as much victim as
possessor of power, since he is not just its master, but also its target:
'Man's power over Nature turns out to be a power exercised by some
men over other men with Nature as its instrument ... Each new power
won *by* man is a power *over* man as well' (Lewis 1947: 48). And that
power is yielded in two directions. On the one hand, each generation
exercises power over the following generations, conditioning the shape
of future lives, and on the other, the possessors of power will exert
their influence on those who do not have it, conditioning the shape of
present lives. Power always throws up questions of justice with respect
to present as well as to future generations.

Without doubt, the power gained through speed today will most
likely leave less power for the generations to come. For it is the
generations of the twentieth century who corner a great deal of the
resources for power that might be indispensable for steering the boat
of humankind through the rapids of the next centuries. The excitement
about speed tends to lessen future chances of leading flourishing, let
alone high-powered, lives. Moreover, what is true with regard to future
generations also holds with regard to present generations. The power
over nature amassed by the high-speed population of the globe fore-
closes opportunities for a large majority of their contemporaries. After
all, only about 8 per cent of the world population have a car at their
disposal, and only around 3 per cent have access to a personal computer. A tiny, privileged fraction enjoys a level of speed that contributes
to depriving most of the world's people of their fair share in the
world's resources. The conclusion is inevitable: whatever virtues justice
might require in the world of today, the search for selective slowness
surely figures among them

From that point of view, the victory against distance and duration carries a heavy cost. Speed does not come gratuitously. Obviously enough, the mobilization of space and time requires the mobilization of nature. Fuels and vehicles, roads and runways, electricity and electronic equipment, satellites and relay stations, call for a gigantic flow of energy and materials. On the one side, the earth is cut open to obtain resources such as oil, gas, coal, iron, zinc, magnesium, silicon and bauxite, while on the other, it is used as a refuse dump where polluted waters, broken rocks, oil-spills, toxic substances and green-house gases are left behind. Certainly, this throughput can be reduced through technologies and innovative design strategies that aim at minimizing the use of nature at each step along this cycle. But gains in eco-efficiency will never cancel out the basic law that governs the physics of speed: to beat friction and air resistance requires a dispro-portionally increasing amount of energy. An average car, for example, which consumes 5 litres of petrol at a speed of 80 km/h, will need not just 10 litres when it runs up to 160 km/h, but 20 litres. The high-speed French TGV train and the German ICE consume not 50 per cent but 100 per cent more energy when they jump from 200 to 300 km/h. Generally speaking, the more speed outdoes natural timescales, the more environmental resources – at a rather exponential rate – have to be expended.

Some hope that the advent of electronic communication will lead to the end of resource-heavy speed. Indeed, quite a few champions of the information society proclaim that electronic impulses, travelling at the speed of light, will finally square the circle: simultaneity and ubiquity can be achieved without any cost to nature. They are, more likely than not, mistaken. To be sure, the data highway can be travelled without noise and exhaust fumes, but the electronic networks require quite a lot of equipment. Preliminary results of a study undertaken by the Wuppertal Institute on the resources used by desktop computers show that electronic equipment is environmentally much more ex-pensive than is usually assumed. What counts is not the electricity used, as one might expect, but the amount of nature to be moved for the production of the hardware. In particular, numerous components require the use of an array of high-grade minerals that can be obtained only through major mining operations and energy-intensive trans-formation processes. As it turns out, between 8 and 18 tons of energy and materials – calculated over the entire lifecycle – are consumed by the fabrication of one computer (Malley 1996: 48). When one con-siders that the production of an average car requires about 25 tons, it is clear that the ecological optimism surrounding the on-line future is misplaced. On the contrary, there is no reason to believe that mass computerization will weigh drastically less heavily on nature than mass motorization.

In Remembrance of Time Gained

Looking back into the history of transport and telecommunication, one remains uncertain as to whether the battle against the shackles of time and space was really worth the effort. True, nothing is more frustrating than waiting in the slow line, but is faster always better? Does more acceleration make our lives richer? There is obviously no straightforward answer to this kind of question, but it would be a possible point of departure to wonder why it is that despite the ever expanding number of time-saving machines we feel more pressured and driven by the lack of time than ever before.

The automobile can serve as a case in point. Right from the beginning, it was hailed as the utimate time-saver, marvellously shortening the time to reach a desired destination. What has happened to that promise? Indeed, contrary to popular belief – and this is proved by a multitude of studies from many countries – car-drivers do not spend less time in transit than non-drivers. Nor are drivers more frequently on the move: they leave the house slightly less often than non-drivers. Where has the time gained been lost? Those who buy a car do not take a deep breath and rejoice in extra hours of leisure. They travel to more distant destinations. The powers of speed are converted not into less time on the road but into more kilometres travelled. The time gained is reinvested into longer distances. And as time goes by, the spatial distribution of places changes and long distances become the norm. People still go to school, to work, to the cinema, but are obliged to travel longer routes. As a consequence, the average German citizen today travels 15,000 km a year as opposed to only 2,000 km in 1950 (Schallaböck 1996). The automobile is not a special case. Across the board, from mobility to communication, from production to entertainment, time saved has been turned into more distance, more output, more appointments, more activities. The hours saved are eaten up by new growth. And, after a while, the expansion of activities generates new pressure for time-saving devices – starting the cycle all over again. Time gains offer only transitory relief, because they encourage further growth of all kinds. In this way, the Utopia of affluence undercuts the Utopia of liberation. Acceleration is therefore the surest way to the next congestion.

Counter-productive Effects

As acceleration drives growth and growth in turn drives acceleration, speed permeates society. Speed impulses have an epidemic effect: they spread across all social worlds and into the individual sphere. Under the beat of acceleration social and individual timescales begin to tremble, just as industrial time collides with bio-physical times on the macro level. All social worlds, particular situations and individuals have a time of their own. Different rhythms and tempi co-exist in society. The spread of speed unsettles these timescales. Children have to hurry up. Students are expected to learn more quickly. No breaks are allowed during work. Sickness has to be supressed until the time clock runs out. Even orchestras are supposed to condense their performance. Most conspicuously, the gap between the so-called productive sectors on the one side and the reproductive sectors on the other widens. The times inherent in activities like studying and researching, caring and helping, growing up and growing old, cultivating friendships and doing art, are at odds with the speed of the economy. Acceleration thus both enhances and undermines the good life.

On the level of personal experience, the shady side of acceleration makes itself felt. If pursued thoroughly enough, acceleration will cancel itself out. We arrive sooner at places where we stay for ever shorter periods of time. With all the effort concentrated on quick arrival and departure, we are tempted to devalue the stay. The attention devoted to moving reduces the attention devoted to staying. The more people are on the move, the more difficult it becomes to meet them. Great efforts at scheduling and synchronization come in the wake of increased circulation. Especially for the harried classes in society, acceleration beyond a certain threshold generates counter-productive effects that undermine the very goal to be achieved. The goal – coming together – is threatened with being overwhelmed by the means of acceleration; whoever wishes to protect that goal will have to opt for selective slowness.

Selective Slowness

In the nineteenth century, as society was slow-paced and settled, it was only natural that speed and acceleration appeared as the promise of a bright future. At the end of the twentieth century, however, as society has become restless and high-speed, Utopia changes its colour. Desires are cropping up that define themselves in contrast to the dominating model of time. Where hustling mobility rules, a taste for slowness grows. Who hasn't dreamed of quitting the 'rat race'? Where acceleration is the everyday norm, slowness becomes a non-conformist adventure. Gradually there will come a change in what was long taken to be the logic of progress: that improvement always means reducing the resistance of duration and distance. Countless bridges, tunnels, highways, cables and antennae are the heredity of that belief. Instead, the suspicion grows that progress could perhaps also imply deliberately leaving the resistance of time and space unchanged, or even increasing it. To leave behind the battle against the hindrances of time and space at any cost, such a change would prove that our society has outgrown the compulsion to carry the nineteenth-century world of desires right into the twenty-first century.

It is unlikely that a society that always moves in the fast lane can ever be environmentally or even socially sustainable. It is therefore not going to be up to the challenges of the next century. In a recent study, entitled 'Sustainable Germany', we have called attention to the need to consider a reduction in speed levels for traffic if one wants to move towards a sustainable future (Sachs et al. 1998). Given the fact that peak levels of speed consume a disproportionate amount of energy, we suggest that cars and trains should be designed to reach a lower top speed. More specifically, we envisage a moderately motorized automobile fleet where no car can go faster than 120 km/h. As materials, weight, comfort and design would follow this criterion of construction, a new generation of 'gentle cars' would be in the offing. A similar logic holds for trains. We propose to design fast trains for speeds not higher than 200 km/h, a limit beyond which the disadvantages of speed accumulate much faster than its advantages. Reduced speed levels for physical transport could be an example for a politics of selective slowness, which is born out of an appreciation for a plurality of social times and aims at a lean consumption of resources. The twenty-first-century Utopia of living with elegance inside limits finds its technical expression in the design of moderately motorized engines.

Above all, well-measured speeds for physical transport are the condition for a sustainable information society. True, electronic transmission will sometimes become a substitute for physical transport, but the high-flying hopes that on-line communication will eventually solve the transportation problem are probably illusions. One is well advised to expect ambivalent effects. As the history of the telephone demonstrates, technical communication becomes a substitute for traffic on the one hand, but stimulates new traffic resulting from the extended network of contacts on the other. It will not be different with the telematic infrastructure – both effects, substitution and expansion, are to be expected. The latter, however, will wildly outrun the former, as long as high speed remains an unquestioned dogma. It can be taken for granted that electronic interactions in real time across the globe will, on balance, sooner or later lead to an explosion in physical traffic as closer electronic contacts extend the radius of action and evoke the desire to meet physically face to face. In short, without the deliberate design of a plurality of timescales, the on-line society will turn into a traffic nightmare. Slow, it turns out, is not just beautiful, but often also reasonable.

12

The Power of Limits: An Inquiry into New Models of Wealth

In the course of European history, different ruptures can be identified as having unleashed the dynamics of economic expansion. In the context of the ecological predicament, the watershed that separates the fossil age from the age of living energy is of particular significance. Only since the fossil reserves deep under the surface of the earth were tapped have the gates to an age of apparent limitlessness been open. It is also for this reason that with the beginning of the decline of the fossil age in the last decades of the twentieth century the question of limits surfaces again in the public debate. Even the very idea of unlimited economic growth was able to take hold only after the steam-engine had entered the imagination of economists (Wrigley 1987: 21). For all observers before 1800, economic production was linked into the regenerative cycles of growing corn, cotton, timber and animals, which made limitless growth in output unthinkable. The large-scale mobilization of coal, iron and oil spurred the freeing of the economy from a whole array of constraints. The more the economic circuit was fired with fuel and minerals, the easier it became to take down various limits to expansion. Removing forms of resistance to expansion – physical, social and cultural – has been the chief effect of the ability to draw on the low-entropy islands located in the earth's crust.

Today, at the end of the fossil bonanza age, an inquiry into sufficiency should, among other things, revisit the institutions and world views that have come into bloom with the rise of the fossil-intensive society. The transformation of geologically highly organized low-entropy materials, such as coal, oil, iron and magnesium, has allowed the economy to overcome limits in many dimensions, including the dimensions of human power, the time and space of movements, the scope of economic activity and the volume of consumption. In each of these dimensions, specific technologies and cultural forms have emerged in the nineteenth century. They have subsequently turned into certainties of modern life – and have now become ecological liabilities. Often, however, they have not just become ecological liabilities, but also exhibit socially and culturally counter-productive effects. It is out of this blend of ecological, social and cultural frustrations that the discovery emerges that today limits can be productive.

Eco-intelligent Goods and Services

Modern systems of production still operate on the hidden assumption that nature out there will be for ever abundant. This assumption is a legacy from the early nineteenth century, when economic activity was minuscule with respect to the annually renewed wealth of nature. Such experiential evidence, along with long-established notions about the generosity of the natural world, made economic thinkers forgetful of the role of nature in value creation. Considering nature abundant, they built theories that located wealth creation in the increasing productivity of labour, disregarding losses incurred by nature. This style of thought – along with the capitalist's interest in controling the work of labourers – was largely responsible for the direction technological progress has taken. With one wave of innovation after another, machinery and organizational skills have been devised for decreasing the input of labour per unit of output, paving the way for massive relocation of labour across economic sectors. To a large extent, technology – driven by natural resources – has replaced labour, expanding labour productivity at the expense of resource productivity. However, as progress concentrates on how to produce more with less people, a contradiction comes to the fore that can once again be witnessed today: the objective of doing things with fewer and fewer people may be attractive at the level of a firm, yet it is bound to be ultimately self-defeating at the level of society.

After one and a half centuries of industrial progress, the hidden assumption about nature's never-ending generosity has collapsed. The environmental crisis has revealed the scarcity of nature. With respect to the gigantic volume of economic activity in the world, nature has turned fragile. Before this backdrop of changed historical conditions, the direction of economic progress is bound to change. In response to the vulnerability of nature – and consequently the vulnerability of economic systems – progress must be geared towards boosting the productivity of resources rather than the productivity of labour. As the world of tomorrow appears to be running out of nature rather than out of people, priorities must shift: it is much more intelligent to lay off unproductive kilowatts, barrels of oil, tons of material, pulp from old-growth forest, and water from aquifers than to lay off more and more people (Weizsäcker et al. 1997). The scope for doing so is enormous if one considers not just the final product, but its entire lifecycle from the cradle to the grave. After all, 94 per cent of the materials extracted for use in manufacturing durable products become waste before the product is finished – waste of heat that escapes from power plants, waste of land that has been mined, waste of irrigation water that has evaporated or waste of biomass that has been discarded. However, a post-fossil economy will have to be light in terms of resource use; its historical mission will be to provide welfare to people, using an ever decreasing amount of natural resources. As a consequence new standards of excellence for managers and engineers emerge, which will be measured by their ability to design production systems that create value out of a modest supply of nature.

The most immediate entry point for sketching the contours of resource-light manufacturing is product design. Each product constitutes a claim on resources; products will therefore be made in such a way as to minimize resource content, utilize biodegradable materials and extend durability. Laundry detergent from Proctor & Gamble provides an illustrative example for the first approach. Eco-efficient innovation (Fussler 1997) some years ago has reduced the volume of detergent needed for a given level of laundry power. While in the old days customers carried home bulky barrels of detergent, they have now the same cleaning power contained in smaller packages. The second aproach can be exemplified by a credit card, introduced by Greenpeace, made out of plant starch and plant sugar. Millions of plastic cards can now be composted without residues instead of being incinerated, releasing carcinogenic substances into the air. Finally, the third approach aims at increasing the longevity of products by making those parts interchangeable that wear out quickly or are subject to fashion. The modular office chair, for instance, consists of structural elements including the mechanics of the seat and visible elements such as cushions and cloth (Stahel and Gromingen 1993). The first elements are built to maximise durability, the second to maximize recyclability. Both classes of components are designed to obtain full utility out of a shrinking flow of energy and materials.

Product design, of course, focuses attention only on the final stage of the entire lifecycle of a product. Another set of approaches for enhancing resource productivity attempts to refashion production processes. In this endeavour, the crucial step is to move from the nineteenth-century conception of a linear throughput growth, in which materials flow through the economy as if through a straight pipe, to a closed-loop economy where as many materials as possible are fed back into the same or another production cycle. One way to close cycles is to utilize fully the entire throughput, allowing as little waste as possible. Examples abound. Juice manufacturers may utilize lemon peel for perfume instead of throwing it away, chip manufacturers may re-utilize waste water along with treatment chemicals, power producers may co-generate electricity along with heat for industrial or residential purposes. And, of course, ecological agriculture follows similar principles. This logic is carried further, much more ambitiously, by attempts to set up industrial clusters modelled after ecological food webs. Just as in an ecosystem waste produced by one species turns into food for another, so in an industrial cluster the waste products of an industry become the raw material for another. Such an arrangement is often referred to as 'industrial ecology' (Tibbs 1992). Aiming in the last instance at zero waste emissions (Pauli 1998), it represents the ideal type of an industrial production system for an age of limits.

Furthermore, the move towards higher resource productivity triggers a new understanding of the kind of business that business is in when it produces utility and value. According to conventional wisdom, business caters to the demands of consumers by offering products in ownership. The focus on ownership, however, impedes systemwide responsibility on the part of the company for the entire lifecycle of its products. It encourages more throughput rather than optimal administration of stocks. Shifting the entrepreneurial focus from the sale of hardware to the direct sale of the services through leasing or renting would make the full utilization of hardware, including maintenance and recycling, profitable. For example, Rank Xerox has moved from selling products to selling functions. Photocopy machines are not sold but leased, and the customer pays for the amount of copies required. Such an arrangement changes the strategic interest of the company. The firm now profits from managing its assets carefully through repair services, upgrading or re-manufacturing. A similar shift in entrepreneurial strategy is the transition from energy production to energy services (Hennicke and Seifried 1996). Energy companies move into the business of demand-side management, selling consulting and managerial services for saving energy rather than focusing exclusively on the expansion of energy supplies. Generally speaking, in an environmental service economy money flows not for adding as much hardware as possible to the world, but for providing a particular service to customers through the temporary use of a piece of hardware. As producers turn into providers, and consumers into users, the eco-efficient design, management and disposal of material assets becomes part of the economic logic.

In all of these cases, 'production', in the nineteenth-century meaning of transforming raw materials into useful objects, loses in importance. Instead, a truly post-industrial vision of economic activity emerges where intelligence, social innovation and an attitude of care largely substitute for the accumulation of hardware. Such an evolution, at any rate, is imminent when the golden rule of an eco-intelligent economy takes firm hold: don't expect the Earth to produce more. Expect humans to do more with what the Earth produces (Pauli 1998: 20).

Lower Speeds and the Plurality of Timescales

'Faster' and 'Further' – alongside the principle of 'More' – can be considered as the main leitmotifs of fossil-powered progress. It was towards the middle of the nineteenth century that the first railways revolutionized the human relationship to time and space. Contemporaries were both alarmed and excited as they watched the trains running and running across valleys and mountains without any sweat or fatigue. While living beings can be fast only in proportion to their organic powers, the railroad bursts the bounds of nature and races tirelessly at high speeds, threatened by neither exhaustion nor weakness. In the machine age, neither the body nor the topography any longer defines a natural measure for speed. As a consequence, the modern conception that human motion is set on an infinite path toward ever increasing acceleration takes hold in the popular imagination. In a nutshell, the rush for higher speeds is a cultural fallout of the steam engine.

Since the appearance of the locomotive, our societies have devoted an enormous amount of energy to accelerating the movement of people and goods (and, more recently, information). Engineers have supplied constantly changing generations of locomotives, automobiles and aeroplanes, while planners have transformed the face of the land with railway tracks, roads and airports. Indeed, the assumption that higher speeds are always better than lower ones has prevailed until the present day (Kern 1983; Sachs 1992a). However, it is only against the backdrop of a slow and sedentary society that the Utopia of acceleration could appear as the signal of a bright new world. Where mobility is tiresome and exhausting, mechanized transport appears as a promise to paradise. But in the setting of today's restlessly high-speed society, such a Utopia easily becomes exhausted and stale. New conditions are bound to produce new desires. In this sense, the over-motorized society creates the conditions that give rise to feelings of disenchantment with the car. Where unceasing mobility turns into a stressful burden, a desire for leisureliness and unharriedness is likely to grow. The fact that new wishes are increasingly being articulated in contrast to a high-speed society makes it progressively possible to speak publicly about slower speeds and shorter distances.

Quite apart from environmental problems, pleasure in mobility is today increasingly intermingled with frustration. The biggest setbacks of universal motorization spring from its success. For the automobile offers most of its advantages only as long as there are just a few individual motorists. However, since most people have now become motorized the advantages of being faster and being able to travel further than anyone else have declined. Being faster than your neighbour only takes you more quickly into a traffic jam, just as the desire to get away brings you to remote places crowded by those you have just tried to escape. With mass motorization the situation has changed, and the relative advantages the car once conferred have dwindled: the more cars, the less joy. Moreover, as soon as speed is a general expectation, gaining time is no longer a pleasure, but becomes an obligation. The power over space and time granted by transportation is becoming a duty rather than a privilege, so the fascination of the motorist's Utopia vanishes with its triumph. In short, disillusionment is built into the process of mass motorization. This shift in the emotional base of motorization is an important ingredient in the search for environmentally sound ways of transport.

Moreover, transport experts know that the cures for congestion often result in worsening the illness. They have realized for years that the politics of opening up bottlenecks and expansion of supply – as has predominated in the decades after the Second World War – only provokes new flows of traffic. Any expansion of capacity leads into a vicious cycle: more streets and faster vehicles make more people travel longer distances, which in turn, after the streets have filled up, increases the pressure for more streets and faster vehicles. Indeed, none of the usual 'more of the same' prescriptions help against systemic over-development. Computer-backed monitoring of traffic flow, planning systems for an efficient modal split, or other schemes of traffic management do not strive for anything except optimization of the unsustainable. It is intelligent self-limitation that seems most likely to bring relief. Contemplating limits to further growth is a rational strategy against systemic over-development, because restraint slows down the dynamics of expansion, avoids additional financial and social burdens, and opens space for planning alternatives. Not opting for further acceleration and interconnection will offer a range of opportunities for creating a socially appropriate transport system for the twenty-first century.

The speed Utopia of the nineteenth century still governs the development of automobile technology. Engineers can design cars to be robust and spacious or economical and durable, but their main emphasis has been on making comfortable and high-powered limousines (Canzler 1996). As a consequence, the average power of engines in German vehicles shot up from 34 to 85 hp between 1960 and 1993. Acceleration capabilities and top speeds are treated as if cars had to withstand long-distance races every day. Yet on average, cars spend 80 per cent of their operating time in city traffic, at an average speed of about 25 kilometres an hour. In actual use, automobiles are means more of short- than of long-distance travel and need to be capable of no more than a cosy cruising speed: to send speed machines out onto the streets is about as rational as shooting at sparrows with cannons. Today's fleet of automobiles is grotesquely overpowered, with all the consequent waste of energy, high materials consumption and loss of security. The rules of optimization demand matching the vehicles much more efficiently to their real purpose – a certain amount of self-limitation in machine power would not only be liberatory, but simply rational.

It is at any rate obvious that the victory against distance and duration also carries a heavy environmental cost. The easy availability of speed does not come without a price-tag. The mobilization of space and time requires the mobilization of nature. Fuels and vehicles, roads and runways, electricity and electronic equipment, satellites and relay stations call for a gigantic flow of energy and materials as well as for a massive use of land. In particular, higher speeds are fuel-intensive. The increase in a vehicle's energy throughput (inclusive of emissions) is not simply linear; it rises disproportionately because of air resistance and friction. An average car that uses 5 litres of fuel at 80 km/h needs not 10 but 20 litres at 160 km/h. Similar laws apply to railways. Energy consumption is almost doubled for ICE and TGV trains when speeds are increased from 160 to 250 km/h, and again from 200 to 300 km/h (Zängl 1993). So anyone who is concerned about long-term reduction of energy turnover by a factor of 10 is well advised to contemplate a lowering of technically available speed levels before striving for more efficient motors, new materials or a rational choice of means of transportation.

For these and other reasons, there are indications that beneath the official compulsions of acceleration a cautious interest in greater slowness is beginning to stir – not as a programme, not as a strategy, but rather as a subversive demand viewing the glorification of speed as somewhat old-fashioned and out of touch with the times. If such experiences accumulate, then the familiar trend might conceivably be reversed, and affluence becomes associated with deceleration. Out of the disenchantment with traffic, a social aesthetics might emerge where moderate speeds and intermediate distances are considered a particular accomplishment.

Nineteenth-century society was driven to haste because it feared backwardness; a self-confident society of the twenty-first century could once again be able to afford slower speeds. For a society seeking sustainability, the performance level of its technologies will emerge as a major political issue. Moderation, which long has been a norm for private virtue, will become a norm for public policy. As the age of fossil fuels draws to an end, political limits to unrestrained growth in power and performance will have to assume the role performed by natural limits in pre-industrial times. Setting upper speed limits as design criteria for cars and railways opens up a considerable potential for saving energy, materials and – indirectly – land. At the same time, such a measure would make everybody – except speed addicts – better off, bringing down pollution and noise, easing the expansive pressure of traffic, slowing down urban sprawl and reducing traffic casualties (Plowden and Hillman 1996; Sachs et al. 1998). Creating a resource-light economy will require thinking about a moderately powered automobile fleet where no car by constructive design can go faster than, say, 120 km/h. For such cars, downsized as they are in power and top speed, standards for security or for aerodynamics would play a minor role. In effect, cars of intermediate performance could be of light, material-saving construction, comfortable in height and size, and innovative in engine design. Eco-technology is lean technology in this sense; it combines sufficiency in performance levels with state-of-the-art efficiency in all components. It is equally so for railways. Fast trains designed for speeds not higher than 200 km/h could offer a considerable amount of speed without the disproportionately growing disadvantages of energy consumption, noise and safety concerns. Reduced speed levels for physical transport are a matter of ecological and social prudence; they indicate a technological progress that combines restraint with sophistication. Designing moderately powered vehicles gives technical expression to the twenty-first century-Utopia of living elegantly within limits.

Shorter Distances and the Plurality of Spaces

In the evolution of modern society, large-scale geographical inter-dependence has grown next to acceleration in the evolution of modern society. As distance is the other side of speed, the availability of fossil fuels for transport and electric impulses for transmission has immensely increased the geographical range of many activities. Since distances are a constraint only insofar as it takes time to cover them, mechanized acceleration has made distances shrink: previously far-away destinations have suddenly been moved into immediate reach. Speed shortens dist-ances and electronic speed finally abolishes space. Evolving along this logic, railways, cars and aeroplanes, along with the telegraph, the telephone and the computer, have brought forth a large-scale geo-graphical interconnection of flows of people, goods and messages. It was on the back of these technologies of interdependence that, on different levels over time, the hope grew that growth and welfare could be best achieved through increasing economic interconnections over ever larger distances. The rise of national and supra-national markets, and eventually the prospect of a planetary economy, are all based on these technologies of space annihilation.

However, economic integration entails transport and ever more transport. The distances between producer and consumer, suppliers and manufacturers are increasing everywhere – flowers from Kenya and shoes from Taiwan are cases in point. Through 'global sourcing' manufacturers gather parts from all over the world, and likewise, the current trend toward lean manufacturing extends the supply lines, and thus the distances covered. 'Lean production' thereby leads directly to 'fat transportation'. Even the assembled elements of a simple German yoghurt carton have travelled a total of almost 9,000 km (Boege 1993). Production and lifestyles based on high volumes of long-distance trans-portation carry an unsustainable load of energy and raw materials. The expansion of networks of economic exchange, eventually to the ends of the earth, is to a great extent paid for by spending the natural capital of humanity.

Therefore, for any 'Factor 10' policy to work it will be important to recognize scale as an ecological issue. Awareness of the bio-physical limits to economic expansion requires one to conceive the economy as evolving in a plurality of spaces – regionally, continentally, inter-nationally – that are connected only partially to each other. However, research into the ecologically optimal scale of different economic operations, from the global to the local level, has barely begun. It is, though, obvious that an ecological policy should aim primarily at the reduction of transport to bearable levels. Such a policy will have to turn away from the long-time priority of eliminating obstacles to long-distance travel wherever possible. Instead, it will seek to maintain, or to increase, the costs in time and effort to reach remote destinations. Slower vehicles, less negotiable routes and higher monetary costs lead to fewer journeys and shorter distances – and thus less traffic. Designing transport-saving economic structures requires an emphasis to be put on shorter distances, thereby favouring regional density over long-distance connections. Higher transport costs, which would render long-distance haulage less attractive, are an obvious condition, but they are only part of the picture. The larger picture is a new perception of economic strength.

While for decades economic revival in cities and regions was pursued to attract competitive industries and to insert them as victoriously as possible into the circuits of national and international markets, the idea of a home-grown economy emphasizes the need to reconnect material cycles, as well as monetary cycles, on the regional level (Douthwaite 1996). Forging more business links in the region can create locally intensified economies, which is also desirable for reasons of economic security and enhanced political autonomy in the places where people live. Because of both ecology and community well-being, strategies of regional sourcing and regional marketing are probably particularly important for food, furniture, construction, repair and maintenance services, as well as for human services. There is evidence that even under present conditions quite a number of things are done best on a small or medium scale. In terms of jobs, quality of services, and regional linkages in the economy, medium-scale actors in business and public administration are often superior to centralized institutions (Morris 1996). In addition, a regionalized economy appears to offer the appropriate scale for the development of core sectors of a restorative economy. Recycling and repairing, both sectors of high importance for an economy of low material throughput, require proximity to the consumer and are therefore most efficient at a medium scale of operation (Blau and Weiß 1997). Moreover, solar power, which relies on the widespread but diffuse resource of sunlight, is best developed when many operators harvest small amounts of energy, transforming and consuming them at close distance. A similar logic holds for biomass-centred technologies: plant matter is widely available and heavy in weight, and is therefore best obtained and processed in a de-centralized fashion. In most of these cases, short distances between points of production and points of consumption are technically most suitable; a restorative economy will in part have to be a regionalized economy.

Seen in this light, the long-held certainty that progress always means reducing the resistance of duration and distance gradually comes into question. Countless bridges, tunnels, highways, airports, cables and antennae are the heredity of the standard belief in progress. Instead, the suspicion grows that progress can also imply leaving deliberately the resistances of time and space unchanged, even increasing them if suitable. There would cease to be a relentless battle against the hindrances of time and space at any cost, and such a change would prove that society has outgrown the compulsion to carry the nineteenth-century world of desires right into the twenty-first century.

Wealth in Time Rather than Wealth in Goods

On what is well-being based? Ever since founding father Adam Smith extolled work (for the production of marketable goods) as the source of national affluence, economists have neglected the sphere of non-commercial activities, before and beyond the market, that constitute community. Their eyes firmly set on the GNP, they have difficulties recognizing any value creation in those activities performed outside the formal economy, such as housework and bringing up children, personal activity and friendship, associative life and civic activity. They have, in short, lost sight not only of natural, but also of social capital – if one wants to use economic language. This oversight is in great part a result of the towering output of the formal economy, fuelled by fossil resources, which cast a long shadow on other sources of well-being. The belief that everything of value is produced by marketable goods has found its complement in the belief that satisfaction derives from objects (and services) available from the market, and therefore from purchasing power. Again, personal pursuits, networks of reciprocity, and public associations disappear from the perception of well-being, leaving just the activity of consumption in the limelight.

However, giving the market so much scope has led affluent societies in an ecologically – but by no means only ecologically – vicious circle. As maximizing consumption is seen as the road to satisfaction, maximizing wage earnings appears to be the only rational behaviour. Income has generally been considered more important than free time, and consumption better than having more leisure. As a consequence, increases in economic productivity were for the most part converted into higher wages and increased production – and thus consumption of resources – leaving only a small part available for the increased freedom from the necessity to work. This pattern has been particularly reinforced by the rigidity of working time – and connected income levels – in most societies; regular work for a long time meant an eight-hour day, five days a week, and a lifelong job (Sanne 1992). Despite all their freedom to consume, people rarely had one fundamental option: the possibility of deciding how much time they wanted to work – and, correspondingly, how much they wanted to earn. Up to the present day, the choice is normally between full-time employment or nothing at all. Intermediate forms such as shorter working weeks, or longer annual holidays, are rare. However, as income levels are fixed, spending power tends to determine the level of consumption. In the process a 'work and spend' cycle (Schor 1995) ensues where rising but invariable incomes leave no other option, apart from saving, than to increase consumption. Simply put, people stop asking how much money they should earn for their needs, and instead get used to pondering what needs they can afford by spending the money they earn. From this point of view, the lack of individual freedom of choice over working time emerges as a powerful incentive for the expansion of consumption in society.

However, it is not unlikely that, if they had the choice, a con-siderable number of people would prefer to work less for a lower income. Indeed, for many, in particular the well-to-do, it is not money that is in short supply, but time. (Hörning et al. 1990). Money and time come to be seen as two resources of well-being that are in competition. Beyond a certain income level, the marginal utility of more available time is higher than the marginal utility of more available income. Seeking more freedom for their own interests, some people are ready to renounce part of their income, and deliberately take on the ad-venture of arranging their life so that they get by with less money. In terms of well-being, gaining time can compensate for loss of income, opening room for satisfying pursuits outside the market sphere. Such lifestyle options could be stimulated by the principle of sovereignty over one's own time – the much more extended right to choose the length of one's working periods. Such a principle would not only be socially welcome for mitigating the employment crisis, but also eco-logically welcome for moderating spending power. This approach would offer an entry point for rebalancing the monetized and the non-monetized spheres of society.

A sustainable community will ultimately be dependent on economic under-achievers who are uninterested in, or even antagonistic towards, a mounting volume of consumption. Economic under-achievers can give rise to a sector of reciprocity and civic life without which the end of economic growth would be a dramatic blow for the quality of life. Since the crucial question for an economy of permanence will be:

'How are social security and a good life possible without a growing economy?' one possible answer lies in devising ways in which the resources of law, land, infrastructure and money can be deployed in such a way that citizens become enabled to do many useful things autonomously by relying on their own forces. Such a shift is greatly facilitated when localities and neighbourhoods develop networks and institutions where non-commercial activities, benefiting those involved and others, can flourish. LETS (Local Exchange and Trading System) schemes, for instance, facilitate networks of modern reciprocity whose members (linked by way of a local office) can supply or demand all kinds of services by utilizing an account based on the local LETS currency (Douthwaite 1996). These experiments respond to the need for creative opportunities that allow people to live agreeably with less money and reduced purchasing power. They point towards a future where a society's competence will be measured in terms of whether it can guarantee well-being without permanent economic growth.

Well-being instead of Well-having

With the rise of the consumer society in nineteenth-century England, a redefinition of the meaning of human happiness took hold that today reveals itself as both environmentally pernicious and socially fragile. The growing volume of objects for thousands of needs make sense only in the context of a world view that sees happiness increase along with larger quantities of goods. Ever new generations of commodities hold out the promise that a further accumulation of goods will again raise human satisfaction. Clearly, this assumption of non-saturation provides the cultural ground upon which the world of high-throughput consumption rises. Its roots reach back to the period of the Enlightenment, when the conception of human needs had changed and they were seen as both infinite and utilitarian. While such a definition of human nature contrasted polemically with the classical view that considered needs circumscribed within the various models of an accomplished life and ultimately directed towards some non-material ideal, today's consumer culture is nevertheless thriving upon it.

Why, however, is there never enough, even in rich societies? Why are they still hooked upon the principle of non-saturation? This question has been lingering on for decades. John Maynard Keynes, one of the master thinkers of twentieth-century economics, wondered if an exceedingly successful economy would not at some point reach a state of saturation. In his *Essays in Persuasion* he speculated that the imperative of productivity might lose significance under conditions of affluence, as abundance makes it less and less important to allocate means optimally. But he underestimated the cultural significance of products in affluent societies. What matters in such a society is the symbolic power of goods and services: they are less than ever simply vehicles of instrumental utility, but serve an expressive function. What counts is what goods say, not what they do. Ethnologists will not be surprised: studying pre-modern societies they have always read material possessions as symbols of social allegiance and cultural meaning (Douglas and Isherwood 1978). In modern societies goods are also a means of communication. They constitute a system of signs through which purchasers make statements about themselves, their families, and their friends. While in the old days of the consumer society goods mainly informed about social status, today they signal allegiance to a particular lifestyle and convey how people are different from each other.

Many products have by now been perfected and cannot be developed any further; new buyers can be found only when these goods offer more symbolic capital. Cars that cannot become faster and more comfortable are designed to be technological wonders. Watches that cannot show the time more accurately take on a sportive flair when they become diving watches. Television sets whose images cannot become clearer take on a cinematic effect with wider screens. In short, products play a part no longer in the struggle for survival, but in the struggle for experience (Schulze 1993). Designers and advertisers are thus continually offering consumers new thrills and new identities, while the product's utility is taken for granted. In such a context, the relationship between consumer and product is shaped mainly by imagination, which is infinitely malleable. Feelings and meanings are anything but stable; their plasticity and ease of obsolescence can be exploited by designers in an unending variety of ways. Imagination, in effect, is an inexhaustible fuel for maintaining a growing supply of goods and services. And for that reason, the expectation that rich societies should one day reach a level of saturation has not come about: when commodities become cultural symbols there is no end to economic expansion.

Yet the promise of growing happiness with growing consumption is fraught with uncertainties. Currently, there is not much empirical evidence that – beyond a certain threshold – the assumed correlation between increased consumption and well-being holds true. Research into the psychology of happiness can find neither within nor between societies any evidence that levels of satisfaction significantly increase with levels of wealth (Argyle 1987). After a certain minimum, the less well-to-do are not unhappier than the rich. This derives in the first instance from the fact that people assess their satisfaction above all in reference to others; the perceived distance to others can be the same independent of the general level of wealth. However, there might also be a deeper reason for these findings, ultimately linked to the finiteness of time. In particular the rich are caught in a time trap.

Consider that, beyond a certain number, things can become the thieves of time. Goods both large and small must be chosen, bought, set up, used, experienced, maintained, tidied away, dusted, repaired, stored and disposed of. Even the most beautiful and valuable objects unavoidably gnaw away at the most restricted of all resources: time. The number of possibilities – goods, services, events – has exploded in affluent societies, but the day in its conservative way continues to have only 24 hours, so a hectic pace and stress have become characteristic of everyday existence. Scarcity of time has therefore become the nemesis of affluence.

In fact, in a multi-option society people suffer not from a lack but from an excess of opportunities. While well-being is threatened by a shortage of means in the first case, it is threatened by a confusion about goals in the second. The proliferation of options makes it increasingly difficult to know what one wants, to decide what one does not want, and to cherish what one has. Many people feel overburdened and constantly under pressure; in the maelstrom of modern life they have lost their clarity of purpose and determination of will. Apart from giving rise to all kinds of personal problems, such a condition tends to undermine well-being in post-industrial societies.

Viewed up close, one can say that well-being has two dimensions: the material and the non-material (Scherhorn 1995). Material satisfaction is obtained by acquiring and utilizing certain objects or materials – for example, buying food and eating a multi-course meal will satisfy the need to fill the stomach. Immaterial satisfaction stems from the way in which the object and materials are used – enjoying Italian cooking and convivial company over dinner gives another dimension of pleasure. Similarly, many objects achieve their full value only when they are put to use, enjoyed and cultivated. However, and this is the dilemma, obtaining immaterial satisfaction calls for attention, demands involvement, and requires time. To a varying degree, the full value of many goods and services can be experienced only when they are given attention and become part of a larger activity: they have to be properly used, adequately enjoyed, and carefully cultivated. The conclusion is obvious. Having too many things makes time for non-material pleasure shrink; an overabundance of options can easily diminish full satisfaction. So poverty of time degrades the utility of a wealth of goods. In other words, material and non-material satisfaction cannot be maximized simultaneously; there is a limit to material satisfaction beyond which overall satisfaction is bound to decrease. As it turns out, having much contradicts living well. Frugality, therefore, is a key to well-being.

It almost seems that after its breathtaking success the consumer society comes full circle to some of the classical teachings about the good life. Teachers of wisdom in East and West may have had different views about the nature of the universe, but they almost unanimously recommended adherence to the principle of simplicity in the conduct of life. In this tradition, the opposite to a simple lifestyle is seen as being not a luxurious but a fragmented existence. An excess of things is seen as distracting attention, dissipating energies, and weakening the capacity to take control of one's life. Advocacy of simplicity is thus more concerned with the art of living than with morality. Just as in art everything depends on a limited but skilful use of colours and sounds, so too the art of living demands a limited but skilful use of material objects. In other words, this tradition suggests a subterranean relationship between pleasure and austerity.

Particularly in an age of exploding options, the ability to focus, which implies the sovereignty of saying no, becomes an important ingredient in creating a richer life. Anyone who wants to keep his or her head above the flood of goods has no choice but to be a selective consumer, and anyone who wants to remain master of his or her wishes will discover the pleasure of systematically not pursuing options for buying. Consciously cultivating a lack of interest in excessive consumption is a very future-oriented attitude, for oneself and by chance also for the world. Henry David Thoreau put that experience in a nutshell, when he scribbled in his journal at Walden Pond: 'A man is rich in proportion to the number of things he can afford to let alone.'

Bibliography

Adriaanse, A. et al. (1997), *Resource Flows: The Material Basis of Industrial Economies*, Washington, DC: World Resources Institute.

Agarwal, A. and S. Narain (1989), *Towards Green Villages: A Strategy for Environmentally Sound and Participatory Rural Development*, New Delhi: Centre for Science and Environment.

Allen, J. (1991), *Biosphere 2. The Human Experiment*, New York: Penguin.

Altvater, E. (1992), *Der Preis des Wohlstands*, Münster: Westfälisches Dampfboot.

— and B. Mahnkopf (1996), *Grenzen der Globalisierung*, Münster: Westfälisches Dampfboot.

Anders, G. (1980), *Die Antiquiertheit des Menschen*, 2 vols, Munich: Beck.

Anderson, S. and J. Cavanagh (1997), 'The rise of global corporate power', *Third World Resurgence*, 1 (97): 37–9.

Argyle, M. (1987), *The Psychology of Happiness*, London: Routledge.

Arndt, H. W. (1981), 'Economic development: a semantic history', *Economic Development and Cultural Change* 26: 463–84.

Ayres, R. U. and U. E. Simonis (eds) (1994), *Industrial Metabolism*, Tokyo and New York: United Nations University Press.

Beck, U. (1985), *Die Risikogesellschaft*, Frankfurt: Suhrkamp.

— (1997), *Was ist Globalisierung?* Frankfurt: Suhrkamp.

Beney, G. (1993), 'Gaia: the globalitarian temptation', in W. Sachs (ed.), *Global Ecology: A New Arena of Political Conflicts*, London: Zed Books.

Blau, E. and M. Weiß (1997), *Die Reparaturgesellschaft*, Vienna: Österreichischer Gewerkschaftsbund.

Boege, S. (1993), 'The well-travelled yoghurt pot: lessons for new freight transport policies and regional production', *World Transport Policy and Practice*, 1: 7–11.

Boeing (The Boeing Company) (1998), www.boeing.com/commercial

Botkin, D. B. (1985), 'The need for a science of the biosphere', *Interdisciplinary Science Reviews* 10: 267.

Brandt, W. (1980), *North–South: A Program for Survival*, Cambridge, MA: MIT Press.

Brown, L. (ed.) (n.d.), *State of the World: A Worldwatch Institute Report on Progress Toward a Sustainable Society*, pub. annually, Washington, DC: Norton.

Brown, L. et al. (1998), *Vital Signs 1998*, Washington, DC: Norton.

Burckhardt, M. (1994), *Metamorphosen von Raum und Zeit. Eine Geschichte der Wahrnehmung*, Frankfurt and New York: Campus.

Buttels, F. et al. (1990), 'From limits to growth to global change: constraints and contradictions in the evolution of environmental science and technology', *Global Environmental Change* 1 (1), December: 57–66.

Canzler, W. (1996), *Das Zauberlehrlings-Syndrom: Entstehung und Stabilität des Automobil-Leitbildes*, Berlin: Sigma.

213

Carley, M. and Ph. Spapens (1998), *Sharing the World: Sustainable Living and Global Equity in the 21st Century*, London: Earthscan.

Castells, M. (1996), *The Rise of the Network Society. The Information Age: Economy, Society and Culture*, vol. I, Oxford: Blackwell.

— (1998), *End of Millennium. The Information Age: Economy, Society and Culture*, vol. 3, Oxford: Blackwell.

Cavanagh, J. (1998), 'Background to the global financial crisis', paper presented at the San Francisco International Forum on Globalization, San Francisco.

Clark, W. C. (1989), 'Managing planet earth', *Scientific American* 261, September: 47.

Clark, W. C. and R. E. Munn (eds) (1986), *Sustainable Development of the Biosphere*, Cambridge: Cambridge University Press.

Cobb, C. and J. Cobb (eds) (1994), *The Green National Product: An Index of Sustainable Economic Welfare*, New York: University Press of America.

Daly, H. (1990), 'Toward some operational principles of sustainable development', *Ecological Economics* 2: 1.

— (1991), 'Elements of environmental macroeconomics', in R. Costanza (ed.), *Ecological Economics: The Science and Management of Sustainability*, New York: Columbia University Press.

— (1996), 'Free trade, capital mobility and growth versus environment and community', public lecture given at The Hague Institute of Social Studies, The Hague, 26 September.

Daly, H. E. and J. B. Cobb (1989). *For the Common Good*, Boston, MD: Beacon Press.

Douglas, M. and B. Isherwood (1978), *The World of Goods: Towards an Anthropology of Consumption*, New York: Penguin.

Douthwaite, R. (1996), *Short Circuit: Strengthening Local Economies for Security in an Unstable World*, Totnes: Green Books.

Duden, B. (1990), *Der Frauenleib als öffentlicher Ort: Vom Mißbrauch des Begriffs Leben*, Hamburg: Luchterhand.

Durning, A. (1992), *How Much Is Enough?*, London: Earthscan.

Ecologist (1972), *A Blueprint for Survival*, Harmondsworth: Penguin.

Ecologist (1992), *Whose Common Future?*, London: Earthscan.

Economist (1997a), 'Schools brief: one world?', 18 October: 103–4.

Economist (1997b), 'Schools brief: delivering the goods', 15 November: 89–90.

El Serafy, S. (1991), 'The environment as capital', in R. Costanza (ed.), *Ecological Economics: The Science and Management of Sustainability*, New York: Columbia University Press, pp. 168–75.

Ehrlich, P. (1968), *The Population Bomb*, New York: Ballantine Books.

Esty, D. C. and D. Gerardin (1998), 'Environmental protection and international competitiveness. A conceptual framework', *Journal of World Trade*, 32 (3): 5–46.

Etymologisches Wörterbuch des Deutschen (1997), Munich: dtv.

Factor 10 Club (1995), *Carnoules Declaration*, Carnoules.

Finger, M. (1989), 'Today's trend: global is beautiful', unpublished manuscript.

Flitner, M. (1998), 'Biodiversity: of local commons and global commodities', in M. Goldman (ed.), *Privatizing Nature: Political Struggles for the Global Commons*, London: Pluto, pp. 144–66.

FOE (1995), 'Action Plan Sustainable Netherlands', in J. Spangenberg et al., *Towards Sustainable Europe: A Study from the Wuppertal Institute for Friends of the Earth Europe*, Luton: Friends of the Earth.

French, H. (1998), *Investing in the Future: Harnessing Private Capital Flows for Environmentally Sustainable Development*, Worldwatch Paper no. 139, Washington: Worldwatch Institute.

Fritsch, B., S. Schmidheiny and W. Seifritz (1993), *Towards an Ecological Sustainable Growth Society*, Berlin: Springer.

Fussler, C. (1997), *Driving Eco-Innovation*, London: Pitman.

Gadgil, M. and R. Guha (1992), *This Fissured Land: An Ecological History of India*, Delhi: Oxford University Press.

— (1995), *Ecology and Equity*, London: Routledge.

Garrod, B. (1998), 'Are economic globalization and sustainable development compatible? Business strategy and the role of the multinational enterprise', *International Journal of Sustainable Development* 1: 43–62.

George, S. (1992), *The Debt Boomerang*, London: Pluto.

Goodland, R., S. Daly and S. El Serafy (1991), *Environmentally Sustainable Economic Development: Building on Brundtland*, World Bank Environment Working Paper no. 46, July, Washington: World Bank.

Goodland, R. and H. Daly (1993), 'Why Northern income growth is not the solution to Southern poverty', *Ecological Economics* 8: 85–101.

Gore, A. (1992), *Earth in the Balance: Ecology and the Human Spirit*, Boston, MD: Houghton Mifflin.

Grinevald, J. (1988), 'Sketch for a history of the idea of the biosphere', in P. Bunyard and E. Goldsmith (eds), *Gaia, the Thesis, the Mechanisms and the Implications*, Camelford: Wadebridge Ecological Centre, pp. 1–32.

Gudeman, S. (1986), *Economics as Culture: Models and Metaphors of Livelihood*, London: Routledge.

Gwynne, M. D. and D. W. Mooneyhan (1989) 'The global environment monitoring system and the need for a global resource database', in D. Botkin et al. (eds), *Changing the Global Environment*, San Diego, CA: Academic Press.

Haas, P. (1990), 'Obtaining international environmental protection through epistemic consensus', *Millennium* 19: 347–63.

Haavelmo, T. and S. Hansen (1991), 'On the strategy of trying to reduce economic inequality by expanding the scale of human activity', in R. Goodland, H. Daly and S. El Serafy (eds), *Environmentally Sustainable Economic Development: Building on Brundtland*, Washington, DC: World Bank.

Hajer, M. A. (1995), *The Politics of Environmental Discourse*, Oxford: Clarendon.

Hansen, S. (1991), 'On the strategy of trying to reduce economic inequality by expanding the scale of human activity', in R. Goodland, S. Daly and S. El Serafy (eds), *Environmentally Sustainable Economic Development: Building on Brundtland*, World Bank Environment Working Paper no. 46, July, Washington, DC: World Bank.

Harbordt, H. J. (1991), *Dauerhafte Entwicklung statt globaler Selbstzerstörung*, Berlin: Sigma.

Hawken, P. (1993), *The Ecology of Commerce*, New York: Harper.

Hays, S. (1959), *Conservation and the Gospel of Efficiency: The Progressive Conservation Movement 1890–1920*, 1979 edn, New York: Atheneum.

Heerings, H. and I. Zeldenrust (1995), *Elusive Saviours. Transnational Corporations and Sustainable Development*, Utrecht: International Books.

Hennicke, P. and D. Seifried (1996), *Das Einsparkraftwerk*, Basle: Birkhäuser.

Hentschel, V. (1984) 'Produktion, Produktivität', in O. Brunner, W. Conze and R. Koselleck (eds), *Geschichtliche Grundbegriffe: Historisches Lexikon zur politisch-sozialen Sprache in Deutschland*, vol. 5, Stuttgart: Klett.

Hildyard, N. (1993), 'Foxes in charge of the chickens', in W. Sachs (ed.), *Global Ecology*, London: Zed Books, pp. 22–35.

Hobsbawm, E. (1994), *The Age of Extremes: A History of the World, 1914–1991*, New York: Pantheon.

Hopper, D. (1988), 'The World Bank's challenge: balancing economic need with environmental protection', Seventh Annual World Conservation Lecture, 3 March.

Hörning, K. H. et al. (1990), *Zeitpioniere. Flexible Arbeitszeiten – neuer Lebensstil*, Frankfurt: Suhrkamp.

IBRD (1950), *The Basis of a Development Program for Colombia*, Baltimore, MD: Johns Hopkins University Press.

Illich, I. (1972), *Tools for Conviviality*, New York: Harper & Row.

International Bank for Reconstruction and Development (1950), *The Basis of a Development Program for Colombia*, Baltimore, MD: Johns Hopkins University Press, p. xv.

Johnstone, N. (1997), 'Globalisation, technology, and environment', in *OECD Proceedings, Globalisation and Environment*, Paris: OECD, pp. 227–67.

Jones, T. and R. Youngman (1997), 'Globalisation and environment: sectoral perspectives', in *OECD Proceedings, Globalisation and Environment*, Paris: OECD, pp. 199–221.

Kehr, K. (1993), 'Nachhaltig denken: Zum sprachgeschichtlichen Hintergrund und zur Bedeutungsentwicklung des forstlichen Begriffs der Nachhaltigkeit', *Schweizerische Zeitschrift für Forstwesen* 144: 595–605.

Kelley, K. (ed.) (1988), *The Home Planet*, Reading, MA: Addison-Wesley.

Kennedy, J. F. (1961), Inaugural Address, Washington, DC, 20 January.

Kern, S. (1983), *The Culture of Time and Space 1880–1918*, Cambridge, MA: Harvard University Press.

Kessler, J. J. and M. Van Dorp (1998), 'Structural adjustment and the environment: the need for an analytical methodology', *Ecological Economics* 27: 267–81.

Keynes, J. M. (1972) (first published 1930), 'Economic possibilities for our grandchildren', in *The Collected Writings of John Maynard Keynes. Vol. IX: Essays in Persuasions*, London: Macmillan, pp. 321–2.

König, R. (1989), 'Produktion, Produktivität', in J. Ritter and K. Gründer (eds), *Historisches Wörterbuch der Philosophie*, vol. 7, Darmstadt: Wissenschaftliche Buchgesellschaft.

Koschorke, A. (1989), *Die Geschichte des Horizonts*, Frankfurt: Suhrkamp.

Kothari, R. (1993), *Growing Amnesia: An Essay on Poverty and Human Consciousness*, New Delhi: Penguin.

Lappé, M. and B. Bailey (1998), *Against the Grain: The Genetic Transformation of Global Agriculture*, London: Earthscan.

Lash, S. and J. Urry (1994), *Economies of Signs and Space*, London: Sage.

Lewis, C. S. (1947), *The Abolition of Man*, New York: Macmillan.

Lovelock, J. (1979), *Gaia: A New Look at Life on Earth*, Oxford: Oxford University Press.

— (1988), *The Ages of Gaia*, New York: Norton.

Lummis, D. (1992), 'Equality', in W. Sachs (ed.), *The Development Dictionary: A Guide to Knowledge as Power*, London: Zed Books.

McCormack, G. (1996), *The Emptiness of Japanese Affluence*, St. Leonards: Allen & Unwin.

McCormick, J. (1986), 'The origins of the world conservation strategy', *Environmental Review* 10: 177–87.

— (1989), *Reclaiming Paradise: The Global Environmental Movement*, Bloomington: Indiana University Press.

McLaren, D. et al. (1997), *Tomorrow's World: Britain's Share in a Sustainable Future*, London: Earthscan.

McNamara, R. (1973), 'Address to the board of governors', World Bank, Nairobi, 24 September.

Mack, P. (1990), *Viewing the Earth: The Social Construction of the Landsat Satellite System*, Cambridge, MA: MIT Press.

Malley, J. (1996), 'Von Ressourcenschonung derzeit keine Spur', *Politische Ökologie*, November–December: 46–9.

Malone, T. F. (1986), 'Mission to Planet Earth', *Environment* 28 (8): 6–11, 39–41.

Margulis, L. and D. Sagan (1986), *Microcosmos*, New York: Simon & Schuster.

Mason, M. (1997), 'A look behind trend data in industrialization. The role of transnational corporations and environmental impacts', *Global Environmental Change* 7: 113–27.

Meadows, D. H. et al. (1972), *The Limits to Growth*, New York: Basic Books.

Menotti, V. (1998a), 'The environmental impacts of economic globalization', draft paper presented at the San Francisco International Forum on Globalization, San Francisco.

— (1998b), 'Globalization and the acceleration of forest destruction since Rio', *Ecologist* 28: 354–62.

Moll, P. (1991), *From Scarcity to Sustainability. Future Studies and the Environment: The Role of the Club of Rome*, Frankfurt: Peter Lang.

Morris, D. (1996), 'Communities: building authority, responsibility and capacity', in *The Case against the Global Economy and for a Turn toward the Local*, San Francisco, CA: Sierra Club Books, p. 434.

Myers, N. (ed.) (1993), *Gaia: An Atlas of Planetary Management*, rev. edn, New York: Anchor.

Nisbet, E. G. (1991), *Leaving Eden: To Protect and Manage the Earth*, Cambridge: Cambridge University Press.

Norgaard, R. (1994), *Development Betrayed: The End of Progress and a Coevolutionary Revisioning of the Future*, London: Routledge.

Nørgård, J. (1995), 'Declining efficiency in the economy, *Gaia* 4: 277–81.

OECD (1998), *Kein Wohlstand ohne offene Märkte, Vorteile der Liberalisierung von Handel und Investitionen*, Paris: OECD.

Oppel, N. V. (1999), 'Aus fünf Kilo Fisch wird ein Kilo Zuchtlachs', *Greenpeace Magazin* 1 (99): 40–1.

Opschoor, J. (1992), *Environment, Economics and Sustainable Development*, Groningen.

Pastowski, A. (1997), *Decoupling Economic Development and Freight for Reducing ist Negative Impacts*, Wuppertal Paper no. 79, Wuppertal: Wuppertal Institute for Climate, Environment and Energy.

Pauli, G. (1998), 'No waste economy', *Resurgence*, 182: 20–3.

Pearson, L. (1969), *Partners in Development*, New York: Praeger.

Plowden, S. and M. Hillman (1996), *Speed Control and Transport Policy*, London: Policy Studies Institute.

Polanyi, K. (1944), *The Great Transformation*, Boston, MD: Beacon Press.

— (1977), 'The two meanings of economic', in K. Polanyi, *The Livelihood of Man*, London: Academic Press.

Pörksen, U. (1988), *Plastikwörter: Die Sprache einer internationalen Diktatur*, Stuttgart: KlettCotta.

Rambler, M., L. Margulis and R. Fester (eds) (1989), *Global Ecology: Towards a Science of the Biosphere*, San Diego, CA: Academic Press.

Reed, D. (ed.) (1996), *Structural Adjustment, the Environment and Sustainable Development*, London: Earthscan.

Reilly, W. K. (1990), 'The environmental benefits of sustainable growth', *Policy Review*, Fall: 16–21.

Riedel, M. (1961), 'Vom Biedermeier zum Maschinenzeitalter. Zur Kulturgeschichte der ersten Eisenbahnen in Deutschland', *Archiv für Kulturgeschichte* 43: 100–23.

Robert, J. (1992), 'Production', in W. Sachs (ed.), *The Development Dictionary: A Guide to Knowledge as Power*, London: Zed Books, pp. 177–91.

Rufin, J. (1994), *Das Reich und die neuen Barbaren*, Berlin: Volk & Welt.

Sachs, I. (1980), *Stratégies de l'écodéveloppement*, Paris: Les Editions Ouvrières.

Sachs, W. (1991/92), 'Natur als System. Vorläufiges zur Kritik der Ökologie', *Scheidewege* 21: 83–97.

— (1992a), *For Love of the Automobile: Looking back into the History of our Desires*, Berkeley: University of California Press.

— (ed.) (1992b), *The Development Dictionary: A Guide to Knowledge as Power*, London: Zed Books.

— (1992c), *Satellitenblick: Die Visualisierung der Erde im Zuge der Weltraumfahrt*, Berlin: Science Centre for Social Research.

— (ed.) (1993), *Global Ecology: A New Arena of Political Conflict*, London: Zed Books.

— (1994), 'The blue planet: an ambiguous modern icon', *Ecologist* 24: 170–5.

Sachs, W., R. Loske and M. Linz (eds) (1998), *Greening the North: A Postindustrial Blueprint for Ecology and Equity*, London: Zed Books.

Sagan, C. (1975), *The Cosmic Connection*, New York: Dell Books.

Sanne, C. (1992), 'How much work?', *Futures*, January/February: 23–6.

Sassen, S. (1996), *Losing Control?*, New York: Columbia University Press.

Schallaböck, K.-O. (1996), 'Verkehr und Zeit', in J. Rinderspacher (ed.), *Zeit für die Umwelt*, Berlin: Sigma, pp. 175–212.

Scherhorn, G. (1995), 'Zeitwohlstand versus Güterwohlstand – Über die Unvereinbarkeit des materiellen und immateriellen Produktivitätsbegriffs', in B. Bievertand and M. Held (eds), *Zeit in der Ökonomie*, Frankfurt: Campus, pp. 147–68.

Schivelbusch, W. (1987), *The Railway Journey: Industrialization of Space and Time in the 19th Century*, Berkeley: University of California Press.

Schmidheiny, S. (1992), *Changing Course: A Global Business Perspective on Development and the Environment*, Cambridge, MA: MIT Press.

Schmidt-Bleek, F. (1994), *Wieviel Umwelt braucht der Mensch?*, Berlin and Basel: Birkhäuser.

— (1998), *Das MIPS-Konzept. Weniger Naturverbrauch – mehr Lebensqualität durch Faktor 10*, Munich: Droemer.

Schneider, M., K. Geißler and M. Held (1995), 'Zeit-Fraß. Zur Ökologie der Zeit in Landwirtschaft und Ernährung', *Politische Ökologie*, Special Issue 8.

Schor, J. (1995), 'Can the North stop consumption growth? Escaping the cycle of work and spend', in V. Bhaskar and A. Glyn (eds), *The North, the South, and the Environment*, London, pp. 68–84.

Schulze, G. (1993), 'Soziologie des Wohlstands', in E. U. Huster, *Reichtum in Deutschland*, Frankfurt: Campus, pp. 182–209.

Scientific American (1989), *Managing Planet Earth: Readings from Scientific American*, New York: Freeman.

Seed, J. et al. (1988), *Thinking Like a Mountain*, Philadelphia: New Society Publishers.

Shiva, V. (1989), *Staying Alive: Women, Ecology and Development*, London: Zed Books.

Sloterdijk, P. (1990), *Versprechen auf Deutsch*, Frankfurt: Suhrkamp.

Sontag, S. (1977), *On Photography*, New York: Farrar, Straus & Giroux.

Spangenberg, J. et al. (1995), *Towards Sustainable Europe. A Study from the Wuppertal Institute for Friends of the Earth Europe*, Wuppertal: Wuppertal Institute.

Sprenger, R. U. (1997), 'Globalisation, employment, and environment', in *OECD Proceedings, Globalisation and Environment*, Paris: OECD, pp. 315–66.

Stahel, W. and E. Gromingen (1993), *Gemeinsam nutzen statt einzeln verbrauchen*, Internationales Design Forum, Giessen: Anabas.

Tandon, Y. (1993), 'Village contradictions in Africa', in W. Sachs (ed.), *Global Ecology*, London: Zed Books.

Thrupp, L. A. (1995), *Bittersweat Harvests for Global Supermarkets: Challenges in Latin America's Agricultural Export Boom*, Washington, DC: World Resources Institute.

Tibbs, H. (1992), 'Industrial ecology: an environmental agenda for industry', *Whole Earth Review* 77: 4–10.

Todorov, T. (1984), *The Conquest of America*, New York: Harper & Row.

Truman, H. S. (1950), 'Inaugural address', in A Decade of American Foreign Policy, Washington: US Government Printing Office.

—— (1956), Memoirs, Vol. 2: Years of Trial and Hope, New York: Doubleday.

Turner, T. (1995), The Conserver Society, London: Zed Books.

UN (1968), 'Preamble to the Charter of the United Nations', New York: UN Office of Public Information.

UNDP (United Nations Development Programme) (1996), Human Development Report 1996, Oxford and New York: Oxford University Press.

UNDP (United Nations Development Programme) (1998), Human Development Report 1998, Oxford and New York: Oxford University Press.

UNRISD (United Nations Research Institute for Social Development) (1995), States of Disarray: The Social Effects of Globalization, Geneva: UNRISD.

Wackernagel, M. and W. Rees (1996), Our Ecological Footprint: Reducing Human Impact on the Earth, Gabriola Island, Canada: New Society Publisher.

—— (1997), 'Perceptual and structural barriers to investing in natural capital: economics from an ecological footprint perspective', Ecological Economics 20: 3–24.

WCED (World Commission on Environment and Development) (1987), Our Common Future (the Brundtland Report), Oxford and New York: Oxford University Press.

Weizsäcker, E. U., A. Lovins and H. Lovins (1997), Factor Four: Doubling Wealth – Halving Resource Use, London: Earthscan.

World Bank (1992), World Development Report 1992, Oxford and New York: Oxford University Press.

WRI (World Resources Institute) (ed.) (n.d.), World Resources, pub. annually, New York: Oxford University Press.

Wrigley, E. A. (1987), 'The classical economists and the Industrial Revolution', in People, Cities and Wealth, Oxford: Blackwell, pp. 21–44.

Wysham, D. (1997), The World Bank and the G-7: Changing the Earth's Climate for Business, Washington, DC: Institute for Policy Studies.

Zängl, W. (1993), ICE – Die Geisterbahn, Munich: Raben.

Zarsky, L. (1997), 'Stuck in the mud? Nation-states, globalisation, and the environment', in OECD Proceedings, Globalisation and Environment, Paris: OECD, pp. 27–51.

Zukunftskommission der Friedrich-Ebert-Stiftung (1998), Wirtschaftliche Leistungsfähigkeit, sozialer Zusammenhalt, ökologische Nachhaltigkeit. Drei Ziele – ein Weg, Bonn: Dietz.

Index